Perspectives on Nigeria's Economic Development Volume II

Perspectives on Nigeria's Economic Development Volume II

Pascal G. Dozie

Safari Books Ltd
Ibadan

Published by
Safari Books Ltd
Ile Ori Detu
1, Shell Close, Onireke Ibadan
Email: safarinigeria@gmail.com

O Pascal G. Dozie
Publisher: Chief Joop Berkhout OON
Deputy Publisher: George Berkhout

Perspectives on Nigeria's Economic Development Volume II

Published 2012

ISBN: 978-978-8431-06-0

Table of Contents

Dedication

This book is dedicated to my family and to all those who, over the years, have selflessly advocated and/or helped in one way or the other to implement policies aimed at unlocking the socioeconomic potentials of Nigeria.

Foreword

Nigeria has experienced significant economic progress since publication in 1999 of the first edition of Perspectives on Nigerian Economic Development. Two main drivers of this progress have been the beneficial return to democratic rule and the implementation of key economic reforms, particularly in pursuing external debt relief, implementing excess crude account to stabilize revenue volatility, introducing contributory pension schemes and taking steps to privatize key sectors such as telecommunications. In each case, the benefits have fostered both internal and external expectations that Nigeria could rank within the top 20 global economies by 2020 or soon thereafter. A more realistic assessment is that the upside potential of Nigeria has been partly demonstrated in the past decade but it is clear that not nearly enough has been done to finally unlock Nigeria's great potential on a sustainable, long term basis.

It has been the lifetime mission of Pascal G. Dozie to relentlessly analyze the causes of Nigeria's inability to breakthrough on the economic front to pursue workable solutions through multiple leadership roles in think tanks, chambers, educational institutions, public sector appointments, charitable organizations and, most importantly, in private sector management and investments in financial services, private equity, telecommunications and other diversified businesses. He truly has been one to practice what he preaches as well as continue to speak out on every facet of nation building, with particular emphasis on the fundamental economic issues which still remain largely unresolved and unimplemented.

Having shared in many endeavours with Pascal, it is clear that what Nigeria needs to do to unlock its potential is well understood by many, if not most leaders in both the private and public sectors. One therefore must ask why so little is done to implement such key reforms as downstream petroleum deregulation, electric power development, harnessing of enormous natural gas resources, provision of key infrastructure such as ports, roads and rail transport, etc. In other words, why does the classic dilemma of a country dominated by a natural resource, such as petroleum, fail to use the abundant opportunities for sustainable nation building, as is the clear case of Nigeria. Pascal has wrestled with this dilemma for more than the three decades that I have known him. His approach has been both educational and practical.

In both the first edition and now this sequel, Pascal recognizes clearly that there is an ongoing battle between two opposing forces – those fostering the reforms necessary for nation building with the interest of the Nigerian people paramount and those protecting the status quo which are driven by narrow pursuit of self interest, perhaps in recognition that they could not compete in an open, merit-driven society.

He has applied the three questions which were used in Vision 2010 to guide his research, analysis, problem solving and definition of practical solutions, namely:

- Where are we now? And Why?
- Where do we want to be? And
- How do we get there?

The result, as amply demonstrated in the speeches and presentations presented in this second Volume, is deep insight into the Nigerian Economic situation, in-depth understanding of global best practices and how to tailor them to Nigeria and proven, practical solutions which produce outstanding, long-term results. He is a role model for those who seek to walk their talk.

In closing, I expect a third volume in the not too distant future which addresses more recent developments in Nigeria, such as the banking and capital markets crisis, the relative stagnation of the petroleum sector, the retrenchment of significant manufacturing industry and the dominant spending on recurrent items at all levels of government – which we have experienced in recent years. Despite these fundamental problems, Nigeria continues to demonstrate relatively strong growth rates which again prove that the right policies and reforms can produce extra-ordinary results. My challenge for his next round is to continue his good work in all his leadership roles but with further emphasis on capacity building, stronger institutions, disciplined governance and adapting best global practices to Nigeria – all in the context of encouraging those that believe in nation building (as opposed to excessive self interest) to follow in his footsteps. The end result just could be a nation emerging as a major global and a recognized leader of Africa on all fronts.

Dick Kramer
March, 2012

Preface

Two decades can mean a great deal in the life of a nation, more so in the rapidly changing world of the last decade of the twentieth century and the first nine years of the twenty-first. We only need to ponder over the following. Up to the 1990s:

· The world wide web (www) and internet, with their enormous instant communication powers, were just arriving on the scene, especially in Nigeria

· Global system of mobile communication (GSM) with its attendant mobility, real time access and add-on communication opportunities, was the preserve of Europeans. Nigerians merely dreamed of it.

· Global cable network television of the CNN, BBC, Sky, EuroNews and Aljazeera vintage and their global reach, were remote possibilities in Nigerian homes and offices.

· Nigeria was still a stronghold of military dictatorship, a somewhat pariah State.

· Some 107 banks, largely managed by Nigerians were in operation in the economy while the Capital Market was just emerging and quite shallow.

It was in this environment that volume one of this book, based on papers delivered throughout the 1990s, was published in 1999. The topic for the prologue of the volume was: 'A nation in Distress – Which way out', in which Nigerians were reminded that 'he profitests most who serves best'. Its epilogue – Performance of and Perspectives on the Nigeria Stock Exchange NSE – was equally apt with the caveat:

'If it (the NSE) becomes investor-friendly and cost-effective, it will become a competitive stock market which will be relevant to the aspirations of Nigerians...'. Sandwiched between these two perspectives, volume one also strove to address other concerns, including:' Visioning and Development'; 'Integrating the Petroleum Industry and the Rest of the Economy'; 'Contractor Financing in the Provision of Infrastructure Facilities'; 'Monetary and Fiscal Policy Dynamics – Implications for Regulation and Profitability of Banking Business'; and 'Restoring Confidence in the Nigerian Financial System'.

When we fast forward ten years to 2009, we imagine that the landscape has changed beyond recognition given the following facts:

- The www, Internet and global cable networks have all penetrated Nigerian homes, offices and the mass market.

- GSM has become the most common means of communication in Nigeria as artisans, rural dwellers, farmers, not to talk of high net worth individuals have become connected. In less than eight years of operation, some 60 million telephone lines (against 400,000 lines hitherto) are in service in what has been attributed to a GSM miracle and the fastest growing tele-density in the world.

- Nigeria is once again a democracy, albeit fledgling. Indeed, for the first time, the nation has experienced a civilian to civilian transfer of power and its longest spell of continuous civilian administration since independence in 1990.

- Following the successful bank reform and consolidation programme of 2005, there are now 25 banks with stronger capital bases, wider penetration and global reach.

It is in this context that the papers that constitute the current volume were produced. Ordinarily, it is expected that the changes of the last several years would have shaped the national economy and discourse. And they have indeed. Yet, as the saying goes, the more things change, the more they remain the same.

This volume is, therefore, focused on issues relating to good political and corporate governance and national development; budget and fiscal policy; the Nigerian financial and capital markets and banking.

Two decades after I started documenting my views on the Nigerian economy, national conversations are still dominated by such issues as:

- The challenges of leadership, visioning, re-branding and national development

- Criticisms of banks, bankers, management and operations of the Nigerian capital market.

- Cross-cutting issues, including financing the oil industry, infrastructure development and education.

This book, which is appropriately structured in five parts, tackles these issues in a series of interrelated papers. Part one deals with the issues of globalisation and how Nigeria can play in the emergent environment. Part two (Managing the Nigerian Economy), Part three (Strengthening the Nigerian Banking Sector and Part Four (Entrepreneurship and Corporate Governance) proffers ways and means of handling these intertwined aspects of national challenges. The final part – Key Sector Issues deals with three vital areas – Education, Transportation, and Oil and Gas.

It is my hope that the book will be useful to policy-makers, political leaders, bankers, educators, students and the general reading public.

Acknowledgements

Success is never a solo effort. It is an achievement of so many people, some of whom one might not even remember let alone their contributions to one's success.

In my own case, it is not easy for me to remember the numerous people whose opinion have, one way or the other, shaped my thought process.

Take, for instance, the several intellectual discourses and economic policy dialogues one was privileged to participate in monthly, through the Nigerian Economic Summit Group or the various discussions, debates that one was involved in during the visioning process of the Vision 2010 – a fourteen-year strategic development plan that was intended to grow Nigeria out of economic doldrums into the league of emerging, successful, developed and developing countries like Malaysia, Korea, Brazil, etc. Although it was not to be, the spirit of Vision 2010 has refused to die and somehow manages to struggle on.

In the production of this book, however, I must acknowledge the contribution of a few people. The first person is my wife, Chinyere, who bore and continues to bear the brunt of my occasional frustrations in life and is always involved in all that I do. Dick Kramer played a very key role and helped to structure the arrangement of the various chapters in order to achieve some semblance of order in the various topics. He also graciously wrote the foreword to this book. Reg Ihebuzor and Stanley Egbochukwu proved to be indispensable, especially in making sure that all editorial issues were taken care of, among other things pertaining to this publication. Of course, my able publisher Chief Joop Berkhout of Safari Books Ltd and his team who put it all together in a splendid well designed book. Without these people, this publication would still be languishing in its manuscript form – uncompleted.

Despite all the contributions of all those who made this book possible, I and I alone, am responsible for any shortcomings and/or errors regarding this publication.

Pascal G. Dozie

March 2012

Part I

Globalisation and the Nigerian Economy

Globalisation And The Nigerian Economy

In the contemporary sense, self sufficiency has ceased to be a relevant economic concept. Globalisation has become both the buzzword for modernity as well as the reality facing every single nation in the world today. But globalisation is also a double-edged sword. The integration of world markets has opened up new avenues for economic growth, with vast potential for improving living standards. However, recent past experiences in Asia and Latin America call attention to the untoward consequences of globalisation. These developments reveal the dangers of playing in the open field with a neighbour who has the flu. Everybody in the field invariably catches cold!

Economies such as Nigeria's that are largely peripheral in the global economic scheme of things are particularly vulnerable to globalisation's less savoury effects. The situation has not been made any better by the continuing lopsided nature of the international trade and exchange relations. There are also the internal weaknesses bedevilling many developing economies, namely, corruption and governance concerns, infrastructure and weak industrial bases. This is probably why, in his treatise "Expand the Debate on Globalisation", Peter Southland referred to globalisation as the phenomenon that spurs expansion but triggers dislocation.

Nigeria must find creative means for making globalisation work in its overall interest. In this, the country does not have the luxury of choice. In the conduct of our national economic policy, we must look beyond the myth, the fears and the stereotypes in order to overcome the barriers to our becoming an active participant in the global economy.

If the examples from other national experiences are enough indication, two economic sectors have often served as veritable

entry vehicles into the globalised world market. The first of these sectors is the banking industry. The second is telecommunications. The ability of these two sectors to work closely toward nurturing and sustaining capacities is almost infinite. If anything, the growth of Nigeria's telecoms sector in the last three years partially buttresses this fact. The on-going consolidation process in the banking industry may well complete the
picture. Indeed, much of the success factor lies in the underlying resilience of regulation. The three chapters that follow examine the issues involved at both the conceptual and the implementation levels.

Chapter 1

Impact of Globalisation on the Nigerian Economy

Introduction

Globalisation is a subject of immense importance, emotive force and currency in the world today. I believe the trend towards greater integration of world markets has opened a new avenue for economic growth, just as it promises to improve living standards. However, recent developments in some Asian and Latin American countries, such as Malaysia and Mexico, call attention to the latent downside consequences of globalisation. These developments reveal the dangers of playing in an open field with your neighbour who has the flu. You may just catch the cold. In other words, if this could happen in these more successful economies, one might begin to wonder how safe it is for developing countries like Nigeria to be part of that integrated world market. This is probably why in his article "Expand the Debate on Globalisation", Peter Southland referred to globalisation as the phenomenon that spurs expansion but triggers dislocation.

I believe an attempt to analyse this problem should begin with the evaluation of the concept of globalisation and its impact on the conduct of our national economic policy. This is what we shall attempt to do today. We shall also attempt to highlight the way forward to mitigate the downside consequences of this phenomenon.

The Concept of Globalisation

The origin of this concept has been traced to the writings of Wendell Wilkie and the Club of Rome, which occurred prior to the collapse of the Bretton Woods system and the development of highspeed communication technology, in the latter years.

But the term globalisation as presently used, appears to have developed from the activities of the Allied nations, following the end of World War II, to support a more open trading and investment system in the world. However, the term globalisation has been described as a process of denationalisation of clusters of political, economic, and social activities for the benefit of human kind. It is a historical process that results from innovation and technological progress manifested in the integration of economies through the free movement of capital, labour and also, advances in technology.

Attempts are often made to distinguish globalisation from internationalisation, which is basically the cooperative activities of national actors, public or private, on a level beyond the nation-state, but under its control. In other words, internationalisation is both a consequence and an appendage of the nation-state's activities, aimed at improving the lot of its people. Comparatively, therefore, we find that globalisation is not necessarily targeted at the citizens of any particular nation but at mankind in general. Its effects are also more diffused, diverse and pervasive.

Globalisation is the denationalisation or, if you like, the diffusion of markets and activities in such a way as to bring humanity into a sort of borderless country. The hallmark of globalisation is the removal of all artificial boundaries, including somehow, and perhaps contentiously, sovereignties that previously defined nations. The driving force behind globalisation has been technology of which telecommunication is a major component. Furthermore, globalisation is principally evidenced by the twin phenomena of international financial flows and technological advancement.

Although international trade and cross-border financial movements have always been with us, they have never been so fast. On their own, financial flows and technological development across nations are not new. After all, the highly developed capitals of the world, such as London, Tokyo and New York, have always been linked significantly through trade. The new thing in globalisation is actually the rate at which the high-and low-income countries are being increasingly linked together within a global system.

Today, over $1 trillion is traded globally each day in a nonstop foreign exchange market around the world. Similarly, computers and telecommunications are rapidly encroaching into every sector of human endeavour, replacing old ways of doing things and rendering labour virtually redundant.

In the face of such frightening changes, the discerning mind must rightly wonder what all these should come to, especially for an economy that is still battling to unravel the sources and consequences of the First Industrial Revolution.

The Challenges of Globalisation

A number of challenges arise from the demands of living in a world that literally has no borders, because that is exactly what globalisation portends. With capital flows moving faster than the world has ever seen, government must earnestly rework its economic and financial architecture to ensure that the structures can cope with these startling demands. Unfortunately, most financial and political institutions in the developing world are lacking both in skilled manpower and current technology for the needs of the present time. It could be very naive therefore to assume that such weak institutions would support these countries to participate beneficially in the unfolding events. An initial challenge of globalization, therefore, is to prepare and position our financial and indeed, social, economic and political institutions, to cope with the expected demands on them, in such a way as to avoid a disruption in the system.

Globalisation is gradually transforming erstwhile domestic matters, be they political, social or economic, into international issues, thereby pushing further the frontiers of bilateral and multilateral relationships. But, sometimes, we focus excessive attention on economic and financial matters when we consider globalisation. That should not be the case. It is like being on the information super highway. Once you get in, you may no longer hide very easily. Thus, all matters concerning a nation- its culture, traditions, politics and public institutions are available for scrutiny in this global village. It is no longer sufficient to talk of national interests in isolation; public or world opinion becomes equally critical as countries pursue their national objectives. It therefore follows that even the workings of the domestic economy are open to scrutiny on account of this phenomenon.

The consequences of such scrutiny would include possible modification or adjustments to traditions and practices. While this may raise living standards for some people, many would be dislocated by the change and may fall into difficulty. The challenge here is to ensure minimum dislocation.

The other challenge of globalisation is to ensure that, whoever falls on account of this change makes as soft a landing as possible. As I noted earlier, globalisation exposes one to the flu of one's neighbour. The global market could be likened to the central nervous system in which information, on every event, is transmitted rapidly to every part of the body. Because information is easily available, and can be transmitted at very high speed, economic decisions become more brutal, to the extent that the growth which globalisation promotes becomes inherently destabilising. It should be a concern, therefore, to ensure that such crises as were recently experienced in Asia and Latin America do not get transmitted to the rest of the world, as it were, in a hurry.

Globalisation will challenge humanity, to a large extent, in the area of the environment, crime and crime-related problems as well as migration and urbanisation. Already, there is beginning to emerge, in different spheres of human endeavour, what might be described as global standards. It is no longer convenient for multinationals to degrade their host environment just to meet their production targets. Nor is child labour any longer the private problems of Asia and Latin America. Sooner or later even those corporations that still practice these ills may find no hiding place but have to conform to the global standards. This is another challenge that all persons, institutions and nations must address.

An area of further challenge which globalisation poses, especially to the weaker economies in the developing world, is the likely increase in unemployment as a result of this unrestricted global interaction. It is already the subject of heated discussion in the leading cities of the world including, Seattle, Washington and Prague that globalisation and trade liberalisation are worsening the already bad state of unemployment in weaker countries. There is, therefore, the need to ensure that adequate care is taken to prevent this side-effect from escalating.

Those of us who attended the IMF/World Bank meeting in Prague last year would agree that this discussion has moved beyond friendly chats to resistance and defiance. It is a challenge on globalisation to allay the fears and address the concerns of those who feel unsettled by the development.

With deregulation, foreign companies can now be quoted on our domestic stock exchanges as demonstrated in the MNET/ Supersports quotation. It is obvious that this development has implications for the regulatory system with regard to control and monitoring. There is need therefore to ensure that we maintain high standards of competence, transparency and integrity for a denationalised capital market. All investors in the quoted shares will be interested even in our domestic environment. The challenge is for us to sustain and grow international confidence to enable us to compete in the market. When we reckon that many US companies are floating Eurobonds to tap into the European capital market, while companies in New Zealand are raising funds from the US capital market, the inevitability of playing according to global standards becomes obvious.

The challenge of globalisation, as it relates to the economy, is not limited to the domestic affairs of any particular nation. The international financial environment, especially as it relates to the roles of the Bretton Woods institutions, such as the World Bank and the IMF, needs to be focused upon. These institutions have, without doubt, served fairly well the purpose for which they came into being (postwar reconstruction, promotion of global prosperity and security, and economic development).

However, the possibility of a complete change in the nature and content of international financial relations, due to globalisation may impose fresh and higher demands beyond the capability of these institutions as presently constituted. The reality of regrouping and realignment on the international front, which has given rise to such blocks as the European Union, NAFTA in North America, MERCUSOR in Latin America and ASEAN in Asia, compels a review of the structure and functions of these international financial institutions.

Although the Breton Woods institutions were originally created to rebuild Europe, and drive the process of economic development, they have effectively handled additional responsibilities that have arisen from the evolution of human society. These responsibilities include the resolution of the debt crisis that climaxed in the 1980s, the integration of former socialist countries into the free market spectrum and the canalisation of resources to needy economies. Nonetheless, the increasing disappearance of the dividing line between domestic and international financial markets has made closer monitoring of their activities a matter of urgent necessity. These institutions may have become even more relevant now but could require to be strengthened in appropriate areas, in line with the dictates of globalisation.

With globalisation, markets are gradually becoming abstract terms and location no longer confers any special advantage to industries. Nearness to markets, which we learnt was a major consideration for industrial location, is gradually yielding place to access to information. What does this portend for the Nigerian economy, especially with its heavy dependence on foreign inputs?

There was a time when parent companies in Europe and America used to spend much time defending their local operations here in Nigeria, through concessions and infrastructure provisions. The objective was to keep the Nigerian market, sometimes at all costs, because this market was large indeed (both in numbers and purchasing power). But that was before the wind of change that blew across Europe and Russia in the 90s. Some new, more profitable and perhaps larger markets have since developed with better infrastructure and legal framework that better facilitate business. Besides, the consistent depreciation of the local currency and the erosion of private purchasing power have narrowed the size of this market. Such hard-nosed pursuit of a place in Nigeria may no longer exist because capital is fungible and would naturally gravitate to the jurisdiction of higher returns with lower risk. This high mobility of capital, as I have indicated, carries the risk of high volatility which destabilises the economy and hurts the exchange rate, especially in a system such as ours with policy design and implementation problems.

Globalisation and the European unification would, therefore, combine with the opening up of Russia and the former communist nations of Eastern Europe to curtail interest in our sub-region. This means that the market attraction, which we used to provide, may no longer be there. Parent companies are now being pulled in different directions and away from us. This is probably a source of the virtual de-industrialisation that has occurred recently with many companies selling off or closing down their Nigerian outlets, as in the pharmaceutical industry.

Our infrastructure is both inadequate and outdated. Corruption is endemic and has proved to be very expensive to business. These elements impose high costs on business transactions with Nigeria. Capital flows are, therefore, not likely to be in our favour for reasons already identified. This situation could present serious challenges to our entrepreneurs as foreign associates now have a wider choice of markets.

Globalisation has also removed much of the tariff barriers that used to hide the inefficiencies of certain business units. Global companies now locate, produce and sell anywhere in response to and for comparative advantage reasons. This brings competition closer and makes it fiercer. It means that competition has become a real issue both for companies and nations. But this competition would be most intense in the financial sector where capital seeks only the best returns, both in terms of earnings and security. This also has implications for our local enterprises and their capacity to expand through foreign capital injection.

The economic and political re-organisation, now pervading Europe, has continued apace at a rapid and, indeed, unpredictable speed. The recent political changes in Yugoslavia and Russia are bound to provide a veritable vortex for capital, technology and finance, which could in the end, encompass the whole of Europe. The consequences of this, and the fact that we are still immersed in the murky waters of political and economic uncertainties, could be daunting. Already, the opening of the vast Russian and East European resources to Western capital is proving to be a problem to us here at home. While this is happening, India's Bangalore is carving a niche for itself as the California (Silicon Valley) of the Asian world; China is becoming even more aggressive and has finally joined the World Trade Organisation. These are all players in the global village to which we now belong. We cannot afford to underrate the challenges ahead!

In simple terms, the challenges of globalisation to us in Nigeria begin with the search for an answer to the question "what are we offering to the world?" We must adopt genuine policies to increase domestic production and hence our share of the global market. This should necessarily imply a departure from the present 'monoculturism' to economic diversification. It also includes the preservation of our environment and the control of crime and other social ills that would increase as globalisation hots up.

The phenomenon of e-commerce is threatening to revolutionise the market concept. Virtually all commodities can be bought and sold from the comfort of the living rooms of the parties concerned. Recently, the story of a couple who "bought" a set of two kids, put up for adoption on the internet, was relayed on the BBC following the development of a quarrel between two families contending over the kids in two different countries. Are we going to be able to maintain those good African traditions of respect for family life and the dignity of the human person, that have helped to sustain our vital extended family system? These are indeed, some of the major challenges to be faced.

The Positive Effects of Globalisation

The challenges of globalisation may be daunting but they are not insurmountable. Besides, there are certain benefits that would arise and impact positively on the Nigerian economy as a result of this phenomenon.

Depending on how we position ourselves, globalisation will encourage the inflow of foreign investments in the country. Nigeria has returned to the comity of civilised nations, following the installation of a democratic government. Although we are yet to fully establish the structures requisite for effective participation in world trade and financial flows, such as functional utilities and political-social stability, the country stands to reap foreign investments from this global interaction, if we sustain the political progress so far recorded.

The inflow of direct foreign investment means more than financial investment. It brings not only an increase in the physical stock of capital, but also enhances technological progress. As new techniques of production accompany such foreign investments, new production management skills also develop. Additionally, new sales techniques and strategies are explored in new markets, including the export market. Inevitably, a body of knowledgeable people would definitely grow on account of such inflow of capital and technology. Every developing country needs to continually improve its stock of skilled manpower and Nigeria is not an exception.

Globalisation will afford workers the freedom to move across borders in search of better remuneration and job satisfaction. Nigeria may not immediately provide a substantial proportion of the skilled labour requirement of the world for now, but the number will rise over time. The impetus for this is likely to come from the convergence of global wages as labour migrates between the developed and developing countries. Our surplus labour, especially *in* the area of information technology will benefit from the removal of artificial barriers to job openings abroad. Skills are also likely to be transferred to us from abroad in such a way as to cause a rise in domestic wages, thereby helping to raise standards of living, economy will benefit from such.

The most significant and perhaps immediate gains of globalisation would be in the area of capital movements. Nigeria is presently engaged in a massive decontrol and deregulation effort. The monopolies of the energy and telecommunication sectors are about to melt down. The result would be huge capital requirements of the magnitude never before experienced in the country. Numerous international specialists in these areas are already jostling to be part of the massive investment that would be required to set up independent providers of the various utilities. Not only would this resonate positively in the financial system, it will enlarge our coast in various aspects of human endeavour - jobs, skills, incomes and competences.

The huge capital requirements for some of the soon to be deregulated sectors of our financial system will rev the capital market. Certain functions of the banking sector, such as loan syndication, which has remained unexplored due mainly to the absence of big - ticket transactions will come alive again and with it, innovation and improvement.

Let me say that one major advantage of playing in the global market is the inherent pressures or drive towards the equalisation of standards and procedure. A lot has been said about the lack of standards and procedures in many areas of our national life and the toll it has taken on our relationship with the rest of the world. We have been noted as a haven for discretionary conduct, especially among public office holders, and this has fuelled corruption until we excelled in the whole world. Globalisation will demand that business be done in accordance with global standards which any country can disregard at its own peril. Competition which deregulation and liberalisation will produce would enhance transparency and good governance both in the public and private sectors of our economy.

Globalisation will also draw attention to certain aspects and resource endowments of our country that are presently unexploited, thereby adding to the productive capacity and robustness of the economy. It might, therefore, assist the cause of economic diversification in Nigeria.

It is common knowledge that the newly industrialised countries of Malaysia, Hong Kong, Thailand, Indonesia, and such, have made tremendous progress spurred by technology and their efficient use of natural resources. Today, they have beaten us in areas in which we share common endowments. These same people are going to play in the same market and to the same rules with us due to globalisation. It means, therefore, that all serious countries must learn to adopt policies that will enhance their benefits in the world economy rather than those that isolate them. As I have said elsewhere, we are still wondering why and how the First Industrial Revolution occurred. Therefore, to have the added burden of competing in a world without borders, with countries experiencing their Third Industrial Revolution, could be a great challenge. This burden is indeed a tremendous one, especially for our entrepreneurs confronted by several indivisibilities or more precisely, disabilities, not limited to poor technology and infrastructure, corruption and political-social instability. But it is also a call to reform; a call to a new beginning and an opportunity to make a change for the better.

The Downside Effects of Globalisation

There is a necessary structural change in the economy that should follow the opening and integration of markets, due to the impact of technology. There is also the inevitable winning and losing, by economic agents, that arises from this development. As a result, some segments of the economy are bound to face some disadvantages, even if it were in the short-term, while others will benefit. Globalisation will, therefore, bring its casualties among the citizens, corporations and other agents of every participating country.

Among the citizens, the casualties are expected to come mainly from among the less skilled members and all those groups which are unable to quickly adapt to the impact of technology and competition on their work. It is, therefore, probable that unemployment may be exacerbated. What about e-commerce and the elimination of shop-hands? What about the impact of illiteracy on the rapid spread of computer knowledge on which the whole phenomenon largely depends? It is, however, unclear, as to the extent to which this negative impact will be felt, but income distribution may worsen as the less - skilled members of the society become marginalised in the process.

While it is true that properly structured economies, with relevant production capacity and quality output would prosper, but immediate punishment is likely to be handed out for all policy errors. This is where the fear for Nigeria, and indeed all of Africa, lies in the whole process of globalisation. Can we provide the requisite policy credibility that would attract and retain investment capital? This is very critical because investment decisions and, in particular, capital movements, in the face of alternative and more viable choices, will become more heartless, brutal, violent and consistently rapid. Hence, judgment on the international economic front will be rapid against economies that are poorly structured, just as benefits will flow in like fashion to those properly placed to receive them.

It is necessary to emphasise that the rapid capital flows which globalisation promises will bring with it unprecedented levels of volatility in the financial markets. Such volatility is likely to induce high levels of short-term bank lending which may not be the optimal state of affairs for the economy. This is also likely to pose daunting challenges to the regulatory authorities. Appropriate structures, to encourage long-term flows, must be put in place to avoid the consequences of such market shocks.

It may also be useful to note clearly that globalisation implies that we all buy and sell in the same market and be subject to the same rules. But we do not all have the same infrastructural status and other capabilities. Our products for instance, have no quality equivalents. This will surely have an impact on prices, volumes and quality. But again, what are we producing for this competitive market? Apart from oil, are we offering anything else to this global market? Perhaps, the danger of dumping may never have been more apparent!

Globalisation will, therefore, expose countries, with poor and inconsistent policy frameworks, to the harsh realities of unequal competition, because that is what it is. Both capital flows and technology will pass them by unnoticed. Sadly, we are still deeply rooted in the messy environment of socio-economic insecurity. This is partly due to the fact that we are yet to be seen to remove the sense of uncertainty currently bedevilling our polity. Our national institutions are still far from reputable. Transparency in public policy and leadership is still a rarity, while accountability is still novel. Above all, discretion is waxing stronger as the leading instrument of governance even though the whole world knows that the only thing that results from unaccountable discretionary power is corruption. No system is likely to survive the global environment without a departure from these vices.

But globalisation will surely insist on verifiability and clarity of policy decisions rather than discretion and arbitrariness. It will also insist on the removal of undue privileges, especially for public functionaries. Here lies the danger of marginalisation; this time at the international level. Indeed, countries without integrity and transparency would not only be marginalised but would be structured out of the economic system or, at best, to the periphery of the global village. In this regard, barring any sudden development on the anti-corruption front, Nigeria is certainly on the high-risk track of marginalisation on account of globalisation.

It has been argued that globalisation may impact negatively on the sovereignty of the country by limiting the choices open to policy makers, both in the public and private sectors. For instance, wage and price increases, which would reduce the ability of the country to compete internationally, are automatically precluded, even if they are genuinely necessary.

The past few years have shown that short-term capital flows may harm macro-economic stability. The risk is, therefore, very high for countries to follow externally generated financial policies that do not promote their own internal stability, just because they belong to an integrated finance market. This is a risk of globalisation which some have interpreted to mean a loss of sovereignty. Viewed positively, however, it is only an incentive for political leaders to pursue sound economic policies, and for industry captains to evaluate properly their project choices. But undoubtedly, such limitation on a country's room for manoeuvre is a real and present danger bordering on loss of sovereignty.

The Way Forward

Globalisation is undoubtedly anchored on technology, and the correlation between a country's technological capability and its socio-economic development has been shown to have become positively stronger. We are presently technologically backward and our access to information is still very limited. The use of computers is just catching on. This situation will invariably hinder our growth in a number of areas, including participation in the new fad e-commerce. The need has, therefore, become very urgent for steps to be taken in order to mitigate the expected problems.

In this regard, the need for functional educational institutions and practical programmes, especially in the field of information technology, cannot be over emphasised. To enable our people to compete internationally, their skills must be both current and extensive.

There is now no doubt that traditional market structures, such as boundaries and locations, will become less significant in the years ahead so also will old allegiances, to forms and processes in international trade relations, wane. Every nation must, therefore, review its game plan and strategies for surviving in this very competitive environment. Economic management may become more difficult as shockwaves from one end of the market are instantaneously translated to the other. The successive regimes of crises witnessed in Mexico and other South American countries and also in South-East Asia are direct results of an interconnected financial market. We must develop strategies to enhance the stability of our financial markets.

There is also now a greater challenge for government to create the requisite enabling environment for industry to take advantage of the developments in the technology sector. In this regard, certain preconditions are to be noted, chiefly among which is the need to strengthen the private sector, imbue integrity and transparency in our national institutions and an insistent pursuit of the anti-corruption agenda in a new economy whose public utilities work. Financial capital may be inanimate; however it will only reside in a location where, among other things, the comfort and security of its owner can be guaranteed.

Undoubtedly, globalisation will test the degree of cohesion in an economic system. Therefore, there must be evident commitment, on the part of both government and the Nigerian private sector, to mutual co-operation and trust. In this regard, it may be useful to call attention to the concept of Nigeria Incorporated which, though a product of the dictatorial era, was fashioned after the successful Malaysian experience.

We have earlier acknowledged the fact that Malaysia, among many of the newly industrialised nations, has out-performed us in all areas of mutual endowment. Although we share common bio physiographical possibilities, Malaysia has succeeded where we have failed. The last evidence of our failure, and I think it was colossal, was the failure of the National Agricultural Land Development Authority (NALDA) - a bright idea we copied from Malaysia's Federal Land Development Authority (FELDA) - which was scrapped recently after several billions of naira had been wasted. There is an urgent need for a return to orderliness in our economic and political management.

Much of Malaysia's success has been traced to the vibrancy of its private sector. Our national competitive strategy must be revised and anchored on tested structures, which should include a willing and able private sector. Privatisation, though fraught with a lot of imperfections, must continue apace. The private sector must seek and find the requisite financial ability to stand in for a failed public sector adventure in economic activity.

Government must begin to learn how to establish effective supervision in all sectors of the economy to curtail possible excesses and unwarranted abuse of power and opportunity.

To deal successfully with the competition which globalisation entails, we must begin by identifying our strengths and weaknesses, or as we say in business, do a SWOT analysis of ourselves. Can we say presently what the strength of the Nigerian nation is? Competition is about the application of one's strength to the best of uses while playing down, and possibly obliterating, one's weaknesses.

Let us be reminded that globalisation is akin to a Trade Exhibition in which all participants showcase their best in different areas of human endeavour. All nations will, therefore, be called upon to show good cause why they should continue to be relevant in the affairs of men. For the umpteenth time, I ask, what are we taking to this "open market?" The quality of our products, be they human or material, must meet world standards. That is the only way we can hope to get a stand in this global exhibition. This is where quality control and the integrity of our local standards authorities come into focus. The quality check must apply to all products, including the output of our educational institutions, to enable us to survive in the world market place. And the quality control must be real, transparent and serious.

It is perhaps an act of God that we now have a democratic government. This guarantees that at least, we shall discuss and agree strategies and also, with some doggedness, achieve their implementation. Without any doubt, the present world has no place for a country run by one man in the name of military dictatorship, as witnessed in Nigeria's recent past. Let us support a return to the rule of law and sustain it!

Our starting point is to assess our possibilities, marshal our best team, irrespective of tribe or tongue, and insist on probity and accountability. It is possible to insist on probity and accountability. Such insistence may curtail some temporary comforts we enjoy. It may even bring down governments. However, our trajectory must be, and remain, the future of this country; not our individual comfort of today.

Conclusion

I would like to say that our country has come a long way from the dark days of military misrule. Today we gather and freely make pronouncements for the healthy progress of our people and nation. I am convinced that we are in a position to save our children and indeed, future generation, the shame of irrelevance which globalisation may bring to the unprepared.

While globalisation promises to further our chances of improved living standards in a free world economy, the dangers of unequal competition, which that phenomenon represents as far as the developing world is concerned, must be recognised and efforts made to ameliorate the effects.

Our government and people must come together to share knowledge and experience. The spirit of sacrifice must be renewed in all of us. Leadership must return to the old quality of transparency and good example.
Let us do it for Nigeria.

Being speech delivered on the occasion of the Golden Jubilee Anniversary celebration of Boys Secondary School, Gindiri, January 2001.

Chapter 2

Globalisation and Reforms in the Telecommunications Sector

Introduction

I am glad of the opportunity to contribute my views to a forum such as this and, in particular, on the important subject of telecommunication. The place of telecommunications (telecom) in the modern economy is so pervasive that I believe it deserves more than a cursory look.

When the British Administration established the first telegraphic system in what later became Nigeria in *1895,* the purpose was to facilitate the interchange of information in the territory it controlled and to contain incursions by the competing conquering powers. This system spread rapidly to various parts of the Northern and Southern Provinces and by 1950, functional telephone exchanges had been put in place. By 1962, Nigerian External Telecommunication was established to focus on communication with the outside world. Internal communication was left to the Post and Telecommunications Department (P&T).

Unfortunately, this rapid development and the great importance of the sector seem to have waned. Otherwise, one may ask how come that, in a world that has become increasingly integrated, many of our cities are still without access to telephones. Among those that are lucky to be connected, most of them are still using rustic 18th Century analogue equipment.

Our position in the telecom ladder is, to say the least, not enviable. At the 49th position among the least developed, we are struggling with, several smaller and less endowed countries such as Mali, Zimbabwe and Morocco, for this lowly position. While the International Telecommunication Union (ITU) recommends one telephone line per 100 persons, we barely have one line to 200 persons.

The Concept of Globalisation

The concept of globalisation appears to have originated from the activities of the allied nations, following the end of World War II, to support a more open trading and investment system in the world. However, globalisation as presently used, according to Jost Delbruck (1993), is a process of denationalisation of clusters of political, economic, and social activities for the benefit of human kind. Attempts are often made to distinguish globalisation from internationalisation which Delbruck defines as cooperative activities of national actors, public or private, on a level beyond the nation-state but under its control. In other words, internationalisation is both a consequence and an appendage of the nation-state's activities aimed at improving the lot of its people. Comparatively, we find that globalisation is not necessarily targeted at the citizens of any particular nation but to mankind in general. Its benefits are more diffused.

Globalisation is, therefore, simply the denationalisation or, if you like, the decolouration of markets and activities, in such a way as to bring humanity into a sort of borderless country. The hallmark of globalisation is the removal of all artificial boundaries, in eluding somehow, sovereignties, that previously defined nations. The driving force behind globalisation has been technology of which telecommunication is a major component.

Globalisation carries with it a number of consequences for humankind. In the Wealth of Nations, Adam Smith spoke of the possibility of informed choices which would arise when there is a free flow of information. This, according to him, would happen when every buyer becomes aware of the price every seller will accept and similarly, every seller knows the price each buyer is willing to pay. If Adam Smith was speaking at our time, I believe he would have used the terms information age and globalisation. This, according to him, would lead to a more efficient use of society's limited resources. Electronically based markets are today providing traders, worldwide, with instantaneous information on such items as stocks, bonds and commodities.

With globalisation, markets will gradually become abstract terms and location no longer confers any special advantage. Nearness to markets will gradually yield place to access to information. At the hub of all these is telecommunication, reflected both in the international information superhighway and in high efficiency digital telephony.

Global Realities

There is a certain level of compulsion which globalisation emits. It imposes a compelling demand on every nation - the need to belong to the global family. It is difficult to contemplate the efficient functioning and, perhaps, survival of any nation which remains cut off from the global family. Unfortunately, the process of globalisation appears to be taking place to the exclusion of most developing countries including Nigeria. This situation is the consequence of a combination of factors including poor and corrupt leadership, lack of vision and financial constraints, among others.

The Nigerian Situation

The state of telecommunications in Nigeria, to say the least, is despicable. It might, therefore, be useful to consider a few of the notable features of the state of affairs in this vital sector of our economy, perhaps, as a guide to the needed reforms, which have become imperative in the industry.

For its nearly 120 million population, Nigeria boasts of an installed tele-network of 700,000 lines, out of which a little above 400,000 are connected by the national carrier, the Nigerian Telecommunications Limited (NITEL), whose lack of efficiency has become second to none. The situation is worse still in the mobile cellular network sub-sector. There are just 20,000 lines for the same population. To further compound matters, the technology used by the national cellular operator is the most out-of-date. Ours is the analogue system that has long since been discarded in all developed economies and in most forward-looking developing nations.

Until recently when a government statement reduced the official connection fee for a NITEL fixed line, from ₦50,000.00 to ₦20,000.00 and mobile line from ₦80,000.00 to ₦60,000.00.00, it used to cost as much as ₦150,000.00 for NITEL lines and ₦200,000.00 for mobile lines. But most observers view the price reduction as nothing short of political gimmickry. The reason being that there are no lines to meet the demand of 6 to 7 million applicants on the waiting list for NITEL lines and over 500,000 for mobile lines-a field day for market forces.

The state of affairs in the Nigerian telecom sector is not only below world standard but also depicts the country as a people who are unconcerned about the direction of world development. Many countries in the world have passed through difficult stages like this. They are now cruising on the information super-highway. We too, should get over these inadequacies but there are basic actions which are requisites for success.

The concept of deregulation is no longer esoteric to many. In Nigeria, however, it remains a difficult step to take. The telecom industry is currently going through considerable confusion, while

Nigerians' continue in their suffering, because of our half-hearted approach to deregulation. The potential of the sector, to vastly improve the fortunes of the country, have been put on hold, while conflicting signals are emitted to the world on our decision to deregulate the sector. Something has to be done urgently to bring the sector up to world standards for the many benefits it promises.

It must be understood that telephone access has ceased to be a luxury in most countries at our level of development. It has rather become a necessity both for the individual and the society.

Efficient communication has become key to the efficiency of nations because it is a liberating factor. Time is freed by instant communication thereby saving man-hours, usually lost in travelling from one location to another. Stress is reduced, health is preserved and productivity is increased.

The impact of telecommunications on resource mobilisation is tremendous. It is no wonder that our national orientation and mobilisation efforts have practically failed to change a thing. How do you re-orientate people with whom you cannot communicate? Are you even sure they know what you have embarked upon?

The importance of telecommunication is felt in all aspects of our national life -be it education, business, health and social life. For those of us that use the services of banks, have we ever stopped to ask what life was like before the introduction of on-line real-time banking, when money could only be withdrawn from the branch into which it was paid, and when money transfer used to take several weeks to materialise?

Telecommunication streamlines our daily life and helps to keep the environment friendly. The massive traffic jams around our cities are a reflection of our poverty in the telecoms sector. Something must be done. It is only in Nigeria that elders show off their mobile phones. Elsewhere, school children use them to hold conversations in their free time.

The African Telecom Think-tank led by Nigeria's Mr. Shola Taylor of INMARSTAT recently sent a memorandum to the Federal Government. In that memo, the group counselled that in order for Nigeria to improve and expand its telecommunications network, the government should initiate the following action plans:

· Roll out a policy of one million lines yearly in the next five years;
· Encourage direct foreign investment in Nigeria, in both the fixed and cellular markets, by foreign investors/operators, who have the financial strength and experience to develop the Nigerian Communications sector. These foreign investors/operators will be encouraged to team up with local investors/operators;
· Promote the provision of efficient, effective and affordable communications services for all sectors of society, including the rural communities;
· Protect the integrity and viability of public telecommunications services; and
· Develop a regulatory framework to support the achievement of the policy.

The think-tank believes that one way of redressing the situation is for the government to have a clearly defined telecom policy that sends "a strong signal to the global telecommunications community" regarding its determination to develop this growth industry.

Overall, NITEL's overwhelming presence in the industry has not helped the cause of growth in the sector. Frustration has been the lot of those private companies that have dared to come on-stream to offer commercial services.

NITEL should ordinarily serve as a rallying point for these other satellite operators. But its monopoly of telecom transactions, of both local and international traffic has, willy-nilly, created more problems than it has solved.

In 1992, the government of General Ibrahim Babangida scored a major point towards the deregulation of the economy by promulgating Decree No. 75. Although the statute could not be regarded as perfect in its entirety, its key highlight was setting up of the NCC as the flagship of the deregulation train.

Essentially established to issue licenses to operators in the sector, the NCC has so far offered licences to companies to provide various services, including private network links, internet, public mobile communication, cabling, repairs and maintenance, provision of community telephones, Very Small Aperture Terminals (V-SAT), amongst others.

But the NCC has issued more licences than the network can accommodate. In reality only a few of such licensed operators have come on-stream. The reason is that the sector is capital-intensive. The cost for terminal equipment is high; so are tariff charges. A number of factors can be blamed for the peculiarly high cost profile in the Nigerian telecom industry: NITEL's lack of commitment to reform; the somewhat ambiguous statute establishing NCC which enables it to bark without biting; inconsistent government policies that discourage foreign inflows of capital; ineffective use of frequency spectrum; use of wrong technology; and lopsided interconnectivity pacts that are heavily biased in favour of NITEL.

Tariffs are high because NITEL dictates what should be charged instead of accepting accounts settlement, as is the practice amongst global carriers like British Telecom (BT), Mercury, Vodacom, etc. under the regulatory aegis of the British Office of Telecommunications (OFTEL) established by an act of Parliament;

and in the U.S. amongst carriers like AT&T, MCI Sprint, Bell Brothers, Atlantic Bell, etc.

All these issues have so stifled progress in the sector that, since 1992, when the sector was supposedly deregulated, only five private companies have effectively opened shop with a total capacity of just 50,000 lines. This is like the proverbial drop in the ocean. No wonder then that tele-density remains very low indeed (less than one line to 200 persons as against an ITU standard of one line to 100 persons).

Ideally, NITEL should be brought under the purview of the NCC to ensure the effective reform of this vital sector and to create a level playing field in the process. Under the envisioned regime, the NCC will dictate the rules of the game and all players (NITEL inclusive) will play by these rules. This is what obtains in Britain under OFTEL and in the U.S. under the Federal Communications Commission (FCC).

It takes between ₦100,000 and ₦150,000 for a line in Nigeria, ₦25,000 in Ghana and ₦5,000 in South Africa. NITEL's famous inefficiency, which has fed on its monopoly status, is largely responsible for this sad situation. Until this behemoth is brought under the truly neutral umpire, that the NCC is supposed to be and subjected to unambiguous rules for competitive behaviour, the problem of high cost of telecom service in Nigeria will remain very much with us and, perhaps, even worsen.

Besides bringing NITEL and M-Tel under the purview of the NCC, a well thought-out reform of the sector should also be one way of bringing about efficient services. For now, NITEL and M-TEL are run as state parastatals and subject to the whims and caprices of existing government bureaucrats. So, whichever government is in power dictates to NITEL what it should do. And this includes allocating lines to public offers free of all charges at the expense of the tax payer. If there is weak legislation on how these utilities should be run, the entire economy, which depends on such infrastructure, ultimately suffers. We need a strong regime of public sector reform that will ensure that there is equity in every material particular. Above all, there should be a requisite injection of funds by institutional or strategic investors.

The matter of systems interconnectivity has remained one of the sore points in the Nigerian telecom sector. NITEL's dominance and monopolistic status has, thus far, enabled it to dictate the pace even in the interconnectivity and tariff regime. The present interconnectivity pacts have been criticised as lopsided, and biased in favour of the state monopoly, NITEL. By the pacts, private operators get only 30 per cent of their gross earnings while NITEL keeps 70 per cent. This is seen as draconian and does not give room for the survival of the smaller operators as going concerns in their own right.

The V-Sat Controversy

In May 1997, the government withdrew the international V-SAT licenses it had awarded several private companies including Systems Worldwide, and made this important telecom vehicle the exclusive preserve of NITEL. Two years earlier, Systems Worldwide had been licensed to provide this service using the Intelsat Satellite transponder and had, accordingly, entered into a technical pact with Telkom of South Africa.

Earlier in June 1997, Systems Worldwide and others lost their licenses to government order and the government blackmailed Telkorn S.A to terminate its existing contract with Systems Worldwide.

By a meeting held among NITEL, NCC and Communications Ministry officials on June 24, 1997, Systems Worldwide among others were ordered to stop offering international V-SAT services. The same applied to Omnes, and Schlumberger Company, among others.

In July 1997, the Prince Eddy Ugbodaga-led Systems Worldwide went to a Federal High Court in Lagos to challenge the government's position. The matter is still pending. Essentially, allegation of lopsidedness is rife. There are allegations that the government deliberately offered the rights to foreign stakeholders at the expense of Nigerians. If ever there is a clear example of how government policy has become investor-unfriendly, then this is it.

The Need for Reform and Consistency

Open liberalisation, consistent policies to attract foreign investors and the need to create a level playing field should become the hallmark of policy conception and implementation in this all-important sector. It is no longer a discovery that competition brings out the best in all. In this regard it will not only impact on services but also prices. If more network operators should be appointed, a privatized NITEL would be forced to compete effectively.

Privatisation is the twin brother of deregulation. These two are already working perfectly well elsewhere in the world and are, in the process, improving the lot of many nations. Through private sector initiatives, deregulation has lifted the telecommunications sector in several countries from historical decline to varying levels of compliance with the International Telecommunications Union (ITU) prescription of one telephone line to 100 persons. In Nigeria, despite being a part of the global telecom community since 1897, it has an unenviable 700,000 lines out of which only 400,000 lines are actually connected to a population of about 120 million.

This is a good reason to augment deregulation with privatisation of state-owned telecom agencies, including NITEL and M-TEL. Government thinking is that if deregulation must be made to work and a level operating environment created, NITEL and M-TEL must be privatized and brought within the ambit of those same rules governing other operators in the sector under the control of

NCC. Already, the National Council on Privatization (NCP) through the Bureau of Public Enterprises (BPE) is working to ensure a smooth privatization process for the state-owned telecom companies, including NITEL and M-TEL but the pace could be quickened.

The enabling legislation for privatization under Part I of Decree 28 of 1999 states in section 2 (1) that: "subject to the provisions of Section 1 1(F) of this Decree, an offer for the sale of the shares of a public enterprise shall be by public issue or private placement as the case may be". This may be made to Nigerians via the capital market [section 2 (2)]. Part 3 of the Decree establishes the BPE and prescribes its functions to include, amongst others:

- Implementing council's policy on privatization; and
- Preparing public enterprises approved by the Council for privatization.

A new Telecommunications Policy prescribes for four digital mobile cellular companies to be licensed by public auction on or before December 5, 2000. These companies are expected to deploy a minimum of 300,000 lines each, in 24 months. All attention is currently, therefore, focused on this magic date in December when the industry is expected to take the important first step toward freeing itself from years of bureaucratic shackles in the telecom sector.

The ambition of the government is to ensure that no fewer than 1.2 mobile lines are available by 2002. This will augment almost two million landlines within the same period. The policy equally prescribes a level playing field for all operators and strengthens NCC to enable it the play the requisite oversight role in this growth sector. The policy is technology neutral; thus putting paid to the controversy over whether the standard technology should be the Global System of Mobile Communication (GSM) a Pan European standard or the American Standard Code Division Multiple Access (CDMA). It may be necessary to mention here some of the features of the GSM.

Global System of Mobile Communication (GSM)

* GSM is a well developed standard supported by around 400 operators from *150* countries and used by in excess of 340 million users world wide. With this state of development both in the technical and operational standards, incremental costs for new products and services are at an all time low due to infrastructure and terminal economies of scale. Furthermore, the pace of leading edge developments within the standard means that the practical quality and speed of deployment are maintaining GSM as a competitive technology, despite newer technological developments.

* GSM is an open standard, covering interfaces between the major switching and radio network components, as well as the air interface to the customer. The open nature of the standard means that many vendors can develop systems without the need to pay prohibitive royalties (IS-95 is commercially owned), resulting in more vendor competition and consequent choice and lower pricing for operators. Open and standardised interfaces also mean that an operator can attach network elements from one supplier to those from another supplier. In practice, this means that an operator can go out to tender for a new supplier at any time, forcing prices lower (with CDMA, the operator is stuck with the same supplier and consequently its pricing).

* International roaming is integral to the GSM design with bills sent back to the home operator. The GSM Association standardises all this and operators in 150 countries have agreements with each other for roaming (this capability is only now becoming available in some form with CDMA and the number of countries is very limited because the CDMA footprint is very limited).

* Smartcard based identification of the customer offers an important level of security, thus largely avoiding unauthorised use of a phone.

All licensed operators have a flexible choice in deploying technology, in line with their individual strategies. After several failed attempts in the past to get started on the liberalisation route, the open bid/auction process has emerged as the only logical option to guarantee rapid progress in the sector.

Let me add at this point, that government should take bold steps to encourage indigenous participation in the cellular telephone business. I believe one way of doing this is to make a clear distinction between network operators and service operators. In my view, license holders and service operators should be separated to encourage local participation.

The Need for a Regulator

There is certainly no doubt that the industry needs a strong regulator. To propose otherwise would be preposterous in view of the strategic nature of telecom and its pervasive influence on the society. However, regulation must be distinguished from control. The regulator is basically concerned with making sure that licensees comply with the terms of their licenses. Its responsibilities include the prevention of unethical practices such as collusion against consumers. The regulator ensures that things are done professionally by the operators by establishing guidelines, policies and procedures and making these known to all concerned. It imposes sanctions for breach of procedure and maintains a level-playing field in the industry. The purpose of regulation is not price control or tariff determination.

A Global Growth Industry

Opportunities abound in the Nigerian telecom sector as it is said to potentially command about 20 per cent of the African market. This is an enormous attraction to foreign as well as local investors. With such a large market potential coupled with a telecom-hungry population, there is a great deal of opportunities for investors.

While Nigeria is inching towards the auction for the second generation of mobile phones (G2), the global trend will alter significantly beginning from 2002 in favour of the Universal Mobile Telecommunication Systems (UMTS) known as the third generation (or 3G). The 3G is an improvement on the GSM, and will take-off in year 2002 in Germany, Italy (2003), Netherlands, Belgium and Britain (2002), and Ireland (2004).

The GSM providers club already has 369 members in 137 countries and the membership will definitely increase in the coming years. At its conference last February in Istanbul (Turkey), the ITU proclaimed UMTS the global standard for the future. Since then, Germany, through the auction process, licensed six companies and raised over £30 billion in the process. What this clearly means is that the opportunities are not only for private sector investors governments also stand to reap huge financial gains from the opening up of the telecom sector.

Alliances are, therefore, being struck in several parts of the globe in recognition of this singular fact.

Only recently, regulatory authorities in West Africa established the West African Telecom Regulatory Association (WATRA) to harmonise their plans for a telecom network of the West Africa sub-region. Investment in the sector being capital intensive and since government cannot do it alone; it must enlist the private sector to align with it.

Only recently, NITEL rolled out a four-year investment plan whereby about five million lines will be added to its current capacity. The expected total capital expenditure for this project is put at N625 billion, to be provided through contractor-financing, the Build Operate and Transfer (BOT) option and through loans. Citibank of New York is leading a consortium of banks to source the requisite credit while Siemens AG of Germany is handling the BOT aspect of the plan. This ambitious plan, if successfully implemented, will help to correct the grave shortfall in telecommunication services in the country.

Telecommunications remain the major catalyst for the transformation of human societies into one big global village. Failure to be a part of this global village could spell doom for the unfortunate country that excludes itself. The political, social and economic future of any nation in today's world is hinged on the existence of a universal, efficient, and modern telecommunication infrastructure supporting inexpensive and high quality service. To succeed as an individual, corporate body or nation state, people and machines must be able to exchange information quickly and accurately. This is the imperative of reform in our telecom industry.

The Future of the Nigerian Telecom Sector

At present, Nigeria's telecommunications infrastructure and services is not up to the universal standard. It is not efficient and it is not modern. The service is expensive and of low quality. However, this is the challenge for those wishing to participate in the Nigerian telecommunications industry. The prospects and opportunities for potential investors are indeed great, especially with a population of over 100 million, abundance of human and natural resources, and a new democratic order.

Already, the Federal Government is showing encouraging signs that appreciates the importance of telecommunication to national growth and development. In this regard, a revised National Telecommunications Policy (NTP), that will soon be released, is expected to set the pace, and give direction and purpose to the expansion and modernisation of telecommunication networks and services in Nigeria.

The possible future of telecommunications in Nigeria can best be envisioned from the short (3years) and medium (5years) objectives of the NTP.

The objectives include the following:

i) To implement network development projects that will ensure the country meets up with and exceeds the ITU recommended minimum tele-density of 1 telephone to 100 inhabitants. Government intends to provide a minimum of 2 million fixed lines and 1.2 million mobile lines in the next 2 years.

ii) To develop and enhance endogenous capacity in telecommunications technology by establishing a National Institute of Telecommunication (NIT).

iii) To ensure that the government divests its official interest in the state-owned telecommunications entities.

iv) To promote competition to meet growing demand, through the opening of the market to additional National Carriers.

v) To ensure that all telecommunications operators are brought under the control of the regulatory authority.

vi) To ensure that telephone facilities are brought to within 5km distance from any community.

vii) To create the enabling environment, including the provision of incentives that shall attract investors and experts, among others.

These objectives are laudable but to join the global village, Nigeria must come out of the doldrums of a poor nation status. We must work our way back to international regard. This would require our embarking on a serious growth path within the region of 5 -6 per cent per annum. And we are capable of doing this if we address some of the following requirements:

(i)   Pursuit of sound fiscal and monetary policies which guarantee little or no budgetary deficit and, by extension, keeps inflation low;

(ii)   A well developed and stable financial system;

(iii)   A commitment to private sector leadership of the economy in a highly deregulated setting;

(iv)   Enthronement of due process and the abandonment of discretion and arbitrariness in public policy;

(v)   Pursuit of the rule of law and the sanctity of contracts; and

(vi)   Security of life and property.

Conclusion

I would like to say that the future of telecommunications in Nigeria is indeed very bright. Some areas that should be of interest to investors would include (but are not limited to) the following:

* Capacity building, training and development of core competences in regulatory functions;
* Advisory and consulting services in the deregulation of the telecommunications industry, global trends and the convergence of information, communications and broadcasting technologies;
* Increasing the capacity of basic telephone services and lowering of rates;
* Increasing the number of public pay-phones particularly in the rural areas;

* Provision of more value added services such as Voice Mail, Operator Assistance, Billing Assistance and Verification Confirmation, etc.

* Introduction and implementation of new technologies that will add value to national development such as Internet related services (e-business, e-services, e-commerce, etc), Voice Over Internet Protocol (VOIP), Digital Subscriber Lines (DSL), Integrated Services Digital Network (ISDN), 3rd Generation Mobile Systems) etc.

* Satisfying the telecommunication needs of business, particularly in the area of data and multi-media applications

* Human Resource Development in the management, operations and maintenance of telecommunication networks and services

* Manufacturing and assembly of telecommunication equipment, components

* Setting up research and development facilities

All these areas and more require huge investments and should offer the investor commensurate returns on his investment.

Being paper presented at the Forum on Nigeria Telecom: Investment Opportunities and Challenges, October/November 2000.

Chapter 3

Taking Nigeria to the World:
The Builders' Analogy

Let me begin by confessing that I like the way good construction companies set out to do their work at building sites. They begin by shielding the site from unauthorised interference. They also deploy appropriate scaffolding as enablers. I am told that in addition to security, construction companies shield their sites to prevent the public from exhibiting a *déjà vu* attitude about the building when the facade is eventually removed. Yet, despite this 'shielding' from the public, builders allow stakeholders – owners, suppliers, creditors, sub-contractors, city officials – access to sites

Now, taking a country to the world is somewhat like construction. A nation needs to get its acts right, its scaffolding and infrastructure appropriate and its governance to be in sync with the rest of the world. Like construction, it is not being suggested that the nation has to shut itself from the rest of the world while getting its acts right. Rather, while building the nation, stakeholders – citizens, trading partners, investors and the like – are allowed access to the economy.

I would like to suggest that getting five related areas right are necessary conditions in taking Nigeria to the world. These areas, to my mind, are - education, agriculture, infrastructure, governance and appropriate branding.

In today's knowledge economy, Nigeria needs to aggressively and innovatively pursue an educational agenda that will sustain the present achievements, equip the citizenry to compete in a globalised world and prepare future generations for leadership. Such an educational agenda needs to focus on science and technology, especially Information Communications Technology (ICT), which connects the world into a global village and drives innovation and productivity. This educational agenda must emphasise applied research and medical sciences to combat diseases and aid agriculture. On this score, the current educational system which is forcing many young Nigerians to seek education outside Nigeria does a lot of disservice because many of these young people do not settle in Nigeria to contribute to development. Whereas they might remit funds back home, their knowledge is largely lost to the economy.

The current world food crisis has, once more, drawn international attention to the fact that a nation that cannot feed itself cannot lead in a sustainable manner. We now know that countries can and have refused to export their agricultural commodities such that a nation that is a net importer of food is at great risk. Food security, it must be emphasised, exists when all people, at all times, have physical and economic access to sufficient, safe and nutritious food to meet their dietary needs and food preferences for an active and healthy lifestyle'.

To achieve food security in Nigeria, there is a need for a new agricultural policy that will lead to increased yields per acre through an appropriate combination of human, mechanical and agricultural inputs; that will enhance modernisation of storage and processing; and enthrone efficient markets for agricultural produce.

The role of infrastructure in economic growth and development can no longer be over emphasised. It is now well documented that the adequacy of infrastructure helps to determine one country's success and another's failure in diversifying production, expanding trade, coping with population growth, reducing poverty, or improving environmental conditions.

The current situation where only 30 per cent of Nigerians have access to electricity; where Nigeria's road network falls below that of other emerging market; where Nigerian ports are comparatively inefficient and where railways contribute to only 1 per cent of transport, collectively impair Nigeria's development. It is, therefore, gratifying to note that the government has infrastructure in its seven-point agenda. It is equally noteworthy that Public Private Partnerships (PPP) would be adopted in the provision and management of infrastructure in Nigeria.

The point being made is that, if Nigeria gets these acts right, we would be in a pole position in competing with the rest of the world for investment, export and leadership. In investments for instance, investors go where government is stable, where infrastructure is adequate and where local labour is cheap but skilful. For export, good education is a *sine qua non* for producing goods and services that are globally competitive. For instance, there are about 2,000 Indian firms in the United Kingdom alone. These companies are known to provide employment for Indians, provide huge remittances back to India thereby enabling mutually rewarding synergy between the United Kingdom and India.

When these areas are right, branding Nigeria becomes easier and believable. And, following our builders' analogy, it would be easier to remove the façade, dismantle the scaffolding and invite the rest of the world to appreciate brand Nigeria. It must be noted that, besides being brands, countries can also be products, particularly when they serve as tourist destinations or factory sites. In many cases, the country brand must serve as an umbrella, in much the same way that a good firm serves as an umbrella brand for all of its subsidiaries. Once an umbrella brand concept, that is unitary and clear, is established, states and local governments can go their merry separate ways within it, without the risk of inconsistent messaging. I believe that achieving this will take a lot of doing. There might be a steep learning curve and, therefore, a great need to devise approaches for coordinating within and across diverse constituents.

Finally and most importantly, it must be reiterated that good governance would be the driving force in taking Nigeria to the world. Good governance will produce good elections and will fight and reduce corruption. Good governance will implement an appropriate education agenda, and ensure food security and infrastructure development in an open, transparent and accountable manner. In all, good governance will breed confidence in Nigerians to engage with the rest of the world.

Part II

Managing the Nigerian Economy

Managing the Nigerian Economy

Good political governance has been adjudged the major difference between development and underdevelopment; between economic growth and stagnation or decline, and between enabling and constraining policies. Whereas good governance fosters growth and corporate development, poor governance stifles the national economy and, *ipso facto*, weakens industries, corporations and the citizens.

The low performance of Nigeria's economy over the years is ultimately attributable to poor governance. Perhaps, the best way to assess governance is through the budgetary process and implementation thereof (at the political governance level) and the role of the private sector (at the corporate governance level).

Since the return to democratic rule in 1999, three issues have been quite dominant in political economic management. First, there is the challenge of budget processes and implementation of the annual appropriation acts. Whereas, during military regimes, budgets were largely annual rituals that were handed down by the dictatorship of the day, budgeting under the new dispensation should be more open, democratic and accountable. This proposition is borne out of the notion of separation of powers and checks and balances, which enjoin the legislature to enact laws (including appropriation, with attendant oversight roles); the executive to implement enacted laws and the judiciary to adjudicate and interpret laws should there be conflict between the first two arms of government. Also, under a democracy, it will be imagined that the fourth estate of the realm (the media) will play a more active role in the budget process by fearlessly appraising good performances and exposing infractions of the Appropriation Act.

The second issue that has engendered great controversy in the last several years is the role of government as an enabler versus direct engagement in the production of goods and services through state-owned enterprises (SOEs). Following consistently poor performances by SOEs and suspension by the Abacha regime of 1994 to 1998, privatisation was reinstated as a tool for economic management in the year 2000. The 1999 Privatisation and Commercialisation Act is quite comprehensive as it provides for the reform and divestiture of government interests in virtually all sectors of the economy – manufacturing, services (banking, insurance, tourism), the downstream oil sector, telecommunications, power, transport and associated infrastructure, etc.

The third issue, that has assumed paramount importance since the return to democratic rule and in an era of divestiture of government interests in SOEs, is the role of the private sector as a major driver of economic growth and development.

Part II of this book, appropriately dubbed "*Managing the Nigerian Economy*", examines these three issues under four interrelated headings:
·   Budgeting as a tool for economic growth and development
·   The effects of the 2001 budget on commerce and industry
·   Privatisation, economic growth and technology transfer
·   The role of the private sector in economic development.

Chapter 4

Budgeting:
Tool for Economic Development and Growth

Introduction

Between 1970 and 2000 Nigeria earned about $350 billion from the export of mainly crude oil. This income is mainly supposed to be used for economic and social development programmes and for investment in the development of other non-oil sectors so as to diversify the income base of the economy. Most economic commentators believe that only about 40 per cent of this sum is today represented tangibly on the ground as programmes and projects put in place to benefit the ordinary citizen of the country. The bulk of the country's foreign exchange earnings ended up as either:

    a.   Abandoned white elephant projects or

    b.   Misappropriated by private citizens and some companies.

It is to be noted that the income earned was well budgeted for use in the execution of various projects and programmes. The problem is that our budgeting process is so weak that we are yet to get any closer to our long-term economic development goals. Most people blame the military establishment for the failure to realise the dreams of our budgets, as there were not enough checks and balances in the system. However, could this failure still be possible in a democratic setting where budgets are debated openly by the representatives of the people who are also responsible for monitoring to ensure full implementation?

Nigeria still has quite some way to go if budget implementation and monitoring operations are to make any meaningful impact on national economic development. In spite of years of planning and annual budgeting, oil still remains the prime mover of the Nigerian economy. The economic base is still import- oriented; the industrial and technological infrastructure is still weak. The economy is still largely public sector-led. And the national currency is yet to stabilise. To address this problem, the government adopted market-oriented policies that seek to place the private sector as the engine of economic growth. Consequently, it is not the role of government to impose any development project for the country. The role of government is to provide a vision for the country, which reflects the national aspirations of all the citizens, and to provide an enabling environment for private sector growth. The budget is then used to fashion policies and programmes that will lead to the realization of the vision. The budget is thus an implementation tool that guides the private sector as to the direction the government wishes the economy to follow.

The State of the Nigerian Economy Today

To put our discussion in proper perspective, it will be beneficial to start by reviewing the performance of the national economy in the year 2000. Despite the improvement in oil revenues, the economy continued to perform below the budgetary expectations. The key performance indicators reveal the following:

Growth in real GDP remained sluggish at 2.8 per cent, compared with the target 3.0 per cent for the 2001 year and the 7.0 per cent minimum required in order to reverse the poverty trend.

Although some macroeconomic indicators showed marginal improvements relative to 1999, the overall performance of the real sector continued to fall below potential, as persistent structural bottlenecks constrained output and employment growth.

Monetary policy targets could not be met owing largely to expansionary fiscal operations with resultant strain on domestic prices. In particular, against a projected Broad Money (M2) growth of 14.6 per cent, a growth rate of 38.8 per cent was recorded.

The inflation rate remained largely subdued but its acceleration from 0.9 per cent in June 2000 to an estimated 7.5 per cent in December 2000 should be a matter of great concern.

The pressure on the balance of payments abated developments in the international petroleum market surplus, while gross external reserves rose to US$9.4 billion in December 2000. Substantially, as a result, the current account recorded a surplus from US$5.4 billion in December 1999 to US $9.4 billion in December 2000.

The foreign exchange market, however, remained persistently under pressure, reflecting the effect of excessive growth in demand for imported goods and services.

Overall, economic growth has not resumed, the level of unemployment has remained high, manufacturing capacity utilisation remained low at 34.8 per cent (34.6 per cent in December 1999) and non-oil export receipts continued to be low.

One of the major reasons for our failure to improve the economy is our failure to develop and/or adhere to an economic policy that will guide our budgeting process. To fully appreciate this problem, we need to review our efforts in planning for our national development and its linkages with the budgetary process.

History of National Economic Development Plans in Nigeria

The preparation of National Economic Development Plan started well before independence. A summary of these efforts is as follows:

1946-1956   First National Development Plan

1955- 1960   Revision of FNDP to accommodate Regional
Plans

1960- 1990   Four Development Plans implemented

1990- 1997   National Rolling Plan introduced: 15-20 years

1998- 1999   Perspective Plan combined with a 3-year Rolling
          Plan

1998 -1999   Vision 2010 launched and its implementation
          started with the 1998 budget.

1999   The 1999-2003 Nigerian Economic Policy and the
          Obasanjo Economic Direction launched.

The Vision 2010 is a formalisation of the Perspective Plan with
each annual budget being a step toward its realization. It analysed
the socioeconomic and political position of the country and clearly
states the target socioeconomic and political position by the year
2010 and then gives the strategies and policies that will lead to
the realisation of these dreams. All our medium term plans and
budgets are supposed to be drawn from the Vision. However,
policy inconsistency and political expediency have not allowed
for continuity in government programmes. For example, the 1999-
2003 Nigerian Economic Policy and the Obasanjo Economic
Direction were Rolling Plans that do not claim any relationship
with the Vision 2010 or any Perspective Plan. Thus the global
direction is not clear.

Vision 2010 and its Linkage with Development Plans and Budget

The Vision provides focus and inspiration for all future plans; be
it long term, medium (rolling) or short term (including annual
budgets). These have to be linked and harmonised with one another
at all levels. The imperatives of effective coordination and

monitoring of the vision require the following relationships to be sustained:

a. The perspective plan should be adapted in line with the objectives, strategies and action plans of the Vision.
b. The Rolling Plan should be based on the Vision and the Perspective Plan.
c. The annual budgets should be based on the Vision, the Perspective Plan and the Rolling Plan.
d. The Private Sector, NGOs and IGOs should also base their plans and programmes on the main thrust of the Vision, the Perspective Plan and the budget.
e. Policy and programme formulation, implementation, monitoring and evaluation should be co-coordinated and done appropriately in collaboration with relevant stakeholders as much as possible.

Coordination and monitoring to ensure that our budgets are in line with the long- term vision is the responsibility of the legislature.

The Role of the National Assembly in Making the Budget an Effective Tool for Economic Development

The role of the legislature does not start after the budget speech. The legislature must be involved in the pre-budget consultation, in reviewing the budget and more importantly in monitoring and controlling its implementation. We take these roles one after another.

Pre-budget consultations

The legislature must on continuous basis be getting performance reports from its committees and also other monitoring organs of government. This will place it in a better position to attend to any submission from the executive for a budget review and also for the consideration of the next budget.

For an effective coordination of the budget implementation process the legislature should engage in consultations with various interest groups and citizens on ways of reducing budget variances.

Some of these groups include the Nigerian Economic Summit Group, the organised private sector, the National Economic Intelligence Committee and National Planning Commission.

The legislature should also learn to be pro-active. It should consider submitting its own report on the implementation of the previous budget, which can be a guide to the Executive in preparing the next budget. This will make the budget deliberations easier and more focused, since the executive now has some insights into the thinking of the legislature even before budget submission.

Deliberation on the Budget Speech

The budget speech is a bold statement of government plans, policies and projected performance indicating the direction of government policy, thinking, in line with the long-term expectations of the nation. The speech is the most important part of the budget since the estimates are just the quantification of the projects and programmes outlined in it. The legislature should spend more time deliberating on the speech because any change to the policies and programmes automatically changes the estimates. In its deliberation, the National Assembly should ensure that:

    (i)   Government's own assessment of the performance of the economy of the preceding year is realistic. This budget performance must be supported by a variance analysis showing actual performance against anticipated goals.

    (ii)   The main thrust and objectives of the current year budget are realistic and in line with the Vision of the nation.

(iii)   The special programmes and projects slated for the current year are in accordance with the Rolling Plan and Vision of the nation.

(iv)   The financial position of government is in line with the targets set for the year.

(v)   The fiscal, monetary and banking policies for the current year can adequately lead to the realisation of the budget objectives.

Reviewing the Budget Estimates

The budget estimates are supposed to fully reflect the budget objectives, government priorities and socioeconomic policies as contained in the budget speech. Most often the budget objectives, projects and programmes are influenced by political considerations, thus contradicting the prudence, sacrifice and discipline needed in achieving fiscal and monetary policy objectives of the same budget. For example, a budget that intends to reduce inflation should not be expansionary, while one that intends to reduce unemployment should be expansionary. Hence, it will be contradictory, as we have always been doing, to have both reduction of inflation and unemployment as budget objectives simultaneously.

After deliberating on the budget speech the legislature should review the revenue and expenditure estimates to ensure that:

a)   The revenue projections are realistic.

b)   The projects and programmes are properly priced and not based on guesswork estimates or the rule of thumb.

c)   Current liabilities and existing commitments/obligations of government are properly provided for.

d)   The expected outputs and results of the projects and programmes are clearly specified.

Legislative Approval

The annual budget is a control tool for the legislature over the executive and for the Chief Executive over his subordinates. The NASS is vested under the law with the ultimate power of approving and passing the Budget bill into an Appropriation Act. The legislature may alter materially the proposal submitted. The legislature, being the watchdog over public funds, should exercise its powers to:

a) Ensure that the budget is in line with long-term national goals as contained in the national vision. As a prelude to the budget, the vision and long-term goals should be debated and approved by the NASS.

b) Debate and agree on budget policies and programmes to ensure that only the best emerges in terms of development targets, projected programmes and operational policies. This debate will usually follow party philosophy, development targets, agreed programme priorities.

c) Audit revenue and expenditure estimates,

d) Query allocations, and

e) Approve the budget and pass it into the Appropriation Act.

The Appropriation Act passed by the legislature is a contract entered into with the executive, which must be implemented in both a legal and efficient manner. Thus, the duty of the Executive is to ensure that accounting systems are put in place to prevent misapplication of assets and illegal expenditure, ensure use of proper methods and procedures, and also ensure executive control of rates of expenditure and purposes of expenditure. On the other hand, the duty of the legislature is to monitor implementation to ensure that this contract is not breached. The presence of legislative checks and controls is the main difference between a democratic system and a dictatorship hence, unchecked breaches of the Appropriation Act indicates either the presence of dictatorial tendencies or abdication of statutory responsibility by the legislature or both.

Post-budget Monitoring and Control

The budget is a working document, which should guide the activities of government. Being a law, the government should keep track of its performance so as to minimise variance. Hence, if the variance between budget expectations and the actual performance is getting wider, reviews will become necessary. In an ideal case, the government should ensure quarterly reviews of performance and appropriate amendments to the budget. However, effective and efficient budget monitoring can be greatly facilitated by the following factors:

a) The monitoring system should be timely, comprehensive, simple, routine and corrective.

b) Few agencies are used with a proper allocation of well specified responsibilities. For example, the National Planning Commission should provide reports based on actual government expenditure and revenues; the National Economic Intelligence Agency should provide intelligence reports to enable proper determination of the quality of the government analysis as presented by the NPC; the National Assembly should ensure that the NPC and the NEIC submit not only timely but also true and fair reports, which are supported by the constituency reports.

c) There must be wide public enlightenment on public projects in order to mobilise all stakeholders to be involved in informal monitoring and reporting.

d) There must be a strong and demonstrable political willingness at the topmost government levels to take the necessary corrective actions, dictated by the results of monitoring.

For the National Assembly to really appreciate the task of monitoring the implementation of our national budgets, I wish to briefly outline some of the major reasons why past efforts have failed and map out new strategies to address them.

Reasons Why Budgets Fail To Bring About Economic Growth

Despite the seemingly simple budget process, our past efforts in mapping out our economic development plans have not yielded much dividend. For years the key objectives have remained elusive. These include:

a) Enhancing capacity utilisation in agriculture, manufacturing and mining industries.

b) Encouraging diversification of foreign exchange earnings through increased export activities.

c) Reduction of inflation, unemployment and stabilisation of the exchange rate.

d) Provision of incentives for attracting foreign direct investment.

Our failure to achieve these objectives is strong evidence against the efficacy of our budgets as tools of economic development. The reasons for these are not far- fetched: the general conclusion, in assessing past development planning efforts, is that the plans were largely in the right direction, but the implementation was often faulty, monitoring weak and evaluation poor. The major causes for this situation include the following:

* Linkage failures: Except in 1998 and 1999, our budgets were hardly drawn from any Vision or Perspective Plan.
* Overemphasis on expenditure allocation rather than revenue generation.
* Overemphasis on politically motivated projects rather that economically viable ones.

* Overindulgence in projects that could best be handled by the private sector.
* Lack of focus on the creation of an enabling environment for private sector growth.
* Poor work ethics: The culture of productivity, patriotism and excellence are nonexistent in the thinking of the average Nigerian worker.
* Corruption and Leadership crisis: Leaders failed to lead by example. Hence the followers feel cheated, used and abused, leading to a situation where both the leaders and the led are busy sabotaging all development efforts.
* Poor and untimely budget monitoring reports.

Strategies for Effective Control of Budget Implementation

Control involves monitoring and regulating government activities so that they accord with the expectations established in the plans, policies and targets. The whole responsibility for performance or failure of the budget lies primarily on the NASS. However, effective control of the implementation of the budget requires the commitment of all citizens. Below we suggest some strategies that the NASS should adopt in order to succeed in this task.

The Need for a New Budget Culture:

There are two types of budget: The political budget and the rational budget.

Rational Budget:

a) Starts with the vision.
b) Locates current performance within the vision and notes variance against the desired performance targets.
c) Notes constraints/problems that led to negative variances and fashion out mitigating strategies.

d) Draw up budget policies, programmes and projects that will meet performance targets given the constraints that are being faced.

e) Programme Performance Budgeting System (PPBS).

f) Compute budget estimates, using established cost standards with emphasis on project and programme performance to obtain maximum efficiency.

g) Set timetable for evaluating budget plans and reappraisal of programmes, projects and budget targets and strategies.

Political Budget

a)   Starts with the status quo.

b)   Draw up budget policies, programmes and projects that seek to improve the status quo. This is done through political bargaining and horse-trading with other interest groups.

c)   Assign budget estimates.

In practice, the budget is a political document that has been influenced by rational economic considerations. However, in the long run, economic realities do prevail over political considerations. It is, therefore, recommended that economics not politics should be the basic rationale for embarking on government projects and programmes. Our past failure to approach budgeting from the rational economic perspective is what led to the litany of uncompleted political projects throughout the country. Political projects always suffer abandonment when there is a change in either the decision makers or change in their personal priorities.

Sharpening Budget Monitoring and Implementation Procedures

For long, we have had the Financial Regulations, Financial Instructions and Financial Memoranda, which provide the basis for budget implementation and monitoring. However, these have been taken as mere procedures. Very little attention is paid to using them to achieve the objectives of government. There is a need for:

a) More rigorous monitoring process for every government project and programme.

b) Clearer cost standards and properly defined standards for acceptable performance.

c) An effective orientation that ensures that projects fulfil not only the objective for which they are set up, but also complement the long-term goals of government.

In short, government needs to borrow a leaf from the international agencies that operate in the country. These agencies have rigid standards of monitoring and evaluation of projects and programmes. For example, the programme Management Module of the UNDP clearly sets out an efficient process for monitoring and assessing the progress made in implementing projects and programmes.

Strengthening the Institutional Monitoring Processes

The National Planning Commission is the government organ charged with the responsibility of, among other things, formulating, preparing, monitoring and coordinating the long, medium, and short-term national development plans. Recently, the National Economic Intelligence Committee and the Nigerian Vision have been established to complement the duties of the NPC. Between them, these bodies should be in a position to unearth any uneconomic costing of projects, wasteful spending of public funds, and unsubstantiated claims to the completion of projects. NEIC should be strengthened and equipped to operate more like an underground intelligence outfit, sufficiently ubiquitous to ensure that all government projects and programmes are fully and effectively executed. The NCNV should be the main agency to promote and coordinate the implementation and monitoring of the Vision, in collaboration with other appropriate government agencies and the private sector.

Furthermore, bodies such as the CBN, FOS, Ministry of Finance and NASS Public Accounts Committees should publish monthly, quarterly and half-yearly reports, to highlight the extent to which budget expectations have been met. These organisations should be allowed to freely and independently report on government performance lest they be turned into some kind of propaganda structures.

Sustaining Greater Accountability and Transparency

For the budgetary process to be effective there should be transparency and accountability. This can only be ensured if:

a) There is openness in government structure and functions.

b) The dividing line between public and private domains is clearly evident.

c) There is free access to public information, such as periodic statements of public accounts, policies and targets, so that every interested person can appraise government performance against budget statements.

d) There are fora where key government officials, financial market operators, industrialists, academicians and other stakeholders will meet, from time to time, to brainstorm on major economic and social policies and programmes. In this regard, we note the fora created by the Nigeria Economic Summit, the CBN Monetary policy Forum, etc.

Developing a Culture of Productivity and Proper Work Ethics

Government can encourage a culture of productivity and excellence in the Nigerian worker by taking the following measures:

a) Demonstrate clear commitment to the development of human capital in the country through investment in education, skill acquisition and training.

b) Introduce welfare schemes, tax relief, etc in order to improve the purchasing power of citizens and improve on our misery index.

c) Provide workers with the requisite materials, machinery and funds needed to be productive, and, thereafter, set rigid standards of performance.

d) Prop up the Nigerian middle class through a deliberate policy of wage enhancement and properly rationalised material incentives. The middle class, which is the backbone of the Nigerian economy, is currently non-existent.

Refocus on Growth and Development

Government should continue to pursue the following growth inducing programmes:

a) Creation of an enabling environment by improving the nation's infrastructure. This will stimulate the formal private sector to greater and sustained investment for growth and development.

b) Maintenance of fiscal and monetary policy stability.

c) Provision of long-term funds and research support for small and medium scale industries.

d) Provision of data bank to aid project take-off, project financing, project implementation and project monitoring.

e) Reallocation of public spending towards priority areas, such as health, education, and essential infrastructure.

Conclusion

Most commentators, on the past performance of our economy, blamed the military for all its failures. The main basis for this conclusion is that, by its nature, military government lacks checks and balances. Commentators have recommended a quick return to democratic rule, in which the National Assembly, comprising patriotic representatives of the people, will over-see government activities and hence ensure the attainment of our national goals.

The successful implementation of the budget is a major concern of the National Assembly. However, a proper approach to monitoring and controlling budget implementation is the key to addressing this concern. Poor monitoring and evaluation of budget implementation caused past failures. We have not only identified the reasons for poor budget monitoring but also suggested some strategies, which the National Assembly should use to improve the situation.

Lastly, the obvious way forward is for the National Assembly to consider, immediately, the two major issues raised in this paper:

1. Revisit and, if possible, review the Vision 2010 report and use it as the basis for reviewing the 1999-2003 Economic Direction (Rolling Plan). Budget preparation and evaluation should then be based on the Rolling Plan.
2. Re-examine and re-assign roles to the National Planning Commission and the National Economic Intelligence Committee and, where necessary, provide them with all the resources needed for them to effectively and efficiently provide all the information the National Assembly requires to facilitate its budget monitoring and control efforts.

As Chief Inspectors of banks and other financial institutions, you should rise up to the challenges and prepare yourselves for the 21st Century IT applications. This can only be achieved by continually updating your skills in the dynamic world of Information Technology and, also, by creating awareness among yourselves of the threats associated with Electronic Commerce.

I feel for you. While your part of the world is still battling to understand the sources and causes of the first Industrial Revolution, you are being called upon to fight crime on the Information Superhighway. I am, however, encouraged by your past achievements. I know you are equal to the task. You will surely succeed.

---

[1] *Being a paper presented at the Senate Retreat held in Calabar, Cross River State in February, 2001.*

Chapter 5

Budget 2001:
The Effect on Commerce And Industry

Introduction

After our economy has been in the doldrums for so long, the desire of every Nigerian is for the country to attain a sustainable economic development. Our National Budget is, no doubt, an important tool for achieving this desire. However, government budgets have let us down in the recent past when the act of budgeting was seen as a ritual or ceremony, without any serious commitment to the implementation of budgetary policies. In fact, under the military, there was usually a misplaced priority in extra-budgetary expenditure, which was seen as a more attractive spending mode than the budget itself. Now that we are in a democracy, more emphasis is placed on budgets to determine the economic direction of the government. It is for this reason that we are here today to review the Budget 2001 and analyse its expected impact on Nigerian Commerce and Industry.

I would like to say that the road to sustainable development, in a public sector- dominated economy like ours, is slow and very challenging. This is because economic development requires policies that will rapidly lead to fiscal discipline at all levels of governance. In particular, these policies must enable the government to curb its urge to spend its revenues on non-socially benefiting projects. In fact, the government needs to shift its focus, from activities that the private sector can perform more efficiently, to those that will facilitate the private sector involvement.

The preparation of this year's budget seems to be based on the stated principle, as the President indicated in his budget proposal to the National Assembly that the government will:

- Continue to address the bottlenecks that increase the cost of doing business; and
- Provide incentives for the private sector to be the leading engine of growth through increased investments.

Accordingly, he expressed the hope that the budget will pave the way for revamping the productive sector.

My task in this presentation, therefore, is to examine the extent to which this year's budget will achieve the expressed objectives. In doing this, I will highlight the prevailing situation, as well as the challenges, in Nigerian Commerce and Industry. Next, I will discuss the key issues the Government needs to address to set the economy, especially commerce and industry, on the recovery path, and the measures proposed in the budget to address these issues.

State of Commerce and Industry

For an economy to achieve sustainable development, its commercial and industrial sectors must be very vibrant. In recent times, economic growth is often measured in terms of industrial output as well as the commercial activities of an economy. For most developed economies, industrial contribution (mainly manufacturing) to Gross Domestic Product (GDP) averaged about 40 per cent, while in most developing economies, it contributes dismally to GDP. This is also the case with Nigeria, where our non-oil industry (manufacturing) is currently prostrate, operating at about 34 per cent capacity utilisation and contributing a dismal 5.5 per cent to the nation's GDP. Our economy is mono-culturally based on oil (and recently gas) as the main source of government revenue. Oil (and gas) contributes between 70 per cent and 90 per cent of the federal government's collectible revenue. At this juncture, the question that comes to mind is what are the problems facing our non-oil industry?

The bane of the industry is the lack of infrastructural support from - such as electricity, water, communication and transportation. For instance:

* The power outage ratio is over 60 per cent nationwide, while in the Lagos area alone, it is over 75 per cent. Companies have to rely on generators for power supply.
* Water corporations have become grossly inefficient to the extent that water supply for industrial use is currently about 25 per cent. Virtually every company has its internal source of water supply, i.e. boreholes.
* The communications sector is also riddled with many problems, ranging from obsolete equipment to massive corruption in NITEL. Since private communication operators are still connected to NITEL, their services are also less reliable. As a result, functional telephone lines remain at 4 per 1,000.
* Rail and inland water transportation is virtually non-existent in Nigeria. Road transportation is currently the main mode of transportation. However, the poor state of the roads and the scarcity of petroleum products have led to the high cost of transportation.

These infrastructural deficiencies have made manufacturing costs very high. Many companies' products have been rendered uncompetitive, as their prices are usually higher than imported substitutes.

The companies that are mostly affected by the problems in the industry are the Small and Medium-scale Enterprises (SMEs). They experience more difficulties in overcoming the constraints. Aside from the general problems facing the industry, the SMEs have sub-sector specific problems that require separate attention from the relevant bodies. Despite the fact that they are considered crucial to the future development of the Nigerian economy, the SMEs have become 'endangered species'. This is because the SMEs:

- Generally have a weak presence in external and domestic markets.
- Operate within a hostile financial environment, as banks are most times reluctant to grant them credit facilities due to inherent high risks in their operations.
- Suffer from dearth of manpower skills. Most of them are one-man or family businesses and the 'ownership syndrome' that is common with these types of businesses often prevent the ceding of management control to competent people.

These peculiar problems of SMEs and the general problems facing the industry, mostly contributed to the high incidence of failure/collapses and the inability of most SMEs to transform into large-scale enterprises.

Other problems facing the industry include a weakening consumer demand for manufactured goods. The reason for this is the low living standard of Nigerians, as measured by the per capita income of about $300 currently, compared to almost $400 in 1996. In addition, an income analysis on the economy in 1998 revealed that 41 per cent of Nigeria's income is earned by the top 10 per cent of the population, while 4 per cent of the income is earned by the lowest income group that constitutes 20 per cent of the population. This indicates high income inequality between the few rich and the numerous masses. This is taking its toll on the demand for locally produced goods as we found ourselves in a situation where many Nigerians buy imported second-hand goods because they cannot afford new locally manufactured goods.

The Nigerian non-oil industry is also suffering from a lack of support from the agricultural and solid mineral industries in terms of raw material inputs. Most of the production activities in the economy depend on imported raw materials, and this (coupled with a high taste of Nigerians for imported finished goods) has led to high Marginal Propensity to Import (MP1) at 0.8. The high MPI was responsible for the persistent trade deficits/gap and it is an indication that consumption, which is one of the variables that drive economic growth, is largely a withdrawal in Nigeria. The agricultural and solid mineral sectors also have their peculiar problems. The major problems facing the sector are a low level of mechanisation and a reluctance of private financial institutions to fund the operators due to the high risk of the sectors. Most of the government financial institutions, that were established to cater for the financial needs of these sectors, are moribund.

The commercial sector is the third largest contributor (about 17 per cent) to the nation's GDP, after oil/gas and agriculture. Commerce includes import and export activities. Nigeria, as the largest market in Africa (with about 120m population), has become very attractive to many foreign companies, which have extended their markets to Nigeria directly or through trade intermediaries. It is, however, sad to note that, while the foreign companies have developed markets for their products in Nigeria, our local industries have largely been unable to extend their markets beyond Nigeria. This is, however, not surprising, considering that many of them cannot even compete (in terms of pricing) with the foreign products at home. I wonder how they would be able to compete in the foreign markets, given that they would have to contend with additional costs of excise duties and freight.

It is also important to note that the little exports we do in Nigeria comprise mainly primary products (crude oil and agricultural produce), while imports into the economy mostly consist of intermediate and finished goods (that require little or no value-added). Though importation has broadened the consumers' options, its negative effect is that the consumers' tastes are now skewed towards imported goods, despite the fact that some of the imported goods are inferior in quality.

Given that domestic production is severely constrained, the yearly growth in commerce is an indication of growing volume of imports, at the expense of local industries. The commercial sector is also faced with many other problems, of which the major ones are the cumbersome port procedures; high port and incidental charges; reduction in the scope and use of credit transactions; non-resolution of regional trade disputes; and poor dissemination of trade related information for the domestic and external markets.

Issues to be addressed

Before I start to discuss the issues that the government needs to address to turn around the fortunes of our commerce and industry, and revive the economy, I would first like to discuss the economics of growth. I believe that by discussing the economics of growth, we can begin to identify areas that the government really needs to address.

The GDP, as a measure of economic activities in a country, is the summation of Consumption, Investment and Government expenditures, and Net Exports (Exports minus Imports). The consumption and investment expenditures are both private sector expenditures. While consumption is a function of income, investment is a function of savings. Since an increase in investment (especially in productive activities) leads to an increase in production output, which in turn leads to increase in income, investment is thus the most important variable driving economic growth. When aggregate income rises, people will consume more goods and save more money, which can be channelled by financial intermediaries (like the banks) to further increase investments.

The economic trend in Nigeria is that Consumption is the largest variable of the GDP, followed by Government Expenditure. On the other hand, Investment Expenditure has been very weak. The result has been a dismal growth in GDP, less than the growth in national population. For example, last year, the estimated GDP at 1984 constant market price was ₦119.88 billion, consisting of Consumption- ₦86 billion, Government expenditure ₦23. 5 billion, Investment N7.1 billion and net export ₦3.5 billion. You would notice from the breakdown that investment is the second lowest of the variables. The low investment level was responsible for the low net exports, as it has partly weakened the supply base of the economy. From my discussions on the economics of growth, you would agree with me that the growth that we should all desire for the economy is investment-driven growth as any attempt to focus too much on consumption-driven growth will aggravate our level of growth. The problems militating against investment are the same problems challenging the economic sectors and they have constituted barriers to entries into the sectors.

As mentioned earlier, Consumption Expenditure (which is the largest components of the GDP) is largely a withdrawal from the economy since it is mostly incurred on imported goods. The government expenditure, which is the second largest component of the GDP, has most times turned out to be wasteful expenditures. The government sector is grossly inefficient and riddled with corruption. In the past, the national revenues were squandered on white elephant projects that did not enhance productivity or have any impact on the lives of the average Nigerian. The net effect is that GDP grew at a lower rate than the population. For example, GDP grew by 2.8 per cent, while the population grew by 2.8 per cent last year. With this performance, our per capita income dipped slightly.

From the above discussion, we can deduce that there are three key areas the government needs to work on in order to change the fortunes of the country:

* Redress deficiencies in infrastructure and utilities by privatising key parastatals — this will reduce manufacturing costs and improve the standard of living.
* Encourage local and foreign investment by instituting investor-friendly policies, such as providing more incentives for manufacturing and exports.
* Eradicate corruption in public offices — this will ensure value for money in public expenditure, improve the public image of the country and reduce the cost of doing business in Nigeria. It will consequently boost the attraction of Nigeria to foreign investors.

Year 2000 Experience

The present administration has tried to project itself as a purposeful government by working on some of the key issues. The president has said on many occasions that the main hurdle for him to scale is the eradication of the 'twin devil' of corruption and poverty. The government recognises that poverty is caused by the low level of economic growth and development. It expects that eradication of corruption will result in increased efficiency in the government ministries, parastatals and agencies and will improve the investment environment generally.
. Thus, the government established Anti-Corruption Commission to probe and prosecute cases of corruption in public offices.

To eradicate poverty, the present government has set for itself some economic targets with which its performance can be appraised (as contained in the Economic Blueprint) by the end of its tenure in 2003. Some of the targets are: a GDP growth rate of 10 per cent (from around 3 per cent); inflation rate of 5 per cent (from about 15 per cent); employment level of 70 per cent (from about 50 per cent) and so on. However, the government failed to set specific targets for economic variables, such as investment, exports, savings, etc., that will drive GDP to meet the set targets.

Notwithstanding this, I would want to commend the administration for being prudent in its spending, as budgetary deficits have been curtailed to date. With the good fortune of an increased oil price, foreign reserves have been built to about $ 10.3 billion. The government has also been pursuing market-friendly initiatives, such as deregulation, privatisation and overall economic liberalisation, which are aimed at freeing government expenditures from 'private sector' activities, where it is least competent, to enable government to concentrate more on the provisions of social and economic infrastructure such as health, education and roads. A privatisation timetable has since been released and government shares in some oil marketing and cement companies were sold to private investors last year.

The government has also taken some initiatives to revive the Nigerian industry. The government instituted a tariff reform that conceded an estimated sum of N19 billion on import duties in Year 2000 to serve as incentives to the industry operators. To resuscitate industry financing institutions, the government is merging the NIDB, NERFUND and NBCI to form a new Bank of Industry, which will be adequately capitalised.

In all fairness, the actions taken by the government so far have resulted in a better international image and have improved our credit rating. Last year, the IMF approved a standby credit facility for the country, which enabled the Paris Club of creditors to grant a 3-year moratorium for the nation's debt servicing obligations. The steps that have been taken so far have also enabled the private sector to access foreign credit financing from international agencies such as the International Finance Corporation (IFC), the Netherlands Development Finance Company (FMO) and the US-Eximbank, etc.

Despite the above achievements, Year 2000 performance indicators revealed that the investment level still remains low and the industrial sector performance remains below potential.

Capacity utilisation recorded little or no improvement, poverty level remains at 60 per cent and unemployment level, at 50 per cent. The low industrial performance could be ascribed to the continued dilapidated state of infrastructure. The administration's failure in improving the state of infrastructure was due to the continued inefficiency of the government ministries, parastatals and agencies and the government's slow pace in implementing the privatisation of key parastatals.

On the other hand, the disappointing capital inflow could be adduced to the high country risk still attached to Nigeria, relative to some other developing countries. Some foreign investors still regard Nigeria as a corrupt and unsafe country, as opposed to President Obasanjo's contention that Nigeria is now safe for foreign investment. Even, among Nigerians, there is growing apprehension over the state of security in the country, especially with the rampages of armed robbers. Further, the government is yet to be considered as transparent in its activities. There were insinuations of unprofessionalism in the last oil-bloc allocation exercise and the bidding for the government shares when some oil marketing companies were privatised. In line with foreigners' perception of the security situation in Nigeria, country reports on Nigeria are yet to be favourable. For instance, the recent rating by Transparency International indicated that Nigeria is still one of the most corrupt nations of the world. This has cast doubts on the effectiveness of the Anti-Corruption crusade of the government.

The policy failures should impress upon the government the need to come out with leap frog strategies to ensure a fundamental transformation within a maximum period of a decade. To achieve timely results, the government also needs to concentrate its efforts on the 20 per cent of its strategies that will produce 80 per cent positive change in the economy. What we see today is a government that wastes so much effort at convincing the people on the advantages of the deregulation of the petroleum sector, while it is dragging its foot on the privatisation of NEPA and NITEL, and establishment of the Bank of Industry to start financing the industrial operators, most especially the SMEs.

Let us now examine how this year's budget can minimise the production bottlenecks and provide incentives for the increased private sector investment that is greatly desired.

Budget 2001 Fiscal Measures

The government's desire in Budget 2001 is to address the problems militating against economic growth and development and jump-start the economy. The extent to which the provisions of the budget will be successful in making this desire a reality is the issue for discussion here. In this regard, we will critically examine how the budget addresses the basic issues such as the direction of macro-economic policy, human capital development, social expenditure, stable exchange rate policy, economic diversification and the non-monetarisation of crude oil export proceeds.

The budget 2001 is termed 'the road to economic recovery'. It is a very ambitious budget, with an expected increase in total federally collectible revenue of almost 100 per cent to ₦2, 165.9 billion from last year's actual of ₦1, 092.9 billion. The increase is predicated on an increase in oil revenue by 87 per cent from N89 billion (which was realised last year) to ₦1, 672.6 billion and in non-oil revenue by 149 per cent from last year's actual of ₦197.8 billion to ₦493.3 billion. The expected oil revenue is based on a crude oil price of $22 per barrel and a daily production output of 2, 4112 million barrels per day. This indicates an expected oil production increase of 23.9 per cent.

A review of the recurrent expenditure convinces me that there would be an increase in aggregate demand. This is because over 50 per cent (₦204 billion) of the total recurrent expenditure (₦397.7 billion) is allocated to personnel costs. With the aim of deterring corruption in the civil service, the government planned further increase in civil servants' transport and housing allowances, by 33.3 per cent and 50 per cent respectively. Pensioners are not left out. The government proposes to exempt pension payable to public servants from tax. These fiscal measures will impact on household disposable income of the civil servants on one hand. The increase in the overall expenditure will be inflationary. It should therefore lead to increase in demand with consequent increased productivity and disposable income of the private sector on the other hand.

To complement the expected increase in workers' income, the government proposed a tax relief for all income earners. The upper limits of the taxable income band will be increased. In addition, basic food items would be exempted from VAT. With the expected increase in national disposable income, there will be a rise in savings and by implication, an increase in capital formation, and subsequently, investment. The result will be a rise in capacity utilisation as well as industry contribution to economic growth.

Although I have said that there is need to improve power supply, I doubt if the huge capital expenditure allocation to Power and Steel ministry (15.79 per cent of the total capital expenditure budget of ₦78.4 billion) will achieve the desired result going by the past performances of the ministry. I therefore believe that the most effective route to achieving improvement in power supply is to deregulate the sector. The government has actually promised to privatise NEPA. However, a situation where government is still injecting so much money into the power sector is an indication that the government does not intend to privatise NEPA this year. Past heavy spending on NEPA has failed to significantly improve power supply. Thus, the huge allocation may not guarantee a steady power supply, especially when an estimated $7 billion ($1 billion for a plant) is required to put NEPA in good shape so that it can seriously improve power generation and supply. In view of this, there may be no respite on manufacturing costs for local industries.

In fact, the cost of production may increase further in the face of the impending deregulation of the oil sector, which will increase the cost of fuelling generating sets. What baffles me is that, whereas the government has been foot-dragging on privatising NEPA and NITEL (which will be of immediate benefit to economic operators), it intends to be swift in deregulating the petroleum sector as a way to guarantee a steady supply of petroleum products. This action will further compound the woes of local industries.

The Budget 2001 also proposed a customs and excise tariff relief for industrial operators and adjustments to export promotion schemes. These trade policy changes are significant, as they largely address the concerns of manufacturers regarding tariff anomalies that expose them to unfair competition from imported goods. Among other objectives of the customs tariff changes, the government aimed the relief at:

* Improving the industrial climate;
* Stimulating higher capacity utilisation; and
* Encouraging the diversification of foreign exchange earnings through increased export activities in the non-oil sector.

The tariff reforms are in two sectors — tariff reduction for major raw-material inputs and equipment, and an import duties hike for finished products.

The tariff reforms cut across all the industrial sectors of the economy. Some sectors would enjoy cross-sector relief. The most singular beneficiary of the tariff reform is the Textile and Footwear industry, as it would enjoy relief on chemicals and machinery and equipment aside from the relief granted to the industry itself. The tariff concessions in the textile and footwear industry range between 5 per cent and 20 per cent. The industry would also enjoy concessions of 5 per cent – 20 per cent and 5 per cent – 25 per cent on imported chemicals and machinery and electrical equipment respectively. Agricultural and Paper Mill industries would benefit from concessions of 5 per cent – 30 per cent, while the end-users of base metals (e.g. aluminium, packaging, steel and loose foils companies) will enjoy a tariff concession of 5 per cent – 25 per cent. The transport industry was not left out of these reforms. Transport companies and farmers are to enjoy a concession of 5 per cent -25 per cent on luxury buses, engine-fitted chassis and tractors. This implies double concessions for the agricultural industry operators.

On the other hand, the government also increased import duties on imported goods across the industrial sectors and, for the agricultural sector import duty per cent hikes on edible commodities ranging between 30 and 80 per cent. For the textile industry, import duty on woven fabric was increased by 35 per cent – 40 per cent. The steel industry would also benefit from import duty rate increase of between 35 per cent and 65 per cent on iron rods. End- users of Gypsum can now import the clay mineral albeit at a higher duty rate of 65 per cent.

The expectation is that these tariff reductions will significantly lower manufacturing costs, thereby reducing the prices of manufactured products, while the hike in import duty rates will make imported manufactured goods more expensive. The tariff changes should stimulate domestic production and protect local industries from undue foreign competition in the domestic market. However, there are still complaints of tariff anomalies emanating from such industries as textiles, chemicals, pharmaceuticals, toiletries/cosmetics and carpets/rugs. It is expected that future budgets would address the outstanding concerns of the operators.

The Budget 2001 provides that efforts will be intensified towards enhancing non-oil exports through the use of existing incentives and the modification of Export Expansion Grant (EEG) and Manufacture-In-Bond Scheme (MIBS). The EEG provides cash incentives for exporters that export a minimum of ₦50.000.00 worth of semi-manufactured products. This cash incentive is directed at enabling such exporters increase the volume and value of exports. The basis for computation of this grant has been increased from 10 per cent to 20 per cent of foreign exchange repatriated, in order to encourage production for export in the 2001 fiscal year.

The MIBS has been modified to make participation under the scheme less burdensome. To this end, the requirement of dedicating a separate production line and warehouse to the scheme has been removed. Accordingly, participants under the scheme are now required to maintain separate registers, which will be regularly checked by the Nigerian Customs Service for transactions under the scheme. Other requirements under the scheme, such as the execution and discharge of bonds, are retained.

In the Year 2001 budget, there was a focus on developing the agricultural sector in order to improve its capability to provide agro-based industries with a stable supply of raw materials. In order to achieve this, the government will:

* Expand the Buyer of Last Resort under the Farmers Income Guarantee Scheme, especially as regards grains, palm kernel, soya beans and groundnuts.
* Develop nurseries for tree plants throughout the country.
* Strengthen the Agricultural Credit Guarantee Scheme to ensure access to credit for farmers to procure key agricultural inputs.
* Re-capitalise and restructure the Nigerian Agricultural and Co-operative Bank to effectively perform its functions of a development bank in the agricultural sector.

While the above policy framework for the development of the agricultural sector seems appropriate, the budget allocation for the execution is inadequate. The budgetary allocation was ₦17.6 billion (representing 1.97 per cent of the total budget), including a capital allocation of ₦10.6 billion, which is 2.13 per cent of the total capital expenditure budget. This is a far cry from the Food and Agricultural Organisation's (FAO) recommendation that 25 per cent of a country's budget be devoted to agriculture towards accomplishing real growth in the economy.

As a banker, I know you expect me to comment on the impact of this year's monetary and credit policy and on the role the banks intend to play in the development of commerce and industry. The primary objective of the monetary policy is to ensure stable prices by maintaining the inflation rate at a single digit level. Consequently, the CBN adopted measures that will address the persistent problem of excess liquidity emanating primarily from government expenditures and its negative effects on price and the exchange rate.

In view of the fact that monetary policy and fiscal operations of government have not been well harmonised towards facilitating the achievement of the desired results, we have witnessed upward pressure on inflation and interest rates this year. In view of the production bottlenecks in our economy, it is difficult to contain interest and exchange rates simultaneously during periods of liquidity growth. Thus, one of the two variables will suffer from whatever action is taken by the CBN and that will be deemed detrimental to the development of commerce and industry.

Fortunately, competition in the banking industry will help to moderate increases in interest rates resulting from the CBN's effort to stabilise the exchange rate. The government, on its part, should harmonise its spending pattern in a manner that will facilitate the achievement of the desirable macro-economic indices.

In order to complement government initiative in facilitating the growth of the real sector, banks are required to set aside 10 per cent of their PBT for financing and promoting SMEs, the modalities for the administration of the fund is being worked-out by the CBN.

It is imperative to add that the business of lending to the deficit units in the economy is an integral part of the operations of the banks. Thus, banks have been lending to all viable businesses in the economy, including SMEs. So, if SMEs have not been receiving a significant share of the bank loans, it means that the risk of lending to them may be relatively very high compared to the other category of operator. Thus, the logical measure to adopt in a free enterprise economy is to address the issues affecting the credit worthiness of SMEs and introduce incentives that will improve their attractiveness to banks. These comments are however not meant to take anything away from the need for banks to support the growth of SMEs. In fact, I believe that we will fund more than enough SMEs projects to profitably absorb the target value of bank credit.

Conclusion

As noble as the objectives of the fiscal measures might seem, I still foresee hard times for Nigerian commerce and industry this year. For example, our expectation of appreciable improvement in power supply may not materialise. The huge amount allocated to NEPA may become misplaced spending, especially if the utilisation is not effectively monitored. The industrial operators should brace-up for new bureaucratic bottlenecks and higher replacement/maintenance costs for alternative source of power generation in view of the new directive that generator importers should first obtain clearance from NEPA before they can import generators and the expected increase in pump- price of petroleum products when the oil sector is deregulated. Coupled with the expected volatility of interest and exchange rates, the inadequacy of infrastructure would result in a high cost of production and a continued under capacity utilisation of below 40 per cent.

I am one of the people who believe that remarkable economic growth cannot be achieved overnight, particularly in a depressed and distorted economy like ours. Once the right policies are in place and sustained, the desired results will be quick in coming. The 2001Budget is an improvement over the past budgets in many respects, especially as it affects commerce and industry. Thus, I will enjoin you to optimise the benefits of the incentives provided and be creative in minimising the effects of the constraints on your operations.

Finally, it is my sincere hope that the government will ensure the effective implementation of the budget towards achieving the desired results. The government should also intensify efforts to privatise government parastatals earmarked for privatisation, ensure more transparency in the conduct of its affairs and reduce corruption in the civil service so that every naira of public spending can be justified. This way, the platform for facilitating the development of commerce and industry, and stimulating overall economic growth as provided by this year's budget will be enhanced.

Being a paper presented at the Annual General meeting of Aba Chamber of Commerce, Industry, Mines and Agriculture. March 22. 2001

Chapter 6

Privatisation: A Recipe for Sustainable Economic Growth and Technological Transfer

The objective of every economic system is efficient resource allocation. Two primary mechanisms are relied upon to fulfil this task. First, the price mechanism by which private firms respond to demand and supply levels in individual markets and undertake that level of economic activity which is in their best interest. And second, the public sector or the government, which also makes resource allocation decisions through its activities of taxing and spending, regulation and control and, sometimes, direct production.

Public sector activities sometimes account for a significant share of resources in the economy and this influences the behaviour (and size) of the private sector directly or indirectly. In Nigeria for instance, there were six hundred federal public enterprises in 1990, according to the Technical Committee on Privatisation (now Bureau of Public Enterprises or BPE). At the same time, the various states and local governments of the federation owned about nine hundred smaller enterprises. These enterprises jointly accounted for about 40 per cent of fixed capital investment and the largest share of formal sector employment.

The study of public sector economics seeks, among others, to address the question: What should be the role of the public sector in resource allocation in a market-oriented economy?

The notion of economic efficiency is conventionally used by economists to judge the merits of various resource allocation decisions and, ultimately, to prescribe policy, the production of most goods and services by the private sector.

This model is rooted in the principle of *laissez-faire* developed in the 19th Century by Adam Smith and built around the famous 'invisible hand' doctrine. This doctrine gave rise to the popular saying that "the best government is the one that does the least".

Under this proposition, government is expected to act mainly as an umpire in the economic contest among private sector operators. These operators are believed to advance society to its optimal level of performance through their self- interested deference to the dictates of the price system.

However, it has been recognised that the market-determined model of economic activity may also fail to maximise economic welfare. Consequently, the justification for public sector involvement in economic activity occurs when circumstances exist which prevent the market from attaining the desired level of efficiency (or equity or both) in the allocation of resources. On this basis, certain specific functions, which government must perform, arise. These include, but are not limited to those listed hereunder:

1. **The provision of public goods:** These are goods that the market cannot efficiently provide. They have the basic characteristic that they must be made available equally to all citizens. Since no one can be excluded from their benefits, they cannot be produced and sold on a strictly profit-making basis. Under this category of goods, defence is the most obvious example.
2. **The existence of externalities compels public sector intervention in certain areas of production:** Production activities of firms and consumption activities of individuals are often inter-dependent. The upstream paper firm, polluting

the water supply of a downstream settlement, is a simple example. By educating our children, we increase the overall productivity of the workforce, which benefits society generally. Thus, where private and social considerations diverge because of these interdependencies (or externalities), some form of government intervention is needed.

3. **Some services cannot be produced under competitive conditions:** The efficient production scale is so large that the activity can only be provided efficiently by one or a few enterprises. On this count, a level of subsidy may be needed to ensure economically efficient output.

4. **The market system may not be capable of functioning in a sufficiently suitable fashion:** Unexpected shifts in aggregate demand, may occur, that cause the economy to experience bouts of inflation or recession.

   Accordingly, government may be needed to stabilise the economy through appropriate fiscal and/or monetary policies.

5. **The rate of capital formation may be too low to achieve what is thought to be an acceptable rate of growth:** Government may need to change the parameters that affect the rate of growth saving, investment, productivity, the rate of growth of the labour force, etc to ensure the attainment of the desired levels.

Thus, the public sector basically fills the gap in resource allocation and production in areas where the price mechanism is considered inoperable or inefficient. This was the reasoning behind the establishment of most Public Enterprises (PEs) in Nigeria.

Until the early 1970s, the public sector in Nigeria remained relatively modest in size. The original objectives for setting up most of the public enterprises (PEs) at that time conformed generally with the principles of public sector economics as earlier explained. For instance, The National Electric Power Authority (NEPA) was set up to exploit the huge economies of scale and synergies in electric power generation, transmission and distribution. Similarly, the Nigerian Telecommunication Limited (NITEL) was established to provide telecommunications services which, at that time, was unattractive to private investors and also involved large initial capital outlays both of which most private entrepreneurs could not afford.

The above situation changed after 1973 in the face of dramatic rise in the oil price and in earnings. Specifically, oil export recorded a huge leap from $2.9 billion in 1973 to $8.6 billion in 1974. This was the precise juncture the public sector began its enormous growth. The government did not only dictate the maximum levels of foreign participation in the various economic sectors but also directly acquired majority shares in many businesses, expanded existing parastatals and established new corporations. Government spread its investment tentacles to many industries, including oil marketing, fertilizer production, paper mills, sugar manufacturing, cement, motor vehicle assembly/manufacturing, textiles, insurance, hotels, and even grains, poultry and root crops production.

With the unprecedented mushrooming of PEs in Nigeria came the indiscriminate release of funds to such enterprises, without regard for fiscal discipline. As the enterprises became more dependent on the Treasury, they lost their operational autonomy and were subjected to destructive ministerial interference in their day-to-day operations. Consequently, inefficiency and corruption became the order of business in the PEs.

By the mid-80s when the oil boom came to an end, the Treasury went virtually dry, along with it, the country's foreign exchange resources and reserve holdings. The PEs, like many other agents of government, however, continued their old ways. They continued to base their operations more on expenditure plans without much serious effort to match performance and revenue with expenditure. This led to the accumulation of large deficits by the public enterprises whose performance, as typified by the energy sector, has been nothing to write home about.

Of the twenty countries sampled by the UNDP in 1988, for instance, Nigeria had the highest rate of energy losses of 33% and the lowest generation capacity factor at 20 per cent. Also, Nigeria's power sector had the lowest revenue at 1.56 cents/kwh, *the* lowest rate of return of 8% and the longest average account receivable period of 15 months. This is typical of most PEs in Nigeria.

A generous definition of privatisation would admit any transfer of ownership or control from the public to the private sector. A more appropriate definition would, however, insist that such transfer be sufficiently profound to guarantee the private operators or owners enough independence and power through majority ownership. Privatisation gained wide currency during the sale of British Telecommunications in 1984. The basic philosophy behind privatisation is the efficiency argument. This argument does not always go down well with some analysts who have argued that even in the private sector there is a surfeit of non-performing enterprises. So that inefficiency is not the exclusive preserve of public enterprises. They hold that, but for alien enterprises (by which they refer to subsidiaries of foreign companies), most Nigerian companies are inefficient even if their owners are resource rich. This, they argue, is only a replication or reflection of the state of affairs in the public enterprises, which are making losses while their managers are getting fabulously rich.

The complex nature of the Nigeria society makes privatisation imperative for sustainable development. The dearth of good governance and accountability and the monumental corruption of the many years of military rule had made private discretionary considerations the cardinal principles of leadership in our public enterprises. Consequently, incompetent and unqualified (but 'connected') persons have held sway in these organisations for too long. Most Nigerians have now assimilated the dubious notion that public enterprises are mere compensation packages for government officials and their loyalists. This feeling, therefore, continues to fuel the ever raging competition for public office. All these factors happen at the expense of the public, which neither gets the expected goods or services meant to be offered by the public enterprise at the right time or at the right prices.

Certainly, inefficiency is not the only reason for privatisation. As the statesman and economists of repute Dr. Pius Okigbo puts it, if it were to be the sole rationale for privatisation, then, government itself ought to be the first candidate for privatisation. That is, if it escapes going into receivership.

It is fruitless to expect the public enterprises to improve by merely requiring the managers to operate on the basis of reward and punishment for failure. The question is, can old dinosaurs learn new profit-maximising tricks? This is unlikely!

Moreover, the need to sustain the operations of public enterprises, which are partly social in nature, compels government to continually subsidise these enterprises. But times have changed, and government is no longer able to offer such subsidies hence the call to privatise.

This illustration confirms that, rather than being a catalyst, the operations of the PE have become a cog in the wheel of economic progress in Nigeria.

The services provided by some PEs, including NEPA and NITEL, are so fundamental to the overall efficiency of national economic life that the inefficiency of such PEs becomes a drag on economic growth.

As a result of the drain on the Treasury, the expenditure level for good governance, particularly as regards the provision of basic infrastructure like good roads, can no longer be met.

The situation described above has not changed materially, except that some PEs were privatised between 1988 and 1993. Efforts at commercialising PEs or finding solutions to their problems have not been fruitful. This reinforces the general belief that there is a need to embark on privatisation if sustained economic growth is to be achieved.

The major argument against privatisation is that it turns public assets, painstakingly acquired over a long period of time, to private individuals with the real possibility of exploitation of the public. I believe, however, that with proper valuation of the assets, the public can recover its investment and put it to better use under private equity.

It should be noted, however, that privatisation does not represent a wholesale capitalisation to *laissez faire* in regard to a nation's economic affairs. Government can still play its role by ensuring effective monitoring of the activities of the privatised enterprises.

But what benefits do we derive from privatisation? Let me first outline some of the fears of those against privatisation. Privatisation is always a political issue. Government would always have some goals that are not strictly economic. These include the need to accommodate certain classes of buyers (or even exclude others), maintaining a larger shareholding list or sustaining employment. But all these must be balanced with the economic objectives. A growing array of studies shows that privatised enterprises tend to improve their performance and that the economy as a whole gains from a properly managed privatisation programme. Privatisation adds value, directly in terms of shareholder value for the privatised enterprises and other stakeholders. It also adds value to the economy as a whole through its impact on what Douglas North called "adaptive economic efficiency" - changes in the framework of beliefs, procedures and incentives that are essential to the emergence of the competitive economy.

Transferring PEs to the private sector will expose the enterprises to the discipline of the market, and thereby lead to increased efficiency. To thoroughly examine the efficiency implications of privatisation, we need to distinguish between PEs that are already subject to national or international competition, and those in monopolistic positions.

A number of factors suggest that privatisation will increase productive efficiency. We will emphasise three such factors - the impacts of reduced political interference, a change in property rights, and more effective financial management.

If public enterprise managers are held hostage to political expediency, in their decision-making function, privatisation should improve the quality of such managerial decision-making. The result of political interference in the operations of public enterprises is, to say the least, unhelpful and the fact that government, in many cases, retains a controlling interest in privatised enterprises, implies that considerable scope for political interference will remain, even after privatisation.

However, in their attempt to exercise this power, politicians are likely to face two constraints. The first constraint is the existence of a proper regulatory framework, which is concerned not only with policing anti-competitive practices, but also with eradicating other sources of economic inefficiency, including attempts by politicians to affect economic decisions. To be effective, the regulatory agency should be invested with sufficient autonomy to limit the possibility of it being captured by particular interest groups.

The second constraint is the existence of private shareholders, who can monitor the conduct and performance of the enterprise. While in effect, every tax payer/voter is currently a shareholder in the public enterprise sector; an explicit shareholding may induce those voters who hold shares to take a greater interest in the performance of a public enterprise. Politicians may, therefore, be required to act more responsibly as a result of privatisation. Of course, if ownership is widespread this may not be an effective constraint. There might be better control if the majority shares were in the hands of major core investors, which of necessity must be involved in the management of the enterprises.

In view of the strategic position of most public sector monopolies significant improvement in the efficiency of their operations will, no doubt, have a multiplier effect on the economy as a whole. Privatisation will also remove some financial burden from the government, more so in view of the absence of the provision of satisfactory or commensurate services to the consuming public by the PEs and in the face of inadequate resources to provide the basic public goods.

It follows that privatisation will enable the government to concentrate its resources on providing and improving infrastructure such as roads and power supply in the rural areas. Government should also be able to focus attention on providing security of lives and property for its individual and corporate citizens.

It could also be in a position to give national defence the attention it deserves in the interest of its national sovereignty.

Privatisation will also stimulate the nation's overall economic performance through the development of the capital market. An increased volume of trading can attract greater foreign investment capital as in the case of Telefonos Mexico (Telemex) with the entry of US$12 billion compared to only *$156* million from domestic investors.

Privatisation is not an end in itself. It is a means to an end and perhaps we should examine some of the benefits that are likely to accrue to us — what one may call privatisation dividends.

Privatisation is a means by which capital is accessed and, therefore, a major impetus for capital market development. Recent capital market reforms in Nigeria would certainly profit the nation if the ongoing privatisation exercise, with evident complementarities offers, is made to feed the capital market. The privatisation of the Chilean Telecommunication Company in the late 80's led to the floating in 1990 of the first Latin American equity issue in the international market since the 1960's. Of the US$2.7 billion invested in Chile in 1993, for instance, US$826 million came from the purchase of Chilean stocks abroad. Privatisation, therefore, opens the window to foreign capital for a reforming country like Nigeria by deepening the stock market.

Privatisation seeks, ultimately, to redirect the energies of government away from economic activity to the provision of a level playing field for economic actors. This would, in turn, remove political expediency from the menu of managerial decision criteria, thereby improving the quality of decisions.

As I have said elsewhere, privatisation is not necessarily the total exclusion of government from economic activity. It is only a redirection of government to its proper roles. Thus, government still retains the role of guidance and regulation, which are actually very important if private monopoly is to be discouraged. This is why, in the United Kingdom for instance, OGTEL and OFGAS are involved in the hands-on monitoring of the operations of private telecommunications and gas companies (respectively) to make sure the citizens are not cheated.

To be effective, such regulatory agencies must be imbued with adequate autonomy and powers to insulate them from vested interests. Privatisation is not just a technique for converting public enterprises to private enterprises. It is more than that. The real import of privatisation can be found in the near-term quality of services offered by the privatised institutions.

Given the combination of improved efficiency and effective regulation, privatisation not only increases the quantum and availability of products and services; it also lowers the unit cost of output. Thus, the interest of the consumer would be better served under privatisation. And the reason for this is not far-fetched. Privatisation unleashes the hidden talents of the private sector which are driven by the profit motive and the competitive spirit. The end result offers new ways of doing things better, faster and cheaper. These are the fruits of privatisation.

Privatisation and Technological Transfer

It is generally acknowledged that Nigeria is endowed with abundant human and material resources, which are yet to be fully harnessed. The inability of the nation to tap its resources effectively and develop industrially and economically has been attributed largely to the gap between domestic capital needs and domestic savings. This is the case in most developing countries where the technology and capital required for modern industrial development are in short supply.

Foreign investment, particularly direct investment which privatisation will usually attract, is expected to improve a nation's fortunes in regard to the two vital ingredients which are in short supply in the development process, namely: managerial skills and technological knowledge (in products and processes). To the extent that the transferred factors are scarce in supply locally, they will stimulate employment, output and growth. Furthermore, the inflow of capital is essential for foreign exchange purposes, even in the long run through investment in export-oriented projects.

Given the abundance of material and human resources, in addition to the market potential, there is no doubt that investors seeking outlets in Africa should find Nigeria attractive. There is a large market in Nigeria in particular and the West Africa sub-region; in general. Foreign investors will also derive comparative cost advantage from export-oriented investments arising from the lower cost of available raw materials and cheap labour. In general, foreign investors should expect to earn returns on investments in Nigeria that are comparable to those in East Asia and Latin America.

Finally, given the new democratic dispensation in Nigeria and the consequent openness of the economy to foreign investors, it is expected that the ongoing privatisation programme will attract foreign investments and the accompanying technology transfer that will impact significantly on efficiency, the international competitiveness of Nigerian products and the growth of the economy in general.

Conclusion

Reflecting principally our collective experience in the past three decades, it is my considered opinion that all men of goodwill should strongly support the current effort at privatising our PEs. It is a more reliable way of getting our economy moving forward again and it is a positive step towards dealing with the problems of public enterprises that have contributed in no small measure to the comatose situation of the national economy.

For privatisation, value is not some abstract concept. It refers to real gains for the stakeholders in the process. Viewing privatisation as serving the interest of the stakeholders not only provides some concrete yardsticks for success, replacing the usual lofty statements of objectives, but also represents the first step in structuring privatisation as a participatory process.

Think of the universe of stakeholders as defined by a series of concentric circles, at the centre of which are the two principal partners in the privatisation process - the government and the investor(s). As a principal stakeholder, the government should be primarily concerned with the short and long-term fiscal impacts of privatisation both through the net proceeds of the actual sale of the equity stake(s) and through the net fiscal contribution of the enterprise over time (tax revenues minus any subsidies). But the government should also see itself as an agent for other stakeholders, in particular with respect to the social impact of privatisation.

The second group of stakeholders, at the centre includes all the investors in the privatised enterprise — the strategic investor as owner-operator, the minority shareholders; employees who own stock; and even the government if it retains some equity position, whether temporarily or permanently. The interest of this group is on the financial health and performance of the enterprises, which in turn determines the return on investment.

Much of the recent empirical work on the impact of privatisation has been focused at this level and the message has been remarkably consistent: privatised enterprise show improved financial and competitive performance, resulting in higher shareholder value.

There are also the workers of the privatised enterprises who are primarily concerned with the effects on employment levels and employment-related benefits. The initial concern is likely to focus on changes in employment level (job losses) and in salaries and fringe benefits as a result of the take-over by a private investor and the shift to a commercially viable management. Beyond the transitional stage, workers who stay with the company will be concerned with job security and remuneration (which in turn depend on the financial health and performance of the enterprise). With improved performance, it is expected that privatisation will increase employment in the long run.

Finally, the outer layer of the stakeholder universe is the economy as a whole. The impacts here include changes in economic institutions in the broadest sense. More attention is paid to these institutional impacts as a key to the sustained growth of a competitive economy. If a significant turn-around in the performance of the enterprises, and the productive sector of the economy as a whole, is to be achieved, privatisation must be accompanied by other policies that will promote competition and improve efficiency. Fortunately, the framework for meeting this prerequisite has already been established with the measures taken in recent times to allow competition in the various economic sectors.

Being a paper presented at the National Workshop on Privatisation, February 2000.

Chapter 7

The Private Sector in Economic Development

Introduction

Elsewhere around the world, but more especially in the developing countries, the place of private enterprise in economic development has elicited a frenetic outburst of interest during the past two decades. It has, in fact, provided the single most dominant platform for controversy in economic policy circles in the intervening years.

But that controversy has not necessarily persisted due to a dearth of evidence regarding the relative superiority of the arguments. Instead, the efficacy of the private sector-led economic development model has been well grounded both in empirical findings and in statistical evidence that stares us in the face on a daily basis.

In many cases, Nigeria inclusive, the transition from a state-dominated economic system to market competition has often been agonisingly hard to achieve. This is a reflection of the staying power of entrenched interests at work. It is also the understandable reflex of the well-known resistance to change. But sustainable economic growth has become the central factor in the rise and fall of the wealth of nations. And private enterprise is now globally recognised as the best guarantor of sustainable growth. The catalytic role of the private sector, in achieving economic growth, is perhaps best seen in bold relief in the cases of China, Germany and Korea. Except for Germany, which was re-united in 1989/

90, these nations have been divided during much of the post-World War II years. The economic performance of the parts of these nations, where markets and private capital have been given free rein, has been unquestionably better than those parts where the state maintained a monopoly hold on the means of wealth creation.

The objective of every economic system is efficient resource allocation. Two primary mechanisms are relied upon to fulfil this task:

(i)   The price mechanism by which private firms respond to demand and supply levels in individual markets and undertake that level of economic activities in their best interest; and

(ii)   The government which also makes resource allocation decisions through such activities as taxing and regulation and control and, sometimes, direct production.

Public sector activities sometimes account for a significant share of resources in the economy and this influences the behaviour of the private sector, directly and/or indirectly. It also affects the size of the private sector. In Nigeria, for instance, there were six hundred federal public enterprises in 1990 according to the Technical Committee on Privatisation and Commercialisation (now Bureau of Public Enterprises, BPE). At the same time, the various states and local governments of the federation owned about nine hundred smaller enterprises. These enterprises jointly accounted for about 40 per cent of fixed capital investment and the largest share of employment in the formal sector. The statistics has not changed dramatically since 1990. The same also applies to the effect on the general economy — including, of course, the well known tendency to crowd out all other (private) players.

The study of economics seeks, among other things, to answer the question: What ought to be the proximate roles of the private and public sectors in resource allocation in a market economy?

The notion of economic efficiency, which is conventionally used by economists to judge the merits of various resource allocation decisions, favours the production of all goods and services almost exclusively by the private sector. Under this proposition, government is expected to act mainly as an umpire in the context of economic exchange among private sector operators. These operators are believed to move society to its optimal level of performance through their self-interested obedience to the dictates of the price system.

The Private Sector in Development

Adam Smith's immutable premise for economic progress continues to be a valid proposition in our time. On this, Smith had written: "It is not from the benevolence of the butcher, the brewer, or the baker, that we expect our dinner, but from their regard to their own interest" *("The Wealth of Nations"* — *1776).*

Smith's objective was not to denigrate the role of government. He was himself a principal beneficiary of that institution as a licensed customs tariff officer. Rather it was a bold attempt to put government's role in proper context. He saw three areas of competence for government: Provision of infrastructure (roads, ports, etc); ensuring the nation's territorial integrity (defence); and guaranteeing justice and property rights.

It is my position that these thresholds of comparative competence remain unassailable more than 200 years after the fact of their enunciation.

Sustainable economic development requires the existence of certain basic resources (human and material) as well as some catalysts of growth (legal system, fiscal regime, etc.). Nigeria's economic environment since independence has been characterised by two key trends. First, there has been a dearth of highly skilled managers and administrators. Second, the Nigerian state has pursued socialist-oriented economic strategies involving nationalisation, monopolies and intrusive legislation. Key economic policy thrusts have either been inconsistent, lacking the requisite boldness or plain wrong. The combination of the above factors has conspired to severely curtail economic advancement.

The efficacy of the private sector-led economic development paradigm is founded on strong empirical grounds. Economic activities involving the public sector tend to carry lower rates of investment productivity and return. To bring about sustainable growth, the economic policy thrust must be such that advance the cause of continuing increase in productive investment by the private sector.

It has become evident that the first condition for sustainable growth (especially material resources) would hardly count for much without the catalysts: a sound legal system, a responsive fiscal regime, an intelligent bureaucracy, a stable political environment and good governance. This fact is pointedly buttressed by the Nigerian experience in the past three decades.

Nigeria is abundantly endowed with material resources. The human resource base is also there, especially in terms of numbers. The right complement of skills is, however, lacking. The educational system has not helped much in this respect. But by far the big-ticket issue of the day, in our country, has been the continuing absence of the set of catalysts, as earlier stated, that guarantees sustainable growth.

Nonetheless, the private sector in Nigeria has, in a special sense, taken the initiative in building the bulwark for the continued survival of our economic system. The private sector provides the overwhelming majority of the jobs in the total economy. Out of an estimated 30 million working population (in both the formal and informal sectors) in Nigeria today, the bureaucracy is responsible for just about 4 million jobs. Given the yawning productivity gap in the public service, it may be prudent to assume the figure of 4 million to be well in excess of the public sector's optimal human resources need.

In the above regard, the informal arm of the private sector deserves a special mention here. The exact size and contribution of the informal sector has unfortunately not been subjected to the depth of investigation that it deserves.

But various estimates put it at roughly 60 to 70 per cent of the entire economy. True, there is no doubting the inefficiency of this sector. But it has nevertheless meshed smoothly with the traditional socio-economic way of life to produce what should easily pass as one of the most resourceful alternative economic systems in the Third World (if not in the world as a whole). So much so that a large measure of the credit for the continued survival of the Nigerian economy today should, in fact, rightfully go to this sector.

The private sector has also been the main source of productive credit in the country. Apart from the financial industry, which has stretched its intermediation capacity against the odds of official regulation and interference, there is the communal system of social support involving mostly the widespread culture of micro-credit. Even so, much remains to be done in such critical areas as the mortgage markets, personal and mass consumer financing. Until the per capita income level (currently estimated at less than $300) is significantly improved, not much success would be expected to be registered in these vital areas.

To enable the private sector to play a significant and sustainable role in the economic system would demand that a conscious effort be made to moderate the risk factor attached to investment decisions. In Nigeria, the greatest risk elements are in the form of uncertain macro-economic policies in the key areas of legislation, government monopolies, the foreign exchange market and the tariff structure (among others). This uncertainty limits the scope of private sector initiatives to the short-term. Under the circumstance, the investor's time horizon is significantly shortened to take account of the inherent risk element. For instance, a two-year payback period on investment is usual, with expected rates of return as high as 10 per cent over and above those obtainable in most advanced economies. In such an environment, efficient pricing of financial products and services cannot be taken for granted. In the specific instance of Nigeria, the result has been a severe case indeed of financial repression.

Conditions for Private Sector-Led Growth

Four conditions are necessary for a sustainable private sector-led economic growth.

The first condition is trade with other nations. A key lesson from our years of import-substitution strategy is that the rational for engaging in trade is as much that of encouraging exports as it is to enable a country to import those things it cannot produce cost-effectively at home. Nigeria has for many years erected concentric layers of tariff and no-tariff barriers to trade, in the name of stabilising the trade balance. These barriers have tended to limit not just the cost of imports but also the import of critically needed capital goods.

On the export side, Nigeria's over-dependence on oil for export earnings is set to endure well into the next several decades. But ample opportunities exist, for non- oil products, both to the country's traditional trading partners and to some African markets. For exports to begin to thrive, however, our economic planners must begin to take a more robust view of our system of incentives, while aligning the exchange rate mechanism to the dictates of market forces.

The second condition is the level of investment and the climate for investment activities. Investment is a critical complement to trade reforms in the quest for rapid growth in any country. High investment levels, as underpinned by high rates of domestic savings, exert the strongest influence on economic growth prospects. In Nigeria, investment as a percentage of the gross domestic product (GDP) has declined from about 15 per cent in the 1970s to about 10 per cent in the 1990s (and continues to drop by current evidence). It makes good sense for a country like Nigeria to also worry both about the quality of investments it attracts and the structure of incentives to investors. Our economic landscape is littered with giant industrial projects that are visible testimonies to decades of inconsistent public sector economic activism. In the past few years, we have made considerable progress in the area of macro-economic stability. The fact that little visible gains have so far flowed from this is sufficient proof that macro-economic stability cannot by itself translate to sustainable growth. What would seem to matter most are investment-friendly policies that encourage private entrepreneurs to invest their capital in productive ventures.

The third condition is public sector enterprise reform. The collective patrimony argument has been exploited to the point of clouding the very essence of privatisation in a reforming economy such as Nigeria's. The essence of the provision of public goods lies in how effectively these services are rendered, not in the symbolic existence of institutions of uncertain viability. There is the erroneous notion, held mainly among a rapidly dwindling group of Nigerians, that such institutions as the Nigerian Telecommunications (NITEL) and NEPA are choice national assets that are being covetously eyed by private (foreign and domestic) interests in the run up to the privatisation exercise. Experience has, however, shown that real interest in the privatisation programmes of countries with a tradition of sustained poor economic governance is often slow in building up. It cannot be different for Nigeria. A critical element of privatisation is the sequencing as well as the transparency and openness that is deliberately made an integral process in the exercise.

The fourth and final condition for sustainable economic growth is the existence of appropriate support mechanisms for optimal private sector participation. As already mentioned in this presentation, these mechanisms are the critical catalysts for growth. They include adequate infrastructural support, strong and intelligent institutions (e.g. the judiciary, the bureaucracy, etc.), the fiscal regime, the political environment, and the nature of the social safety nets and the system of conflict resolution. These support mechanisms are the foundation upon which all other conditions for private sector-led economic growth are given full expression.

The New Thinking in Nigeria

The past six years, or thereabouts, have witnessed the emergence of a budding partnership between the public and the private sectors in Nigeria. It would seem that after decades spent in search of a common economic ground, we have arrived at the terminus of a brave new world of mutual inclusiveness. The emerging new thinking has found expression in the build-up of a national consensus as to the proper role definition between the public and private sectors. This shift has not been an easy one. In an ironic sense, it may, in fact, have been facilitated by the precipitate decline in the country's economic fortunes, especially in the past decade or so. In the intervening years, the private sector has been sensitised to its proper role in the economic system. It has mounted an impressive platform to ensure the reversal of the status quo through informed and self-interested advocacy.

The Organized Private Sector (OPS), along with the Nigeria Economic Summit Group (NESG) and key actors within the government itself, has been at the centre of this happy trend. This coalition has initiated an unprecedented dialogue process, aimed at getting the government to accept the logic of the market place, the need for a private sector-led economic development paradigm and the opening up of all sectors of the economy to competition.

In the six years since this collaborative effort began, much success has been achieved. Progress in this regard has yielded a blue print for Nigeria's economic development (the Vision 2010 Report), and brought the government, the organised Private Sector (OPS) and the general public together, in a rare unity of purpose in the interest of national economic progress. Through its annual Summit the NESG has, in addition, fostered a new partnering process as seen in the public/private sector dialogue. This, it is hoped, will reduce the mutual suspicion between the sectors and promote the concept of Nigeria Incorporated. In addition, it has successfully sold the idea of free market, private sector-led growth.

The Vision 2010 project has been the most visible aspect of the success story of the new economic thinking in Nigeria today. The visioning process aims at jump-starting the economy and achieving a reasonable level of sustainable growth by the year 2010. Its philosophical underpinning favours public/private sector partnership in the context of a private sector-led economic growth strategy. The private sector has enormous responsibilities under the new dispensation as the envisaged engine of growth in the next millennium.

The Vision 2010 project has itself given rise to the National Council of Nigerian Vision (NCNV) and the Nigeria Vision Foundation (NVF), both aimed at ensuring the faithful implementation of the recommendations of the Vision 2010 Committee.

These private sector initiatives will help set the pace for sustainable economic growth in Nigeria.

The Future in Perspective

Given positive conditions, the following areas would be expected to attract private sector interest and to flourish in the coming years:

(i)   Oil/Gas and related activities; power supply; telecommunications; construction; IT.

(ii)   Financial industry: with good outlook in the medium/ long-term, the industry will gain both in depth and breadth, enabling the sector to develop new capacities.

(iii)   Small scale and family businesses as Nigerians give expression to their creative spirits.

(iv)   Others (rubber, cotton, health related activities, some minerals, palm oil, etc).

A Continuing Concern

The graphic lesson from the recent experience of many South-East Asian countries is the fact that sustainable economic growth cannot be built on a culture of corruption and lack of due process. Good governance practices, be it in government or in the corporate setting, is a *sine qua non* for orderly and sustainable economic development.

Corruption remains a very strong source of concern in Nigeria. The negative effects of corruption are so pervasive that it has affected virtually all aspects of our national life — be it social life, intellectual development, educational system, creativity, value system and our external image. The gory revelations of the shenanigans of the Abacha years have accentuated this sense of pervasiveness. But by far the biggest victim of corruption in Nigeria is the economy. Not only are foreign investors turned off by the prospects of having to wade through a profusion of toll gates; God-fearing local investors are themselves not always convinced by appeals to patriotism to overlook its overall negative effect.

The efforts of the government of President Olusegun Obasanjo to confront corruption, though commendable, do not in themselves fully address the issue.

We require a holistic and comprehensive assault on the vice of impropriety if corruption is to be obliterated from our national scheme of things. One is encouraged by the fact that the President has sent an anti-corruption bill to the National Assembly. The legislature must act with due despatch to see that this bill is promulgated into law without further delay. This should provide a powerful signal regarding the dawn of a truly new dispensation, both to foreign investors and to their Nigerian counterparts.

Something totally different, even innovative, happened in October at the sixth in the series of annual summits under the aegis of the Nigeria Economic Summit Group. For the first time in this bridge-building process, Corporate Nigeria delivered a pledge to become a full partner with government in its avowed intent to fight corruption. This indeed is as it should be. The war should be waged on all fronts. For, while corruption in government may have acquired a higher profile and visibility, that in the corporate sector has tended to be overlooked for the dubious reason that it is a 'private affair'. The new consensus is that corruption, in whatever form or guise, amounts principally to a diminution on the wealth of the nation.

Conclusion

The number one economic objective of the nation, as expressed in the main report of the Vision 2010 Committee, is unambiguous regarding the new direction for economic governance in the country:

To reduce the dominance of the public sector in the economy and develop a viable, dynamic, highly motivated socially and environmentally responsible private sector. Develop a strong public and private sector partnership which fosters a strong economy that is private sector-driven, with the government as the enabler.

The report goes on to list the strategies for achieving the above goal as follows:

* Make government more efficient
* Increase public/private sector interaction
* Deregulate and liberalise the economy.

What is being envisaged here is a huge turnaround in the way the nation's business has been managed in the past. While presenting his Budget 2000 on November 28, 1999, Nigeria's President, Chief Olusegun Obasanjo, reiterated the envisioned pre-eminence of the private sector. According to the President,

the policy thrust of the Budget for the Year 2000, is to lower the inflation rate, lay a solid foundation for private sector-led economic growth, pay profound attention to education and agricultural production, and consequently reduce unemployment and poverty. Thus, with this budget, the government aims to:

* *provide the framework for taking government out of direct involvement in most economic activities which are best suited for private sector undertaking;*
* *provide the enabling legal, fiscal and monetary environment for the private sector to become the effective engine of growth and development in the economy;*
* *up-grade the performance of major infrastructural facilities;*
* *continue to improve the operational capabilities of the law enforcement agencies at crime prevention, detection and control;*
* *continue with the policy of probity, transparency and accountability in order to reduce the cost of doing business in Nigeria;*

* *fight illiteracy through the implementation of the Universal Basic Education Scheme;*
* *intensify pursuit of poverty alleviation and enhanced food security through fiscal incentives to lenders and borrowers for agricultural production; and by encouraging each state to concentrate on at least one crop for massive and intensive production within the state;*
* *improve the health of the population through the rapid upgrading of our preventive and curative healthcare delivery system, with particular emphasis on HIV/AIDS, etc.*

All of the foregoing notwithstanding, my major concerns are as follows:

1. Is the private sector really willing to take up the mantle of economic leadership?
2. Has the private sector the capacity to deliver, even if it is willing?
3. Will the public sector carry out all these necessary reforms as enumerated by the President with sufficient speed to enable the private sector to perform?

I believe that the private sector is willing. But it is not fully aware of the amount of effort it takes to be the engine of growth. Also, I do not believe it has the capacity to deliver. A lot is yet to be done to build up the capacity in the private sector. One is happy to note that one or two organisations are thinking of setting up entrepreneurial development centres.

Lastly, I hope that the public sector will deliver what it has promised in Budget 2000. This is indeed a critical first principle to securing the new vision of a private sector-led Nigerian economy.

The direction has been set. It will not be easy-going all the way. But with determination, the goal of turning around Africa's potentially most vibrant economy can be achieved. All over the world, nations are boldly shifting the burden of financing economic growth to the market and private enterprise. The hour has equally dawned for us in Nigeria. The private sector had better get its act together so as to fully excel in this new role.

*Being **a** paper presented at the Forum on the Nigerian Economic Development — Private Sector Perspectives at Washington, D. C, USA. December 1999*

Chapter 8

Challenges of E-Commerce to Bank Inspectors

Introduction

It is indeed a great privilege for us at Diamond Bank to host this special session of your committee for the following reasons: it is the second to be held under the present civilian administration and, the last in this millennium.

The banking sector is the fulcrum around which all transactions in the economy revolve. If this fulcrum is unhealthy, unstable or lacks integrity, then the continued economic well-being of the country becomes uncertain. The role of bank inspection, in safeguarding the integrity of the banking industry, cannot be overemphasised.

Undoubtedly, Nigerian Bank Inspectors have operated in a largely unfriendly environment during the past decades. The consequence of this harsh environment has been a whittling down of their effectiveness. Recent bank failures have equally given the impression that Bank Inspectors were probably not alive to their work as such problems could have been nipped in the bud. These perceptions are some of the hazards for Bank Inspectors operating in a defective environment. It is hoped however, that the new political environment will definitely offer great opportunities and major challenges to improve on your contribution to the growth and development of the banking industry.

Today, the world is on the threshold of a great scientific and technological revolution. The spate of the developments in the electronic industry and its speed, scope and impact in the world, and especially the financial sector, are yet to be fully appreciated. Also, by standing at the threshold of a new and very highly electronic millennium, you must be faced with so many questions which you should, by now, be making efforts to appreciate. Today's meeting, therefore, presents a veritable opportunity to re-check your technical and psychological readiness for the task ahead. As a keen follower of your activities for a long time, I have no doubt that you are able to cope with the ramifications of this technological development, as it unfolds in the 21st Century, in order to enhance your contribution to the Nigerian banking industry. This development, while progressive, has its own negative consequences.

In this paper, I shall be highlighting, for you to ponder over, my concerns on the security issues of Electronic Commerce (E-Commerce), which is one aspect of this technological development as it pertains to our industry.

The Growing World of Electronic Commerce

Electronic Commerce involves the exchange of transactions via communication networks. It represents a broad range of technologies, processes and practices, which permit the transaction of businesses through electronic and largely paperless mechanisms. This is also called 'Cyber Trading' and describes automated business-related transactions. It has made life a lot easier for the business community in advanced countries by drastically reducing the use of cash and transaction processing time. There are currently so many forms of E-Commerce (Cyber Trading) among which are Automated Teller Machine (ATM), Electronic Data Interchange (EDI), Point Of Sale (POS), Electronic Card Payment System, Internet, Home Banking, etc.

The transactions carried out in the cyberspace, span from purchase of items via electronic mail message, shopping in an electronic mall on the World Wide Web, to electronic filing of tax returns. What seems to dominate the Nigerian banking industry today are On-line real-time Banking and the Electronic Card Payment System based on the Smartcard technology.

It is believed that in the 21st Century, Electronic Commerce or Cyber Trading will have advanced, and substantially taken over much of the payment system and payments for basic utilities would be by the electronic card system. By this time, it is my belief that Nigeria would join other developing and developed nations in the Intensive utilisation of Electronic Commerce in the next millennium. This would, however, depend on our literacy rate, technological awareness and income levels. Undoubtedly, Inter-bank Trading Systems will depend largely on communication networks.

Security Issues and Challenges to Bank Inspectors

The benefits of Electronic Commerce are numerous. For one thing, it has increased the potential of business to attain greater productivity and profitability. These benefits are, however, not without their own difficulties. In particular, Cyber Trading has increased the vulnerability of mercantile houses to the incidence of fraud, intrusion and outright attacks by unwarranted persons. In this regard, the most exposed sector is the banking industry because of its stock-in- trade, which is money, and near-money instruments.

In reacting to this, therefore, there is a need to highlight the security issues in Electronic Commerce so that Bank Inspectors can find ways of mitigating the risks. This will give the desired assurance of confidentiality, integrity, availability and legitimacy of business transactions to customers, shareholders and stakeholders of banks, and indeed, the entire populace. Here lies, the compulsion to consider the following security concerns in our environment; namely:

(i)   Security of corporate information over free e-mail web sites;
(ii)   Data encryption;
(iii) Firewalls;
(iv)   Non-repudiation in electronic commerce; and
(v)   Downloading from Internet sites.

Security of Corporate Information over free E-mail Web Sites

Electronic Mail, as a way of communication, is gaining rapid popularity in the industry. For all its conveniences, it has security problems. In view of the fact that an e-mail message travels through several different networks until it reaches its destination, you must, therefore, ask yourselves the following questions:

·   Does your organisation allow the transmission of confidential corporate information over free e-mail sites like Yahoo, Hotmail, Microsoft Network or any other e-mail sites?
·   Is the integrity of your Internet Service Provider (TSP) assured?

Data Encryption

One thing that generates a lot of concern in E-Commerce is the interception of vital information. Hackers, sniffers and intruders are everywhere discovering and developing new ways of tapping into network resources. The major way of preventing this act is the encryption of data and information. It involves the transformation of data and information, sent via the network, into a format that will not be understandable. This has been found to be the backbone of network security.

However, in view of the dynamism in the knowledge and skills acquisition in Information Technology, hackers and sniffers are up-dating their skills, on a daily basis, to break into encrypted information. Do banks in Nigeria have adequate equipment to encrypt data transmitted over their networks?

Firewalls

Firewalls are network devices used to restrict connection to an organisation's network from external networks and dial-up links. To a lesser extent, they are also used to restrict access by users on the internal network to external network e.g. the Internet.

If firewalls are not properly configured and maintained, intruders could penetrate the firewalls and access an organisation's internal network.

Therefore, the following questions would aid the assessment of the effectiveness of firewalls:

- Are the firewalls physically and logically configured in a secure manner?
- Does the inspector have the technical skills to audit the firewall?

Non-Repudiation in Electronic Commerce

In today's world of Cyber Trading, a lot of banks are already transacting businesses through the web, while others are planning to follow suit. The consequence of this is that paper documents would be eliminated. How do we then ensure that there is non-repudiation (i.e. inability to deny the initiation of transactions) by concerned parties?

Do banks, that are planning to implement Internet Banking Solutions, have in place authentication schemes that go beyond the traditional system of "what you know"(passwords) to also include "what you have"(cards, tokens, PIN etc.)?

Downloading from Internet Sites

A major area of concern in the downloading of files and software from the Internet is the transmission of computer viruses. Consequently, the following questions are pertinent in checking the menace posed by indiscriminate downloading of files.

· Are there adequate policies and procedures regulating the downloading of files from the Internet into organisations' computer systems? Are they being enforced for strict adherence?

· Does your organisation have well-installed virus protection?

Conclusion

Information Technology changes are in a state of flux, with new developments occurring every moment. The E- Commerce, where trading is carried out in a cashless and paperless environment, is gaining popularity worldwide and with its potential for higher acceptability. This good news is, however, matched by the possibility of high crime.

As Chief Inspectors of banks and other financial institutions, you should rise up to the challenges and prepare yourselves for the 21st Century IT applications. This can only be achieved by continually updating your skills in the dynamic world of Information Technology and, also, by creating awareness among yourselves of the threats associated with Electronic Commerce.

I feel for you. While your part of the world is still battling to understand the sources and causes of the first Industrial Revolution, you are being called upon to fight crime on the Information Superhighway. I am, however, encouraged by your past achievements. I know you are equal to the task. You will surely succeed.

Being text of a paper presented on the occasion of the 84th Quarterly Meeting of the Committee of Chief Inspectors of Banks in Nigeria, December 1999.

Part III

Strengthening the Banking Sector

PART III

Strengthening the Nigerian Banking Sector

The liberalisation of banking licenses was an adjunct to the restructuring of the Nigerian economy of the late 1980s such that, by the turn of that decade, some 110 banks were in operation. In their wake though, there were several challenges, including: competition, capital adequacy, skilled personnel, management and corporate governance. Despite the obvious deepening of banking services at the time, not a few felt that the sector was not doing enough. Banks were accused of a weak capital base, of being elitist in outlook, and a threat to the nation – milking the economy and the real sector dry and, in the process, declaring supernormal profits for themselves and their immediate constituents. And when the burst arrived in the mid 1990s, resulting in the liquidation of about 50 banks, not many outside the industry shed tears for the sector and its managers.

Today, in spite of the banking reforms of 2005, with the attendant strengthening of the capital base, the reduction of the number of banks from 89 to 25, the deployment of relevant information technology and development of various products and services, public perception of banks has not necessarily improved. Indeed, the global financial melt-down seems to have accentuated the criticisms levelled against Nigerian banks and bankers.

The questions that arise therefore include:
·   Are the perception and criticisms of Nigerian banks a reality? Are bankers guilty as charged?
·   How can Nigerian banks and bankers change the public's perception of the sector?
·   What really are the roles of banks in national economic management and growth?

Part III of this book answers these questions via four related sub-titles:

- Macroeconomic environment and the banking sector
- Cross-border cooperation in banking supervision
- Corporate governance in the financial sector
- Ethics and responsible leadership in the banking profession.

Chapter 9

Macroeconomic Environment and Banking System II

Introduction

I will start my address today on a note of appreciation to the nation's preeminent institution for policy and strategic studies and research. The National Institute for Policy and Strategic Studies (NIPSS) has, over the years, acquired an enviable reputation as an intellectual academy of note, not just within the boundaries of our country, but well beyond. Its products, both of the human variety and in terms of research output, would easily rival those of some of the best-known policy academies in the world. It is precisely for this reason that I regard the invitation extended to me by the authority of the Institute to share my thoughts on banking and the larger economy with participants at the Senior Executive Course (SEC) as an honour.

Last year, I delivered a lecture to this august gathering on this same topic. This year I have tried to vary the paper by getting into some greater details in terms of providing some macroeconomic data to support my arguments. The conclusions have remained more-or-less the same, only that, this time, the points have been made vividly visible.

Let me now turn to the theme of my address to this august audience. My original mandate was to discuss the topic "The Macroeconomic Environment and Commercial Banking". I have, however, slightly modified the theme to now read "The Macroeconomic Environment and The Banking System in Nigeria".

With the introduction of universal banking in January 2001, the terms 'commercial' and 'merchant,' as they apply to the banking business here in Nigeria, have become at best nebulous concepts. A more expansive view of the issue would, therefore, seem more relevant to our current realities.

The National Environment

The macroeconomic environment is a sub element of the national environment which, itself, comprises elements, such as the social structure, political setting, the nation's constitutional framework, the rule of law, security of life and property, educational system, ethical standard, religion and culture, population and demography etc., that influence activities and other inter and intra relationships in a country.

The national environment influences the macroeconomic environment, which in turn influences the banking system. The converse is also true: the national environment is affected by the macroeconomic environment, which is also affected by the state of the banking system. Thus, a stable and well functioning macroeconomic environment is impossible unless the whole national environment is stable and conducive. Similarly, without a stable and conducive macroeconomic environment, a sound banking system is impossible.

In this paper, we shall first of all discuss the macroeconomic environment and the interplay of factors that influence it. The paper will then examine the banking system and how the macroeconomic environment affects it, and vice- versa. The main conclusion is that it is the macroeconomic environment that determines the state of affairs in the banking industry, and not the other way round. The rest of the paper is divided into five sections. Section three defines macroeconomic environment and briefly describes the key elements that make up the macroeconomic environment and their linkages. Section four gives an overview of the performance of Nigeria's monetary policy management. Section five details the structure of the Nigerian financial system and the banking industry. Section six tries to highlight the relationship between the banking system and the macroeconomic environment. Section seven gives a brief conclusion.

The Macroeconomic Environment

The macroeconomic environment is the totality of the behaviour of the economy as a whole, this includes: booms and recessions, the economy's total output of goods and services and the growth of output, the rates of inflation and unemployment, internal fiscal balance and external balance of payment positions, level of infrastructure and capital formation, external and domestic debts, etc. In studying our macroeconomic environment we normally focus on the economic behaviour and policies that affect economic growth and development. Whereas economic growth relates mainly to increasing the wealth of the nation, development goes further to emphasise desirable changes in the structure and pattern of the economy, in order to achieve growth on a sustainable basis. To achieve economic growth and development we need to study the behaviour of macroeconomic variables so as to design policies that will enable us to influence the magnitude and direction of such variables. This is the essence of monetary policy management.

In examining the macroeconomic environment, we are looking at the aggregates, whereby all the variables and indices are linked in an intricate cause-and-effect chain that underscores the performance of the entire economic system. As such, investment leads to the creation of real output in the form of goods and services, which in turn leads to the creation of employment which then leads to the creation of income and ultimately savings, which in turn are invested to finance economic growth. All of these variables work in a circular manner to either bring about wealth creation on an ongoing basis or, otherwise, lead to the sustenance of poverty. Hence, either singly or collectively, these variables impact positively or negatively on every aspect of the macroeconomic system. Similarly, a break in the linkage, or weakening of one or more, leads to distortion and instability in the entire economic system.

Issues in Monetary Policy

We cannot do real justice to the theme of our presentation today without some consideration of the foundation on which banking business is conducted. But monetary policy is, indeed, more than just the foundation for the conduct of banking business. It is, in fact, one of the most important macroeconomic policy instruments. The goal of monetary policy in any country will usually vary over time, depending on the level of economic development, the existing financial structure, and the bias of economic policy pursuits. In general, however, the basic objectives of monetary policy are fourfold, namely: full employment, real growth in output, price stability and internal (fiscal) and external (balance of payment) equilibrium. A country is said to have macroeconomic stability when these objectives are achieved and sustained over time. Please note that a prerequisite to price stability is that money supply and real output should grow in tandem. To buttress the imperative of monetary stability, I will paraphrase the words of former US Federal Reserve Board Chairman, Paul A. Voicker at the 1990 monetary conference in Beijing, China: "Without a sense of monetary stability, I do not think we can have a very effectively operating economy ... in which all participants can produce, (are) willing to save, will be willing to invest in the future, and will be able to trade freely with other countries".

The Central Bank of Nigeria has the sole responsibility of monetary policy management. This includes setting the objectives of monetary policy, setting targets for key macroeconomic variables in line with the monetary policy objectives, using market-based measures to ensure the attainment of the targets, review of policy outcomes and possible revision of targets and/or monetary policy measures. In the actual implementation of this policy objective, the monetary authorities use the banking system as their main vehicle. The banking system is, therefore, the main vehicle used by the monetary authorities for the creation of a desired macroeconomic environment.

An Overview of Nigeria's Monetary Policy Management

The specific monetary policy objectives, which the Central Bank of Nigeria has been pursuing for the past decade, include:
  a) Reduction of excess liquidity in the system;
  b) Sustenance of single digit inflation;
  c) Maintenance of exchange rate stability;
  d) Sustenance of a market-based interest rate regime;
  e) Promotion of non-inflationary growth;
  f) Achievement of balance of payments viability; and
  g) Maintenance of financial sector stability.

In line with these objectives, targets for key monetary and credit aggregates were set as shown in Table 1. Before we discuss the result, I would like to comment on these objectives and the targets set to achieve them.

First, if the objective of reducing excess liquidity is taken seriously, the target growth in transaction money supply (Ml) should not exceed the target GDP growth rate, just as in year 2001. In year 2000 and 2002, we are said to be budgeting for excess liquidity and higher inflation by targeting an Ml growth of 9.8 per cent and 12.4 per cent and aggregate credit growth of 27.8 per cent and 57.9 per cent, while aiming at 3 per cent and 5 per cent GDP growth, respectively. These targets are out of alignment: if we know that GDP will not grow by more than 5 per cent, we should have tightened credit and monetary growth to keep inflation under control.

Secondly, we appear to be happy with a situation in which the government gets more banking sector credit than the private sector. Even if this is so, in reality, we should set targets that aim at correcting the abnormality rather than accept it. See Tables 1a and b.

Thirdly, the CBN has sustenance of a market-based interest rate regime as its objective, when it has already imposed an interest rate ceiling.

It is not surprising, therefore, that the implementation of monetary policy faced daunting challenges in 2002 as the problem of excess liquidity persisted, and the demand pressure in the foreign exchange market intensified. The details are as follows:

Growth in Money Supply

The experience of the CBN with monetary policy management, in recent years, has been that of target overshooting. This development is of serious concern, especially as the divergence between targets and actual values have been persistently wide in recent years. The high rate of growth in money supply leads to an increase in demand for foreign exchange, hence exacting downwards pressure on the exchange rate.

The results in Tables 1a and 1b show that the growth in monetary aggregates exceeded targets by wide margins. The growth in monetary aggregates was in excess of the programme targets for 2002, but represented a considerable moderation, compared with the preceding year. Broad money (M2) grew by 21.5 per cent, compared with the target of 15.3 per cent for the year and 27.0 per cent recorded in 2001. Similarly, narrow money (MI) rose by 15.9 per cent, compared with the target of 12.4 per cent and 28.1 per cent achieved in the preceding year. The excessive growth, in money supply, was induced by the expansionary fiscal operations of the three tiers of government.

Fiscal Indiscipline

The deteriorating macroeconomic indicators underscored the need to tighten monetary policy during the period. However, this was not possible due to the fiscal indiscipline of the three tiers of government. As shown in Table 2 the fiscal operations of the Federal Government in 2002 resulted in an overall deficit of N301 .4 billion or 5.1 per cent of GDP, exceeding the deficit of ₦221.1 billion or 4.0 per cent of GDP recorded in the previous year and a budget deficit of ₦103.8 billion or 2.1 per cent of GDP recorded in year 2000. The deficit was financed entirely from domestic sources, including past savings of excess crude oil proceeds and borrowing from the banking system through the issuance of treasury bills.

The state governments have also been recently following the footsteps of the Federal Government. Since the year 2000, they have been running an exponentially increasing budget deficit: from a mere ₦0.59 billion deficit to a huge deficit of ₦54.72 billion last year.

The local governments appear to be more disciplined. They had a deficit of ₦1.98 billion in year 2000 but have been running surpluses since then.

Table 1a: Outcomes of Monetary, Financial and Other Targets

Indicator	2000 Target %	2000 Actual %	2001 Target %	2001 Actual %	2002 Target* %	2002 Actual %	2003 Actual %
M 2	14.6	41.8	12.2	27.0	15.3	21.5	16.2
M 1	9.8	62.2	4.3	28.1	12.4	15.9	12.5
Aggregate Bank Credit	27.8	-23.1	15.8	79.9	57.9	56.6	16.0
Credit (net) to Federal Govt.	37.8	-162.3	2.6	96.6	96.6	6,320.6**	
Credit to Private Sector	21.9	30.9	22.8	43.5	34.9	11.8	
Inflation Rate	9.0	6.9	7.0	18.9	9.3	12.9	10.1
Growth in GDP	3.0	3.8	5.0	4.2	5.0	3.3	

*   Revised
**   Reflecting the substantial draw down on Federal Government deposits
     with the CBN
Source: CBN 2002 Annual Report

Table 1b: Credit Developments (₦ million)

	2000	2001	2002
Aggregate Bank Credit	472,011.7		
Credit (net) to Federal Government	(123,980.8)	(6,006.5)	373,639.2
Of which: Central Bank	(334,003.2)	(185,934.6)	(41,246.8)
DMBs	219,013.4	179,928.1	414,886.0
Credit to Private Sector	596,001.5	854,999.4	955,762.1
Of which: Central Bank	8,001.6	10,513.4	7,298.0
DMBs	587,999.9	844,486.2	948,464.1

Table 2: Analysis of Federal, States and Local Governments Fiscal Balance (₦ billion)

	1997	1998	1999	2000	2001	2002
Overall Fiscal Balance: Federal Government	(5.0)	(133.39)	(285.10)	(103.8)	(221.1)	(301.40)
Overall Fiscal Balance: State	4.27	0.033	1.09	(0.59)	(23.41)	(54.72)
Overall Fiscal Balance: Local Government	1.52	(1.54)	0.36	(1.98)	0.148	2.33

Source: CBN 2002 Annual Report

Growth in Domestic Output (Income)

The real gross domestic product (GDP) increased by 3.3 per cent, compared with 4.2 per cent in 2001 and 3.8 per cent in 2000. Overall, the performance was below the target of a 5 per cent GDP growth rate, which has remained elusive, and the target of double-digit growth as contained in the Vision 2010 document.

In terms of sector contribution, agriculture accounted for 40.8 per cent of aggregate output while the industrial sector, comprising crude petroleum, mining and quarrying, and manufacturing, contributed 16.0 per cent. The sectors, which contributed to the modest growth, included: agriculture, manufacturing, communications, utilities, building and construction as well as services. Mining production, however, declined by 13.6 per cent, due to the reduction in Nigeria's production quota by the OPEC in 2002, as part of its bid to shore-up and stabilise crude oil prices.

There are two factors that have bedevilled domestic productivity in Nigeria. These are: the poor level of infrastructure and over dependence on imported raw materials. Hence, a lower value of the naira always leads to an increase in the cost of production and hence, prices, rather than an increase in the unit of goods produced for exports. In particular, following the depreciation of the naira from ₦84.4/$1 .00 to ₦120.47/$1 .00, among other inflationary factors, the nominal GDP increased from ₦2.76 trillion to ₦5.72 trillion, however, in real terms the GDP only increased from N1.12.95 billion to ₦129.83 billion. See Table 3 below.

Table 3: Cross Domestic Product (Naira billion)

	1998	**1999**	**2000**	**2001**	**2002**
Average Exchange Rate ₦-$1.00	84.4	96.1	102.1	111.9	120.47
GDP at current factor cost	2,765.67	3,193.67	4,842.19	5,545.41	5,726.19
GDP at 1984 Prices	112.95	116.14	120.64	125.72	129.83
Non Oil (GDP)	99.47	103.67	106.77	11.13	117.23
GDP Growth rate (%)	2.3	2.82	3.87	4.21	3.27

Source: Federal Office of Statistics (FOS) & National Planning
*   Commission*

Domestic Prices Stability

Inflation, as measured by the change in the average all-item consumer price index for the twelve-month period ending December 2002, was 12.9 per cent. It represented a deceleration compared with the 18.9 per cent recorded in 2001.

The food index, which is a dominant component, rose by 13.1 per cent compared with 28.0 per cent in the preceding year. However, the core inflation rate, which excludes the impact of food, was 12.5 per cent, compared with 6.0 per cent in 2001. Hence, a situation in which the core inflation rate can double in twelve month is far from being stable.

Interest Rate Stability

Deposit money banks' average deposit and lending rates declined generally in 2002. This was attributable to the downward review of the CBN's MRR, from 20.5 per cent in January to 18.5 in July and 16.5 per cent in December 2002, and the moral suasion employed by the CBN to encourage banks to bring down their lending rates in order to boost investment. With the inflation rate at 12.9 per cent in December 2002, some of the deposit rates were positive in real terms but most were negative. The sharp fall in the call rate, as in the past, was influenced largely by the surfeit of liquidity in the banking system as well as the reduced demand pressure in the foreign exchange market during the second half of the year. From the above, we can see that interest rates are regulated and are very unstable.

External Payments Position

The balance of payments was under severe pressure in 2002 as a result of adverse external shocks, particularly the reduction in Nigeria's crude oil production quota by the OPEC and the external debt service burden (over $3.00 billion since year 2000). Consequently, the overall balance of payments swung into a deficit of US$(4,363.7 million) or 8.9 per cent of GDP, from the surplus of US$261.2 million or 0.4 per cent of GDP in 2001. Consequently, there was a substantial draw down of external reserves and a deferment of scheduled debt service payments. Nevertheless, the current account recorded a surplus while the capital account has been persistently in deficit, mainly due to divestments (minus $8,276.3 in 2002), including private capital outflow (minus $6,917.0). The level of external reserves fell from US$10.42 to US$7.99 billion, which could support 6.4 months of foreign exchange disbursements, compared with the 8.0 months achieved in 2001 (Please see Table 4).

The macro-economic performance below is far out of line with the stated objectives of the monetary authorities. The situation is very bad. We cannot control monetary growth, and hence inflation and pressure on the exchange rate; the growth in our domestic output is negligible; our export earnings are erratic, undiversified and remained below $25 billion since 1980. Are the banks responsible for this? Let us now review the Nigerian financial system, by way of introduction, before addressing this question in Section six.

Table 4: Analysis of FGN Revenues and External Balances (US million)

	1997	1998	1999	2000	2001	2002
Crude Oil Exports	14,850.1	8,564.7	12664.9	18,897.2	17,633.8	14,77.4
Non-oil Exports	357.2	406.5	211.1	244.2	250.3	785.7
Current Account Balance	3,747.7	(4,315.0)	444.80	6,954.8	2,170.7	1,933.2
Capital Account Balance	(3,670.5)	1,519.6	(3,915.4)	(3,760.5)	(1,887.5)	(6,220.5)
Overall Balance of Payments	15.00	(2,873.0)	(3,537.2)	3,090.4	211.20	(4,363.7)
Stock of External Reserves	7,581.20	7,100.00	5,450.00	9,910.40	10.415.6	7,986.7

Source: CBN 2002 Annual Report

Overview of the Nigerian Financial System

The structure of the Nigerian financial system can be seen as displayed in appendix 1. It is important to note that the entire financial system, including the roles of each segment, is defined and driven by the structure.

The Nigerian financial system is highly fragmented and has yet to achieve that robustness that is required to make it globally competitive. Besides, the regulatory regime is too burdensome to allow needed flexibility in the system for growth and development

The Nigerian Financial System comprises the banking system, the capital market and the insurance industry. The National Insurance Commission (NAICOM) is the supervisory body for all insurance companies. The Securities and Exchange Commission (SEC) is the regulatory body for the brokerage firms and the Nigerian Stock Exchange. The Nigeria Deposit Insurance Corporation (NDIC) insures the deposits of all deposit-taking institutions, but is allowed to use its discretion whether or not and when to insure all deposits.

The NDIC, SEC and NAICOM are autonomous from the Central Bank of Nigeria but are all, including the CBN, under the Federal Ministry of Finance. The Chief Executives of all the five institutions are members of the Financial Services Regulation Co-ordination Committee. This body chaired by the Minister of Finance meets to co-ordinate the supervision and regulation of the financial services industry.

The Central Bank of Nigeria is the apex institution in the banking system. It is responsible for controlling and supervising the Deposit Money Banks, Finance Houses, Discount Houses, Community Banks, Primary Mortgage Institutions, Bureau de Change, all of which are deposit-taking institutions. All development banks, though not deposit-taking institutions, are also regulated by the Central Bank.

The liberalisation of the financial sector received a further boost in 2001 with the removal of the dichotomy between commercial and merchant banks, following the adoption of universal banking. Under the system, the erstwhile commercial and merchant banks transformed into Deposit Money Banks and were allowed to engage in both commercial and merchant banking activities, as well as in insurance business, depending on an individual bank's operational preference.

The Development Banking sub-sector has been weak for quite some years. The government, having realised this, set up a committee to restructure the sub- sector. Consequently, the erstwhile NIDB, NBCI and NERFUND were merged into the new Bank of Industry; while the former People's Bank and the NACB were merged into the NACRDB. The proposed merger of the Federal Mortgage Finance Limited with the Federal Mortgage Bank of Nigeria, to form the Nigeria National Mortgage Bank, is yet to materialise. Surprisingly, these restructuring efforts left out the Education Bank and the Urban Development Bank, which are still weak and have had little impact on the economy. Likewise, the problem of dual regulation and supervision, which is being sorted out for the Mortgage Banking sub-sector, needs to be extended to the Community Banking sub-sector. In particular, the position of the National Board for Community Banks needs to be re-examined.

In order to effectively supervise the non-bank financial institutions, the CBN established a new department, the Other Financial Institutions Department, to carry out on-site and off-site surveillance on community banks, finance companies, primary mortgage institutions, bureaux de change and development finance institutions.

The main advantage of the present regulatory framework is that it has, for the first time, brought all deposit-taking financial institutions directly under the supervision of the Central Bank of Nigeria. However, the community banks and mortgage institutions are still under dual supervision.

Structurally, the Nigerian financial system, as at the end of year 2002, comprised the CBN, 90 deposit money banks, which together constituted the monetary system, and other financial institutions, consisting of 769 community banks, 6 development finance institutions, 1 stock exchange, 1 commodity exchange, 5 discount houses, 118 insurance companies, 80 primary mortgage institutions, 102 finance companies, and 83 bureaux de change.

The structure of our banking system has been changed a number of times since independence. This is usually followed by the introduction of a new financial institution and/or a new regulatory body. The basic reason for such changes is the desire to strengthen the channels through which financial resources are injected into the economy. In other words, the changes are brought about in order to ensure that the public policy goals of the government can be achieved. These public policy objectives include:

a) Promotion of efficient intermediation
b) Maintenance of stability and confidence in the system

c) Protection against systemic risk and collapse

d) Achievement of monetary policy goals.

It should be noted that these policy objectives are not mutually exclusive. For instance, unless the banking system is protected against systemic risk, public confidence will be eroded. And, unless there is public confidence in the system, deposit mobilisation will be difficult and hence efficient allocation of surplus resources, to profitable ventures, will be impaired. Thus, without efficient intermediation, the banking system could not bring about any meaningful economic growth and development. Let us now look at this assertion in greater detail.

Relationship between Banking and the Macro-economic Environment

At the end of Section four we wondered whether banks are responsible for the poor state of our macro-economic environment. The puzzle in this question is that the macro-economic environment is affected by the banking system and, similarly, state of the banking system is largely dependent on the macro-economic environment. It must, however, be pointed out that the banking system does not drive the economy or any sector of it. It rather facilitates and renders support to the various sectors of the economy. Indeed, banks generally react to events and decisions emanating from outside the system. In fact, anything that happens within the system is invariably caused by something exogenous to the system. Unfortunately, this is not well understood by the general public which blames the banking system whenever there is a change in some relative prices such as interest rate, foreign exchange rate, or even for such things as absence of long term loanable funds or medium to long-term capital funds in the economy.

How the Banking System Contributes to the Macro-economic Outcomes

The banking system makes significant contributions to the process and magnitude of economic growth in several key ways. These include the following:

· The promotion of growth by raising the savings rate, channelling savings into investment, enhancing the efficiency of capital accumulation and by eliminating costly disruptions to the investment and production process.

· A more efficient allocation of these savings into investment outlets than the individual savers can accomplish on their own.

· It increases the fraction of societal resources devoted to interest-yielding assets and long-term investment which, in turn, augment economic growth. Conversely, it reduces the fraction of societal savings held in the form of unproductive liquid assets.

· It reduces risks faced by firms in their production processes by providing liquidity and enables investors to improve their portfolio diversification by providing insurance and project monitoring information.

· It induces firms to operate more efficiently by monitoring loan projects and by offering financial protection against premature liquidation of their capital.

Clearly, if the banking system enhances the mobilisation of resources, improves the allocation of capital and enhances the productivity of firms, it should make significant contributions to overall economic growth.

How the Macro-economic Environment Drives the Banking System

Financial institutions mobilise savings and allocate credit. The larger and wealthier an economy is, the greater should be the volume of resources that can be mobilised and invested. In this simple way, it can be shown that the size and growth of the real sector influences the size of the corresponding banking system. As an economy develops many different types of financial intermediaries are established, to offer borrowers and lenders a wide range and variety of financial services. The demand driven nature of most financial services implies that real sector economic growth influences the range and type of financial services found in an economy. In general, as an economy develops, its economic agents tend to evolve from self-finance to external finance. Further economic growth stimulates financial development in terms of the development of institutions and markets for direct credit.

In fact, empirical studies have established strong evidence of a positive correlation between the level of real per capita income and the ratio of credit to overall income. This implies that countries with higher incomes have more developed financial systems.

Furthermore, the allocation of credit by the financial system has important implications for economic growth. In particular, empirical evidence indicates that:

- Countries with faster growth rates tend to have financial systems that allocate a larger proportion of total credit to the private sector; and
- The share of credit allocated to the private sector by the financial system is positively and significantly correlated with both the investment rate and the efficiency of investment.

Given the two-way nature of the relationship between finance and economic growth, it would appear that one might not necessarily be used effectively to leverage the other. The nature of the relationship also implies that a country may experience a vicious cycle in which both the financial system and the real sector grow together, in a mutually reinforcing way or in a vicious cycle in which they both stagnate and decline. Hence, financial sector reform and market liberalisation would be more effective if they were accompanied by other policies that directly stimulate real sector growth and enhance overall macro-economic stability.

The point to make here is indeed a rebuttal of the general impression that banks drive the economic system. Nothing can be further from the reality. Banks are not the key drivers of the economy. Rather they play the role typically reminiscent of catalysts. To that extent, banks act as facilitators and generally render support to the various sectors that constitute the aggregate economy.

Banking business takes place in a world of externalities. Banks generally react to decisions emanating from outside the banking system itself. In other words, the banking system's causative capacity is very limited. For instance, the question is often asked as to what extent banking is really responsible for the structure of interest rates, the exchange rate regime or even the paucity of medium and long term capital. Interest rates will rise when the budget spells out a tight money regime; the naira/dollar exchange rate will rise or fall to the extent of the performance of macro-economic fundamentals. None of these realities are set in motion from within the banking industry itself.

Perhaps more important than anything else is the overall structure of the Nigerian economy which, as we all know, is largely public sector driven. Over the years, oil —the nation's primary revenue source has dictated the size of the public sector. By elementary extension of logic, the size of the macro- economy is also determined by this single commodity called oil. So that, in a special sense, the oil sector has historically fuelled the supply side of the economy, while also impacting significantly on the demand side. Crude oil exports account for 94.50 per cent of our exports earning. Oil being by nature highly volatile, the entire foundation of the Nigerian economy is, to that extent, built on a substance akin to quicksand. The question then is: to what extent can a banking system, so dependent on external (and unstable) influences, be expected to then play a moderating role in the economy? Your answer on this matter is as good as mine.

In the rather confused environment, within which the current debate over the role of the banking system, in creating long-tern economic growth, has proceeded, the temptation to place the horse before the cart has been a most noticeable failing. What is clearly happening today is that we are attempting to make banking credit play the role that has historically been the forte of long-term equity. This is wrong! We must first develop the incentive structure and investments that foster the culture of insurance, pension funds, capital markets, direct foreign investments, etc. Our economic management approach has tended to lay emphasis on sporadic and intense spotlights on the pieces of the puzzle rather than the whole. That is why, from time to time, massive national interest is riveted on such matters as foreign exchange, SME funding, interest rates, etc. Until we retract from this set approach, I am afraid that the real solution will continue to elude us.

Banks contribute to the outcome of the macroeconomic interplay only as catalysts would by facilitating the transmittal process of fiscal actions of government. Monetary policy, being largely reactive to signals from the fiscal environment, would then seek the instrumentality of the banking industry to bring a semblance of harmony. A strong and stable macro-economy is ultimately a function of an efficient interplay of fiscal and monetary policies. You cannot talk of a stable macro-economic environment in a situation where the fiscal and monetary policies are working at cross-purpose. The effectiveness of banking in the transmittal process is, therefore, as good as the state of harmony between fiscal and monetary policies. No amount of good monetary policy can ameliorate the adverse effects of bad fiscal measures.

I would like to address one very important issue: that is the limit to which the banking system can be used to ameliorate the adverse effects of fiscal indiscipline. Monetary policies can only be effective if :

a) The banking system is of sound health.

b) The banking system controls a significant proportion of the money supply.

The Health of the Banking System

The oligopolistic structure of the sector remained in the year 2002, as only ten banks of the ninety in operation accounted for 54.5 per cent of total assets, 52.4 per cent of total deposit liabilities, and 46.1 per cent of total credit, compared with the 50.8, 53.1 and 46.5 per cent respectively in 2001. Eleven (11) banks failed to meet the minimum liquidity ratio requirement and 36 banks reported a net loan to deposit ratio of over 100 per cent during the year: that is, they are over trading. Hence, the banking system is not only skewed but has a significant number of problem banks. The existence of distressed banks complicates monetary policy management.

The Level of Money Supply Controlled by the Banking System

The ability of the monetary authorities to control monetary growth and inflation, as well as stimulate savings and investment depends on the degree of banking habit in a given country. In Nigeria, the informal sector accounts for a significant part of the economy. In particular, as we can see in Table 5, about 41 per cent of our money supply is outside the banking system. With such a high proportion of money supply outside the banking system it is very difficult for any monetary policy measure to be effective.

Table 5: The Composition of Money Supply (Ml)

	2000		2001		2002	
	Amount	%	Amount	%	Amount	%
Currency Banks	260.39	41.72	338.7	41.47	386.9	40.89
Demand Deposit	363.72	58.28	478.03	58.53	559.31	59.11
Ml	624.11	100	816.73	100	946.21	100

Conclusion

In concluding, six key points have emerged from our discourse thus far.

1. There is a symbiotic relationship between the macroeconomic environment and the banking system. Like Siamese twins, one cannot succeed without the other - hence there must be alignment and coordination.

2. In Nigeria, government is the dominant player in the economy. While we are in transition to a market-driven, private sector-led economy, this is happening very slowly.

3. The volatility of the oil sector makes both fiscal and monetary policy harder to manage.

4. The banking system itself does not directly drive economic growth and development, but only facilitates and supports it through intermediation between savers and investors. It is much like the blood in the body system. We cannot live unless it functions effectively. Yet, the blood on itself cannot initiate nor execute anything.

5. The banking system controls a little over half the money supply; hence it is not possible to achieve our monetary policy targets using the measures currently in use. Furthermore, some

of the banks are in distress, hence they complicate monetary policy management.

6. A sound and efficient banking system cannot exist in a vacuum. It has to flourish not only within a stable macroeconomic environment; the aggregate national environment must be enabling. These must then be supported by sound monetary policy and banking practice for us to succeed.

Fig 1: *Macro-economic Environment and the Nigerian Banking System*

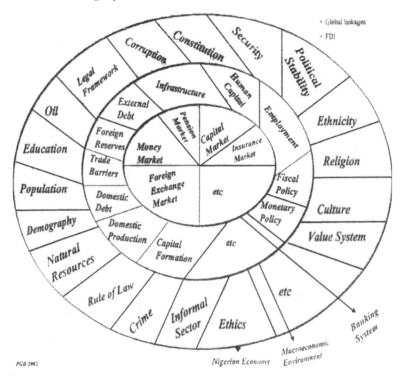

APPENDIX

OVERVIEW OF THE FINANCIAL SECTOR AND THE BANKING SYSTEM

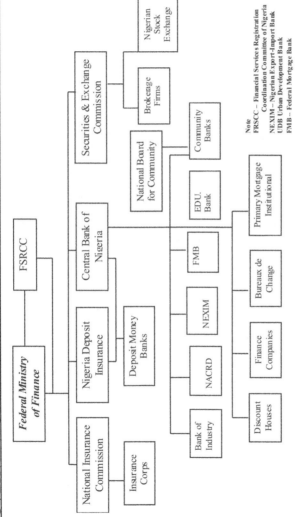

Note
FRSCC – Financial Services Registration
        Coordination Committee of Nigeria
NEXIM – Nigerian Export-Import Bank
UDB Urban Development Bank
FMB – Federal Mortgage Bank

Being a paper presented at the Senior Executive Course of the Nigerian Institute for Policy and Strategic Studies, Kuru on August 2002.

Chapter 10

Cross-Border Co-operation and Banks Supervision

Introduction

On a broad basis, the topic "Cross-border Co-operation and Consolidated Supervision of Banks" has been broken into two major parts. In the first part, I shall be considering the challenges before the regulators/supervisors, the international response to these challenges; and areas of possible and subsisting cross-border co-operation amongst supervisors. In the second part of the lecture, I shall be looking at the core principles for effective banking supervision as set out by the Basle Committee on Banking Supervision.

Preamble

We are living in a world of rapid financial development, which has opened new frontiers for cross-border operations. The contributing factors to this include: the breakdown of barriers to capital movement; the truly remarkable developments in telecommunications and Information Technology; and the growing realisation of just how many ways there are to take or hedge risk efficiently. Consequently, financial organisations have become very complex indeed, with several tiers of operational and proprietary relationships involved. In such a climate, constant vigilance is necessary if a systemic culture of financial crimes is not to flourish unabated.

This raises the issue of how best to effectively supervise banking operations — both domestic and cross-border. In practice, two scenarios present themselves for consideration.

In the first scenario, the banking group's home-country consolidated supervisory authority is also responsible for the supervision of the group's lead and subsidiary banks. In the second scenario, there is one authority responsible for the consolidated supervision of the banking group as a whole (the banking group's home-country authority) and different authorities responsible for the consolidated supervision of individual banks and subsidiaries that are owned or controlled by the group (the bank's home-country authority).

International Standards, as set by the Basle Committee on Bank Supervision, requires that all international banks be supervised by a home-country authority with requisite capacity for consolidated supervision.

What is Consolidated Supervision?

Consolidated supervision can be defined as a group-wide approach to supervision whereby all the risks run by a banking group are taken into account, wherever they may be booked. In other words, it is a process whereby the bank supervisor's purview is the totality of a banking group's activities, which may include non-bank companies and financial affiliates, as well as direct branches and subsidiaries.

A close example of a group requiring consolidated supervision is Union Bank of Nigeria. The group has a merchant bank, a building society in the form of
a subsidiary, and bank branches within and outside Nigeria, including London and South Africa.

Why Consolidated Supervision?

Banking thrives on trust and confidence. This confidence can easily be lost the moment any segment of a bank's total operation runs into difficulties. Typically, we talk of the 'contagion effect' - a situation in which problems in one part of a bank group are transferred to its other segments by a market that is reluctant to deal with a group that it perceives to be tainted.

To protect the integrity of (and confidence in) the typical banking group, therefore, consolidated supervision is *a sine qua non*. Consolidated supervision seeks to achieve the following objectives:

- Support the principle that no banking operation, wherever located, should escape supervision altogether;
- Prevent over-leveraging of capital;
- Ensure that all the risks incurred by a banking group, no matter where they may be booked, are evaluated and controlled on a global basis.

It is necessary, however, to draw a distinction between consolidation as known in the accounting world and the concept of consolidated supervision. Accounting consolidation is purely process-driven, while the concept of consolidated supervision involves both the quantitative and qualitative. The drawing up of consolidated accounts facilitates consolidated supervision but is not necessarily sufficient.

The choice of whether to address risks at local or consolidated level will depend on the risks being addressed. For instance, liquidity concerns can be addressed either on a market-by-market, or currency-by-currency basis, while market risks can be addressed based on whether the bank markets its main risks centrally or regionally. But in terms of control of capital flows, it may not be prudent to offset market and other risks through consolidation.

Challenges before Supervisors

The need for vigilance on the part of supervisors can only be appreciated through an understanding of the following challenges facing them:

- Some banks can create various types of corporate structures across international borders to escape regulation and effective supervision as in the case of Bank of Credit and Commerce International (BCCI), now in liquidation.
- The growing ability of and propensity for banks, to shift their activities to offshore tax havens, present a channel whereby domestic prudential guidelines can easily be circumvented.
- When accounting practices are relatively unsophisticated and disclosure requirements limited, cross-border transactions can be used to conceal problems in the domestic operations by booking problem assets with subsidiaries or other offshore entities.
- Offshore transactions can be used to facilitate or commit outright fraud. Incentives for prudent behaviour are varied across different jurisdictions, leading some institutions to seek out countries in which high-risk activities go unchecked.

International Response to the Challenges

Regulators of financial services the world over have had to work hard to keep up with the process of financial innovation. Bank supervisors have long understood that problems in one part of a banking group can quickly damage other segments of operations within the group. A case in point is the collapse of Barings Bank.

An encouraging development in the post-Barings banking environment has been the effort at improving international co-operation amongst regulators. Across a range of financial services and products, they are working to improve mutual understanding, information sharing and co-operation in normal times as well as in crisis.

The most important of these initiatives is the role of the G10 banking supervisions in the Basle Committee, under the framework of the Bank for International Settlement (BIS), also based in Basle (Switzerland). The Basle Committee on Banking Supervision is a committee of banking supervisory authorities, which was established by the Central Bank Governors of the Group of Ten countries in 1975. It consists of senior representatives of banking supervisory authorities and Central Banks from Belgium, Canada, France, Germany, Italy, Japan, Luxembourg, Netherlands, Sweden, Switzerland, United Kingdom and the United States.

The Basle Committee has come up with three key frameworks:
- Basle Capital Accord — which brought agreed minimum standards of Capital Adequacy in relation to credit risk to internationally active banks based in these countries.

The Accord assigns risk weights (of 0, 10, 20, 50 and 100 per cent) to on- and off- balance sheet exposures according to broad categories of relative riskiness.

The Accord sets minimum capital ratio requirements for internationally active banks of 4 per cent tier-one capital and 8 per cent total (tier-one plus tier-two) capital in relation to risk-weighted assets.

The Basle Committee's capital adequacy formulation attempts to delineate an operational comfort zone for banks by dividing a bank's overall qualifying capital into its total amount of potentially risky assets. The total qualifying capital incorporates the so-called tier-one (core capital) and tier-two capital (revaluation surplus) redeemable preference shares and other long-term borrowing.

- Minimum standards for the supervision of international banks — effectively, this recognises that before a host-country supervisor allows in a branch of a bank located abroad, it needs explicit assurance that the home-country supervisor is up to the job of supervising what may be a complex international group. We will discuss this aspect in detail shortly.
- Supervision of cross-border banking accord — this sets out in detail the appropriate relationship (and flows of information) between home and host-country supervisors.

Under the accord, the main home-country supervisors have due assurance that they could access all the information that they needed to fulfil their obligation to exercise comprehensive consolidated supervision. This means access not just to statistics but, if necessary, the ability to monitor on-site all relevant aspects of the overseas operations of both branches and subsidiaries of "their" banks. In return, host supervisors require assurance that this does not represent the extra- territorial exercise of power by other countries and that information provided would be protected. Host supervisors would also want to receive adequate information and be actively involved in developments which might affect the operations they may have authorised locally.

Minimum Standards for the Supervision of International Banks

The Basle Committee on Banking Supervision in July 1992 issued "The Minimum Standards for the Supervision of International Banking Groups and their Cross-Border Establishments". These standards are to be applied by the individual supervisory authorities in their own assessment of their relations with supervisory authorities in other countries. In particular, a host-country authority, in whose jurisdiction a bank or banking group is seeking to expand, is called upon to determine that the bank or banking group's home-country supervisory authority has the necessary capability to meet these minimum standards. In making this determination, host-country authorities are expected to review the other authority's statutory powers, experience and scope of administrative practices. Some authorities may initially need to make either statutory or administrative changes, in order to comply with these new standards. Therefore, in cases where an authority fails to meet one or more of these standards, recognition should be given to the extent to which the authority is actively working to establish the necessary capabilities to permit it to meet all aspects of these minimum standards.

The four Minimum Standards are as follows:

1. *All international banks and international banking groups should be supervised by a home-country authority that capably performs consolidated supervision.*

To meet this minimum standard, the home-country supervisory authority should:

a) Receive consolidated financial and prudential information on the bank's or banking group's global operations, have the reliability of this information confirmed to its own satisfaction through on- site examination or other means, and assess the information as it may bear on the safety and soundness of the bank and banking group.

b) Have the capability to prevent corporate affiliations or structures that either undermine efforts to maintain consolidated financial information or otherwise hinder effective supervision of the bank or banking group; and

c) Have the capability to prevent the bank or banking group from creating foreign banking establishments in particular jurisdiction.

2. *The creation of a cross-border banking establishment should receive the prior consent of both the host-country and the bank's or banking group's home-country supervisory authority.*

In the absence of the consent of both authorities, cross-border expansion will not be permitted. While the overall safety and soundness of the bank should be judged by its overall condition, particular weight should be given to:

a) The strength of the bank's capital; and
b) The appropriateness of the bank's organisation and operating procedure for effective management of risks on a local and consolidated basis, respectively.

3. *Supervisory authorities should possess the right to gather information from the cross-border banking establishments of the banks or banking groups for which they are the home-country supervisor.*

Consent for inward expansion by a prospective host-country authority should generally be contingent upon there being an understanding with the foreign bank's or banking group's home-country authority, that each authority may gather such information from their respective bank's or banking group's foreign establishments. Similarly, consent for outward expansion by the home-country authority should generally be contingent upon there being such an understanding with the host-country authority.

4. *If a host-country authority determines that any one of the foregoing minimum standards is not met to its satisfaction, that authority could impose restrictive measures necessary to satisfy its prudential concerns consistent with these minimum standards, including the prohibition of the creation of banking establishments.*

If these minimum standards are not met with respect to a particular bank or banking group and the relevant home-country authorities are unwilling or unable to initiate the effort to take measures to meet these standards, the host- country authority should prevent the creation, in its jurisdiction, of any cross- border establishments by that bank or banking group. However, in its sole discretion, the host-country authority may alternatively choose to permit the creation of establishments by such a bank or banking group, subject to whatever prudential restrictions on the scope and nature of the establishment's operations which the host-country authority may deem necessary and appropriate to address its prudential concerns.

Areas of Contact and Co-operation between a Home and a Host Supervisor

The following are areas in which the home and host states can complement one another's efforts in achieving effective cross-border consolidated supervision:

I.   Location of the Licensing and Lead Supervisory Authority

A home-country supervisory authority is responsible for supervising the global operations of a bank or banking group based on consolidated and verifiable financial and prudential information.

The home-country should also be the location of the senior management and the bulk of a bank's business. If the majority of the activities appear to be conducted elsewhere, it would become difficult for the home supervisor to fulfill its obligations, and arrangements should be made with another country involved taking on the role of home supervisor.

II.   Licensing of Internationally Active Banks

Home and host authorities should both give their explicit permission for the setting up of an establishment abroad. The home authority should be able to refuse the establishment of a branch or subsidiary of a bank suspected to be inadequately regulated.

III.   International Implementation of Prudential Standards

The home-country supervisory authority has responsibility for supervising the bank or banking group on a consolidated basis, domestically as well as internationally. The home supervisor will also need to take account of the fact that capital cannot always be easily moved from one part of a banking group to another, across international borders. Host countries are primarily responsible for the liquidity of a foreign establishment, since they will be better equipped to assess liquidity as a function of local market conditions and practices and the establishment's position in the market.

However, they will also be responsible for the solvency and supervision of subsidiaries.

IV.   Cross-Border Supervisory Information

Home-country supervisors have the right to obtain information from their cross- border banking establishments. Host authorities should be able to obtain necessary information from the home authority. This ability to gather information should be a condition for giving consent for the cross-border establishment of a bank, although appropriate safeguards for confidentiality are necessary. Any undue impediments, in the home and the host-country in the area of bank secrecy and confidentiality, to the exchange of supervisory information between supervisory authorities should be removed.

The information to be shared should include both quantitative and qualitative aspects. Qualitative information emphasises credit, market and other financial risks, good organisation and control in the context of ensuring that banks operate prudently and do not take excessive risks that threaten their solvency.

Quantitative information includes data from the cross-border office needed to calculate, for example, the bank's capital adequacy ratios, large exposures or legal lending limits and its funding and deposit concentrations.

Effective consolidated supervision relies on a clear hierarchy of information flows from the local banking activity to the home country supervisor. For example, information should be capable of flowing:

·   From the subsidiary or branch to the head office or parent bank;
·   From the parent bank or head office to the home supervisor;
·   From the subsidiary or branch to the host supervisor;
·   From the host supervisor to the home supervisor.

In addition, for effective comprehensive consolidated supervision, home supervisors also need information on certain qualitative aspects of the business undertaken in other jurisdictions by branches and subsidiaries of banking organisations for which they are the home supervisor. In particular, they need to be assured that:

(i)   The banking group has an appropriate risk management system covering the whole of its global activities;

(ii)   The internal control and audit procedures for controlling the group's overseas operations are of a sufficiently rigorous quality;

(iii)   Changes in ownership and control of partly-owned subsidiaries are monitored;

(iv)   The reporting process by which the home supervisor receives information is reliable;

(v)   The quality of management is adequate, with a "fit and proper" test for individuals where appropriate;

(vi)   The quality of assets and the levels of concentrations are known, and are within appropriate parameters;

(vii)   The liquidity of the institution is being monitored and there is no excessive reliance on a single third-party source (or a small number of sources) of funding; and

(viii)   The statutory laws and supervisory regulations of both the host and home countries are being complied with.

V.   Cross-Border Inspections

The relevant authorities of the host-state should permit on-site inspections by the home supervisor of a prudential nature of establishments of internationally active banks within its jurisdiction. The conduct of on-site inspections on the territory of another state requires the consent of the country receiving the inspection team. The findings of inspections should be shared between the supervisory authorities of both countries, as well as with the institution being supervised.

VI.   Information on Supervisory Systems and Structures

Supervisory authorities of both states should exchange complete information on each other's banking laws, the scope of their respective authorities, and prudential regulations applicable to the establishment on their territory.

The supervisory authority should have adequate powers to obtain the necessary information, including regular financial reports and prudential reports. The quantity and quality of available resources to supervise the foreign operations should be assessed, as well as supervisory techniques, frequency of inspections, etc. These items should provide the basis for a judgment as to whether the supervisory authority is capable of performing consolidated supervision.

A system of routine personal contacts should be set up between supervisors of the host and home countries, including the exchange of names, addresses, and information on language and other skills.

Such information is crucial for building a good and effective working relationship between both authorities and for taking action when necessary.

VII. International Bank Liquidation

When a bank, that has a branch in another country, is closed, liquidated, or declared insolvent, the supervisory authority in the country where the branch is established must immediately be informed by the home supervisory authority. The host authority would then promptly close the branch.

VIII. International Financial Conglomerates

The financial conglomerates (e.g. financial group incorporating banking. securities, and insurance subsidiaries and other financial intermediaries) pose serious problems for supervisors. Some of the problem areas include the overall approach to supervision of financial conglomerates (either on solo basis or group-wide); the assessment of capital adequacy and ways of preventing double gearing; contagion; problem in applying a suitability test to shareholders and a fitness and propriety test to managers; transparency of group structures, etc.

Consequently, supervisors over conglomerates need to establish close contacts and make practical arrangements for the exercise of supervision.

IX. Shell Banks and Parallel-Owned Banks

A shell bank is a loan generation or booking office, licensed or registered in one centre but effectively controlled or managed from another jurisdiction.

Parallel-owned banks are banks in one jurisdiction with the same ownership as banks in another jurisdiction, but where none is a subsidiary of the other.

The host supervisor which licenses a shell branch has the responsibility for ensuring that there is effective supervision of that branch. No banking operation should be permitted without a licence, and no such outfit should be licensed without ascertaining that it will be subject to effective supervision. In the event that any host supervisor receives an application to licence a new shell branch that will be managed in another jurisdiction, that supervisor should take steps to notify both the home supervisor and the supervisor in the jurisdiction where the shell branch will be managed. Before approving the shell branch, the host supervisor should be aware of how the home-country supervisor will ensure the effective supervision of the Branch. For parallel-owned banks, which are not subject to consolidated supervision, the risk exists that funds may be switched from one to the other if problems arise. Home or host supervisors should be vigilant to ensure that operations of this type become subject to consolidated supervision.

X.   Serious Criminal Activities

Investigation into serious criminal activities such as terrorism, theft, kidnapping, drug-trafficking, extortion, money-laundering may often be initiated by a home- country law enforcement authority and proceed with a formal request to the host-country's judicial authorities for information supported by prima facie evidence that an offence has been committed. While banking supervisors are not law enforcement authorities and should normally not be expected to undertake formal investigations into matters that involve apparent violations of criminal law, supervisory authorities need to ensure that their banks remain vigilant for evidence of such criminal activities and that all supervisors should be required to report such evidence acquired in the course of their supervisory activities to the appropriate authorities.

XI.   Year 2000 (Y2K) Issues

For some time, the Year 2000 issue has been perceived as a predominantly domestic issue rather than a cross-border one. Many people have taken the view that if every jurisdiction were to make adequate preparations with respect to its own infrastructure and institutions, the risk of serious disruptions would be significantly reduced, if not eliminated.

Therefore, while putting emphasis on the need for internal and external testing and paying increased attention to infrastructure (telecommunications, power etc), supervisors have focused primarily on their domestic markets in initial reviews of Year 2000 programmes.

Recently, it has become obvious that global implications and cross-border aspects of the Year 2000 issue merit increased attention. Cross-border coordination will likely be more challenging for supervisory authorities, as special issues may arise when the systems involved are in different jurisdictions.

When addressing Year 2000 cross-border issues, bank supervisors have to consider:

- Foreign activities of domestic banks, including the readiness of foreign markets and infrastructures, and
- Domestic activities of foreign banks, including the quality of the head office preparedness and the readiness of the local branch or subsidiary to conduct business, typically within the domestic market.

As a general rule, the Year 2000 compliance of a bank's information systems is probably best evaluated by the supervisors in whose jurisdiction the systems are located or managed. But this is not a principle easily applied since corporate structures and Year 2000 programmes vary considerably and technology permits processing to occur almost anywhere without regard to national boundaries. In practice, cross-border banking establishments have many information systems, some of which are physically located in the host-country, some centralised in the home-country, and some located in third countries. Consequently, supervisory responsibilities will necessarily vary across countries and groups.

These responsibilities should proceed along certain principles as follows:

- As a general rule, the home-country supervisors have organisation-wide supervisory oversight responsibility for the consolidated Year 2000 programme. The home-country supervisor should be prepared to share information with other supervisors on its oversight programme and be prepared to cooperate with host supervisors on issues related to the progress of organisations operating in the host markets.
- The focus of the host-country supervisor is limited to the Y2K readiness of local operations. This includes assessing local preparedness and sharing any possible concern or deficiency of information with the home-country supervisor. Local management should be able to provide appropriate information on the status of any systems upon which it depends, including those supported by the head office or other affiliates. If considered useful, the host-country supervisor should advise the home country supervisor on the extent and status of implementation of the local part of the Year 2000 programme.
- Due to diversified corporate structures and the resulting differences in supervisory responsibilities, situations must be addressed on a case-by- case basis in order to avoid unnecessary (and burdensome) overlaps as well as material under-laps. There should therefore be timely communication of supervisory assessments and report on significant developments which take place.
- Financial institutions should have full responsibility for ensuring Year 2000 readiness, through:

- Developing a strategic approach
- Creating organisational awareness
- Assessing actions and developing detailed plans
- Renovating systems, applications and equipment
- Validating the renovation through testing
- Implementing tested, compliant systems, and
- Developing appropriate contingency plans

The financial institutions are responsible for providing all relevant information to home and host-country supervisors. They are also expected to disclose to counterparts and markets sufficient information in a timely manner to permit an accurate assessment of the actions taken and potential, residual risks.

At this juncture, I want to discuss in some detail the Core Principles for effective bank supervision as enunciated by the Basle Committee. These principles are minimum requirements and in many cases may need to be supplemented by other measures, designed to address particular conditions and risks, in the financial systems of individual countries.

Core Principles for Effective Banking Supervision

1. An effective system of banking supervision will have clear responsibilities and objectives for each agency involved in the supervision of banking organisations. Each of such agencies should possess operational independence and adequate resources. A suitable legal framework for banking supervision is also necessary, including provisions relating to authorisation of banking organisation and their ongoing supervision; powers to address compliance with laws as well as safety and soundness concerns; and legal protection for supervisors. Arrangement for sharing information between supervisors and protecting the confidentiality of such information should be in place.

2. The permissible activities of institutions that are licensed and subject to supervision as banks must be clearly defined, and the use of the word "bank" in names should be controlled as far as possible.

3. The licensing authority must have the right to set criteria and reject applications for establishments that do not meet the standards set. The licensing process, at a minimum, should consist of an assessment of the banking organisation's ownership structure, directors and senior management, its operating plan and internal controls, and its projected financial condition, including its capital base; where the proposed owner or parent organisation is a foreign bank, the prior consent of its home- country supervisor should be obtained.

4. Banking supervisors must have the authority to review and reject any proposals to transfer significant ownership or controlling interests in existing banks to other parties.

5. Banking supervisors must have the authority to establish criteria for reviewing major acquisitions or investments by a bank and ensuring that corporate affiliations or structures do not expose the bank to undue risks or hinder effective supervision.

6. Banking supervisors must set prudent and appropriate minimum capital adequacy requirements for all banks. Such requirements should reflect the risks undertaken, and must define the components of capital, bearing in mind their ability to absorb losses. At least for internationally active banks, these requirements must not be less than those established in the Basle Capital Accord and its amendments.

7. An essential part of any supervisory system is the evaluation of a bank's policies, practices and procedures related to the granting of loans and making of investments and the ongoing management of the loan and investment portfolio. Supervisors need to ensure that the credit and investment function at individual banks is objective and grounded in sound principles.

8. Banking supervisors must be satisfied that banks establish and adhere to adequate policies, practices and procedures for

evaluating the quality of assets and the adequacy of loan loss provisions and loan loss reserves.

9. They should be satisfied that these policies are being reviewed regularly and implemented consistently.

10. Banking supervisors must be satisfied that banks have management information systems that enable management to identify concentrations within the portfolio and supervisors must set prudential limits to restrict bank exposures to single borrowers or groups of related borrowers.

11. In order to prevent abuses arising from connected lending, banking supervisors must have in place requirements that banks lend to related companies and individuals on an arm's length basis, that such extensions of credit are effectively monitored, and that other appropriate steps are taken to control or mitigate the risks.

12. Banking supervisors must be satisfied that banks have adequate policies and procedures for identifying, monitoring and controlling country risk and transfer risk in their international lending and investment activities, and for maintaining appropriate reserves against such risks.

13. Banking supervisors must be satisfied that banks have in place systems that accurately measure, monitor and adequately control market risks; supervisors should also have powers to impose specific limits and/or a specific capital charge on market risk exposures if warranted.

14. Banking supervisors must be satisfied that banks have in place a comprehensive risk management process (including appropriate board and senior management oversight) to identify, measure, monitor and control all other material risks and, where appropriate, to hold capital against these risks.

15. Banking supervisors must determine that banks have in place internal controls that are adequate for the nature and scale of their business. These should include clear arrangements for delegating authority and responsibility; separation of the functions that involve committing the bank, paying out its funds, and accounting for its assets and liabilities; reconciliation

of these processes; safeguarding its assets; and appropriate independent internal or external audit and compliance functions to test adherence to these controls as well as applicable laws and regulations.

16. Banking supervisors must determine that banks have adequate policies, practices and procedures in place, including strict "know-your-customer" rules, which promote high ethical and professional standards in the financial sector and prevent the bank being used, intentionally or unintentionally, by criminal elements.

17. An effective banking supervisory system should consist of some form of both on-site and off-site supervision.

18. Banking supervisors must have regular contact with bank management and a thorough understanding of the institution's operations.

19. Banking supervisors must have a means of collecting, reviewing and analysing prudential reports and statistical returns from banks on a solo and consolidated basis.

20. Banking supervisors must have a means of independent validation of supervisory information either through on-site examinations or of use of external auditors.

21. An essential element of banking supervision is the ability of the supervisors to supervise the banking group on a consolidated basis.

22. Banking supervisors must be satisfied that each bank maintains adequate records drawn up in accordance with consistent accounting policies and practices that enable the supervisor to obtain a true and fair view of the financial condition of the bank and the profitability of its business and that the bank publishes on a regular basis financial statements that fairly reflect its condition.

23. Banking supervisors must have at their disposal adequate supervisory measures to bring about timely corrective action when banks fail to meet prudential requirements (such as minimum capital adequacy ratios), when there are regulatory violations, or where depositors are threatened in any other

way. In extreme circumstances, this should include the ability to revoke the banking licence or recommend its revocation.

24. Banking supervisors must practice global consolidated supervision over their internationally-active banking organisations, adequately monitoring and applying appropriate prudential norms to all aspects of the business conducted by these banking organisations worldwide, primarily at their foreign branches, joint ventures, and subsidiaries.

25. A key component of consolidated supervision is establishing contact and information exchange with the various other supervisors involved, primarily host-country supervisory authorities.

26. Banking supervisors must require that the local operations of foreign banks, be conducted to the same high standards as are required of domestic institutions and must have powers to share information needed by the home-country supervisors of those banks, for the purpose of carrying out consolidated supervision.

Conclusion

The need for vigilance and greater cross-border cooperation amongst bank supervisors has perhaps never been more imperative than now. In 1996, the IMS agreed to allow banks to use their own internal models to measure how much capital they need as a cushion against swings in financial markets. What this means, in essence, is that the BIS is slowly but steadily acquiescing to pressure from global money-centre banks that internal models for determining capital adequacy can produce accurate results for a wider range of risks. Last year, the New York-based commercial bank, Bankers Trust, became the first bank to adopt an internal model following special disposition granted by the Federal Reserve Board.

The challenge for cross-border bank supervision arising from the foregoing is very obvious. Supervisors, both home and host-country, are now faced with the harrowing possibility of a shifting goal post scenario with the implied proliferation of standards. They are now going to be increasingly forced to play catch-up with a highly intelligent and innovation-bound group of operators. How supervisors handle this new state of flux will make a world of difference to the overall health of the global banking industry.

In conclusion, how well we fare in the eyes of host supervisors (and indeed the international community) will be measured, first, by our adherence to the core principles and minimum requirements for effective banking supervision and, second, by the following factors which measure our powers to exercise global oversight:

* Do we (as the home-country supervisors) have adequate power to enable us to obtain the information needed to exercise consolidated supervision?

* Do our banks have their own routine for collecting and validating financial information from all their foreign affiliates, as well as for evaluating and controlling their risks on a global basis?

* Do we receive regular financial information relating to both the whole group, and to the material entities in the group (including the head office) individually?

* Are we able to verify that information (e.g. through inspection, auditor's reports or information received from the host authority)?

* Is there access to information on intra-group transactions, not only with downward affiliates but also if appropriate with sister companies or non- bank affiliates?

* Do we have the power to prohibit corporate structures that deliberately impede consolidated supervision?

*   Which of the following procedures do we have in place to demonstrate our ability to capably perform consolidated supervision?

    ~   Adequate control of authorisation, both at the entry stage and on the changes of ownership?

    ~   Adequate prudential standards for capital credit concentrations, asset quality (i.e. provisioning or classification requirements), liquidity, market risk, management controls, etc?

    ~   Off-site capability, i.e. systems for statistical reporting of risks on a consolidated basis and the ability to verify or to have the reports verified?

    ~   The capability to inspect or examine entities in foreign locations?

    ~   Arrangements for a frequent dialogue with the management of the supervised entity?

    ~   A track record of taking effective remedial action when problems arise?

From my discussions so far, it is evident that there is a multiplicity of areas for cross-border co-operation on banking supervision. The challenges before us, as operators in the banking industry, are enormous. But we can take the first step in exploring the possibilities of building on the foundation laid by the Basic Accord.

In addition, there is a need for consistency in the national monetary policy formulation, particularly in the area of licensing of both indigenous and international banks and foreign exchange policy.

It is my sincere desire to see a very vibrant banking industry in Nigeria that measures up to the high standards obtainable in the developed societies.

The current democratic dispensation has opened a window of opportunities for us to explore all the possibilities, in our increasingly challenging economic environment, for the larger cause of making Nigeria a truly great nation.

Being text of a lecture delivered at the 6th Bank Examiners Annual Conference at CBN Training Centre, Lagos November 1, 1999

Chapter 11

Status of Corporate Governance in the Financial Sector

Introduction

The theme of corporate governance has come under greater international focus in recent years. The highly publicised collapse of the American energy giant, Enron has contributed in no small measure to this new attention on the subject. Enron's demise has caused serious ripples in diverse economic sectors across the world. But as is only to be expected, the financial services industry has suffered disproportionately from the fallout from the largest collapse in America's corporate history (For instance, Korean banks that extended credit to the company are currently reeling from the after-shock).

The Enron debacle has caused global investor attention to shift from the traditional analysis of financial numbers with emphasis on profitability ratios and shareholder value. The new rage is on corporate governance and corporate responsibility. Investors now investigate and analyse companies in these new areas to ascertain their soundness as a first principle in the investment process. The traditional priority, given to the interest of directors and shareholders in the management of organisations, has come under serious review. A clear paradigm shift is taking place in favour of managing corporate organisations for the benefit of a much diverse stakeholder constituency.

Enron has indeed only helped to accelerate a process that had begun to emerge with the globalisation of economies around the world. With globalisation there has been a growing consensus that the competitiveness of businesses, especially in emerging and developing economies, will be enhanced the more they are perceived to be fair, transparent, accountable and socially responsible. In order to grow and to compete effectively in the global marketplace, therefore, it is imperative that all businesses are run on the principles of sound corporate governance.

The level of compliance with corporate governance principles, required of organisations, would normally vary from one country to another. In the developed economies, with strong judiciaries, powerful institutional investors and stable national institutions, corporate governance issues are more generally taken for granted, although events like Enron's have exposed the danger of complacency. This is especially so given that the knock-on effect, from the consequent catastrophes, is potentially more global and pervasive. On the other hand, concern over corporate governance has grown in intensity in respect to emerging economies which are typically characterised by weak judicial/legal systems, institutions and smaller capital markets. In their eagerness to attract investment (both foreign and otherwise), developing countries are generally more likely to ignore certain issues of potential consequence for corporate governance. The level of corporate governance required of companies would equally vary from sector to sector. We shall return to this subject presently.

What is Corporate Governance?

There are various definitions of corporate governance. But this variety belies the underlying consensus. The Cadbury Report, for instance, defines corporate governance in largely unsentimental terms as "the system by which companies are directed and controlled". But Professor Cohn Tricker, who conceived the term 'Corporate Governance' back in 1984, made the very important distinction between management and control/direction in taking the position that " if management is about running business, governance is about seeing that it is run properly". This distinction has been further summed up by the international civil servant and diplomat, Chief Emeka Anyaoku, as the "difference between doing things right and doing the right thing".

Corporate governance is characterised by transparency, accountability, probity and the protection of stakeholder rights. It requires that business entities use sound ethical and moral judgment to ensure the survival of the firm as a going concern. In general, corporate governance refers to the manner in which the power of a corporation is exercised in the management of its total portfolio of economic and social resources with the aim of increasing shareholder value and safeguarding the interests of other stakeholders in the context of its corporate mission. This definition essentially embraces the three important element of:

*   Power   - how the authority at the disposal of an organisation is deployed to facilitate the progress of the entity in the desired direction.

*   Inclusion - the corporate governance concept involves a wide spectrum of issues affecting decisions and views of different stakeholders e.g. shareholders, management, employees, creditors, host communities, etc.

*   Compliance - it requires that an adequate legal and regulatory framework be put in place, and that not only the letter but also the spirit of the law be followed and respected.

The imperative of corporate governance was highlighted in 1997 by the Commonwealth Business Forum when it passed a resolution to the effect that "capacity should be established in every Commonwealth country to create and reinforce institutions to promote best practice in corporate governance and, in particular, codes of good practice establishing standards of behaviour in the public and private sectors should be agreed to secure greater transparency and to reduce corruption. At this juncture, let us examine the various players in the governance process in the context of the corporate organisation by asking the question: Who are Involved in Corporate Governance?

One critical point stands out clearly from our analysis so far, and that is the fact that the board of directors of any corporate organisation is the focal point of the corporate governance process. The board is ultimately accountable and responsible for the affairs and performance of the company. It has the collective responsibility to provide effective corporate governance of the company in such a manner that best serves the legitimate interests of shareholders, while giving due regard to the interests of the larger stakeholder constituencies.

Besides the board of directors, senior management led by the chief executive officer is involved in the corporate governance process. Paramount among the requirements of management in the good governance process is the implementation and enforcement of decisions taken by the board. Management must also:

* Protect the interests of the organisation, including trade secrets, technology, franchises, etc.; and
* Ensure that the organisation's clients are honestly and well served.

The generality of staff members of the organisation are equally involved in corporate governance, and their responsibility would typically involve:

- assisting management in fulfilling its obligations to the board and other stakeholders;
- avoiding waste of corporate resources;
- respecting confidentiality arising from corporate business dealings and

- ensuring honesty and fidelity in line with their terms of employment

The powers of the board are set out in the company's Articles of Association. The authority of the directors, to take actions that are binding on the company, is equally covered by the Articles of Association. The company's Article also outlines the context in which elements of that authority is delegated to senior management under the leadership of the managing director and chief executive officer. Finally, in entering into a formal employment contract with the company, the individual staff members sign on to uphold those broad principles on which the organisation is run.

In general, the release in South Africa of the second King's Report, with the Code of Corporate Practices and Conduct, has reinforced the global emphasis on sound corporate governance practices. The Report identifies the key roles and functions of the board as follows:

i.   To direct the company both as to strategy and structure;

ii.   To give strategic direction to the company, appoint the CEO and ensure that succession is planned;

iii.   To ensure that executive management implements the company strategy as established from time to time;

iv.   To ensure that the company operates ethically;

v.   To select managing directors, ensure succession and give guidance on the appointment of senior executives;

vi.   To monitor the activities of executive management;

vii.   To ensure that the company complies with all relevant laws, regulations and codes of business practice, and that it communicates with its shareowners and relevant stakeholders (internal and external) openly and promptly and with substance prevailing over form;

viii.   To develop a corporate code of conduct that addresses conflicts of interest, particularly relating to directors and management, which should be regularly reviewed and updated as necessary;

ix.   To identify and monitor the non-financial aspects relevant to the business of the company and the board should have an agreed procedure whereby directors may, if necessary, take independent professional advice at the company's expense

x.   To find the correct balance between conforming to governance constraints and performing in an entrepreneurial manner.

The Commonwealth has broadly adopted a similar position in the Principles of Corporate Governance in the Commonwealth as articulated by the Commonwealth Association for Corporate Governance (CACG). Of equal importance, perhaps, is the matter of content and scope of the corporate governance principle itself. The traditional preoccupation of most corporate governance is on conformance, which tracks how company managers adhere to high standards of transparency, probity, accountability and responsibility. For inclusiveness, however, the Commonwealth and the other global bodies in the corporate governance vanguard have taken the position that the process must also embrace performance of the board in providing the strategic leadership that sustains their companies' competitiveness as a going concern while guaranteeing orderly leadership succession. It must also be concerned with consensus which delineates the state of harmony between the company and its host society/societies.

Of paramount significance for corporate governance is the matter of distribution of power within the board as well as the composition of the board itself. The board must ensure that no one person or block of persons has unfettered power and that there is an appropriate balance of power on the board. There should always be a good balance between non-executive and executive managers so as to ensure that independent judgement and decisions are brought to bear on the affairs of the organisation. Major investors may be placed on the board only if they have demonstrated capabilities. To do otherwise may lead to lack of transparency or adversely affect the rights of minority shareholders. Friends and associates should, typically, not be placed on the board unless they have demonstrated experience and capability hence their participation will enhance the quality of board's decision-making process. The board chairman should, as much as possible, be non-executive. But we must make the exception here in a situation where the person occupying the chairmanship position has proven expertise in the requisite field and has substantial proprietary stake in the business. Other non-executive board members should be selected on the basis of their high competence in their various vocations.

To the undiscerning mind, it would appear that, in singling out the financial sector for special examination in this gathering, undue attention is being directed at the industry. In the section that follows, we shall attempt, among other things, to explain why the attention on the sector is in fact called for.

The Financial Services Industry

We had earlier in this presentation looked at the pervasive effect of bad corporate governance processes from the angle of the collapse of the Enron Corporation and its aftermath. Without doubt, the knock-on effect of distress in a financial institution of similar size and importance would almost certainly prove more disastrously pervasive. We witnessed the more vicious type of this phenomenon when crony capitalism combined with other factors to cripple the financial sectors of the Asian Tiger economies in the late 1997 and much of 1998. So that whereas sound corporate governance practices are a universal imperative for all business organisations, the financial services industry clearly presents a case for distinction. Let us examine the basis for this claim.

The reason why corporate governance is more imperative in the financial sector than it is for the other sectors of the economy, can be summarised in three ways. First, the financial industry is very central to economic development and progress by virtue simply of its critical intermediation role in the economy. It has often been said that the financial system is the fulcrum around which the economy revolves. This is by no means a trite claim. When the industry is healthy, the economy can be expected to be equally strong; if the banking system is bedevilled with poor corporate governance, the entire economy is potentially in danger of being infected with the distress syndrome.

Secondly, in many developing countries banks have taken over by default the role that is ordinarily played by the formal equities markets. This is because the capital markets are relatively smaller in developing countries than they are in developed economies. Most companies wishing to raise capital, therefore, rely quite heavily on debt financing by the banks. In the absence of institutional investors to perform the critical role of encouraging good corporate governance within the individual organisations, this function has effectively devolved to the banks. But banks can only become important platforms for the inculcation of sound governance principles to the extent that they themselves are imbued with the requisite capacity and conviction to that effect.

Thirdly, central banks exert direct influence on financial institutions in the normal discharge of the oversight mandates of the apex regulatory institution. The aim of this 'policing' function is precisely to ensure that banks are run on the basis of acceptable global principles. These self-same principles are known to be generally complimentary to the tenets of good corporate governance. Where the central bank's oversight role is transparent, effective and well diffused, the banks are able to take the message of rectitude down to their corporate clients, the private and family businesses that are usually more inclined to cut corners. In doing this, the incentive for banks lies in the resultant reduction of business risks and in better performance by their clients, which ultimately translates to better operating prospects for the banks themselves.

What this clearly means is that for the financial industry, the imperative of sound corporate governance is much higher than would ordinarily be the case in any other sector of the economy. Therefore, due diligence collectively on the part of the board of the financial institution as well as personal integrity on the part of individual board members of a financial institution, cannot but be taken as basic minimum requirements for the industry. The position of executive chairman in the industry must be objectively and critically examined in the light of its implication, both real and potential, for conflict of interest.

The Nigerian financial system comprises banks and non-bank financial institutions. In line with extant universally accepted principles in banking, the
industry operates as a closely regulated environment. Entry into and exit from
the market is closely monitored and managed by the monetary authorities
essentially to ensure the stability and security of banking assets which would in turn guarantee confidence on the part of investors and the general public. The
regulatory institutions within the financial sector include the following:
* Central Bank of Nigeria (CBN);
* Nigeria Deposit Insurance Corporation (NDIC);
* Securities and Exchange Commission (SEC);
* National Drug Law Enforcement Agency (NDLEA);
* National Insurance Commission (NAICOM);
* Federal Mortgage Bank of Nigeria (FMBN);

*   National Board for Community Banks (NBCB); and
*   Corporate Affairs Commission (CAC).

Let us examine these major regulatory institutions and their relevant functions.

i.   CBN: As the apex regulatory institution in the banking industry, the CBN promotes monetary stability and a sound financial system, acts as banker and financial adviser to the Federal Government as well as banker of last resort to the banks. The powers of the CBN include the supervision, examination of the operations of banks and the approval of products and advertisements as well as the application of sanctions against non-complying banks, including the revocation of licences where necessary.

ii.   SEC: SEC is the apex regulatory organ of the capital market. Its major objective is the promotion of an orderly and active capital market. In doing this, the SEC has the major functions of ensuring adequate protection of securities, registering all securities dealers, investment, advisers and the physical markets such as the stock exchanges and their trading floors/ branches, in order to maintain proper standards of conduct and professionalism in the securities business. The Commission also approves and regulates mergers and acquisitions and authorises the establishment of unit trusts.

iii.   NDIC: The NDIC complements the regulatory and supervisory roles of the CBN. NDIC was established to provide deposit insurance and related services to banks in order to promote confidence in the industry. The Corporation is empowered to examine the books and affairs of the insured banks. Licensed banks are mandated to pay 15/16 of 1 per cent of their total deposit liabilities as insurance premium to the NDIC. In the event of a bank failure, a depositor's claim is limited to a maximum of ₦50, 000.

iv. NAICOM: NAICOM is charged with the effective administration, supervision, regulation and control of the business of insurance in Nigeria. Its specific functions include the establishment of standards for the conduct of insurance business and protection of insurance policy holders. It also ensures adequate capitalisation and reserves, high technical expertise and judicious fund placement in the insurance industry.

v. NDLEA: The NDLEA was established to facilitate the Money Laundering Decree 3 of 1995 which is aimed at ensuring that information relating to movement of large volumes of funds that may be crime-related are reported for investigation. All cash transactions exceeding N500,000 for individuals and N2,000,000 for corporate entities must be reported to the agency by the bank concerned. NDLEA may also place many banks under surveillance if it has reasons to believe that drug monies are being routed, knowingly or otherwise, through the bank.

vi. CAC: The CAC is charged with the administration of the Companies and Allied Matters Act (CAMA) of 1990, including the regulation and supervision of the formation, incorporation, registration, management and winding up of companies pursuant to the Act. The agency maintains a register of companies in all the states of the Federation and undertakes investigations into the affairs of any company in which the interests of shareholders and the public so demand.

Having examined the myriads of agencies and institutions collectively responsible for ensuring sound governance practices in the financial industry, let us now review the current state of affairs in this regard in the sector

Corporate Governance in the Financial Sector

At this juncture, the question must again be asked, perhaps more directly this time: why do we now worry about the state of governance in our corporate sector? The answer is quite simple. The forces of globalisation are pushing inexorably in the direction of universal harmony in the application of best practice principles. The impetus here is none other than competition within the context of a globalising world economy.

To locate the precise nexus of the financial sector, in terms of performance in corporate governance, would indeed be a tall order. Such a course of action would necessarily involve a scientific survey of the institutions and agencies charged with ensuring proper conduct in the operations of the industry's various sub-sectors, perhaps even using the OECD Corporate Governance Assessment Criteria. This would definitely lead us beyond the scope of this presentation. But we shall, nonetheless, attempt to wade through the obvious maze, using as a compass the more generally settled nuances and experiences in (and of) the industry. In terms of relative size and, therefore, significance, the financial services industry is dominated by the banking sub-sector. With universal banking, this dominance is bound to become even more noticeable so that in the rest of my presentation, the banking sub-sector will form the basis for much of our argument.

We shall examine how well the industry has fared in corporate governance on the basis of the three yardsticks we had established earlier in this presentation namely, Conformance, Performance and Consensus:

Conformance: As stated earlier, conformance has been the traditional area of focus in the debate on corporate governance. But how has the industry fared in this specific regard? At least, going by the public opinion rating of the industry, it would appear that much needs to be done in this regard. The industry stands convicted in the arena of public opinion for a multiplicity of misdemeanours ranging from insider abuses both at the board and management/ staff levels, foreign exchange violations, questionable people management and ethics, bursting of single obligor limit to fraud perpetrated both from within the individual financial institution and in collaboration with sundry actors operating from outside the industry. For completeness, however, such a verdict must not be delivered in isolation of the societal milieu within which banking business is conducted in our country.

Financial institutions in Nigeria are constrained to operate within the confines of our peculiar counter-cultural environment that is in many ways disdainful of the tenets of sound corporate governance.

Also, one has to go back to the onset of the economic reform process in the country in the second half of the 80's. As would seem only too natural, financial sector liberalisation was a key ingredient in the macro-economic reform agenda. With liberalisation came a massive expansion in the industry. And with expansion came an enormous stress on the industry's resource capacity, especially the human capital aspect. In such a situation, there is bound to be a residual discount on the quality of leadership within the industry.

My position here should not be mistaken for an argument against the inculcation in its entirety of the corporate governance principles in banking and indeed all facets of our economy. Rather I am pointing at the peculiar pitfalls and challenges that we face in the process.

Performance: In terms of performance, the financial services industry has acquitted itself reasonably well in the past decade or thereabouts. The sector has virtually led the rest of the economy in respect of technological innovation, improved service delivery and a generally more responsive attitude to the needs of the market. This fact is increasingly evident in longer service hours, a greater array of available product/service types, shorter transaction turnaround times, etc. Whereas the first generation banks have maintained leadership in terms of asset sizes, equity bases and branch networks, the new generation banks have led the pack in the equally important areas of service innovation, efficiency, profitability and shareholder value. The industry has bravely thrown its weight behind major national economic initiatives such as the privatisation programme, with special emphasis on the growth sectors of oil and gas, telecommunications and even infrastructure development.

Consensus: To what extent has the financial services sector been able to identify with the larger aspirations of its stakeholder constituencies in the context of the Nigerian project? My candid opinion is that the industry has also done reasonably well in this regard, in spite of the widespread vilification it has been subjected to in recent time. The usual criticism of the industry, for failing to support the real sector, rings hollow when viewed from the standpoint of the short-term nature of the resources at its disposal. A cursory look at our socio-cultural landscape will reveal the fact of the industry's support in bringing to fruition such institutions of national pride as the MUSON Centre and the Lagos Business School (LBS), amongst many others. But perhaps more significant is the almost heroic role that banks have recently assumed for the financing of the small-scale enterprise sector of the economy.

Conclusion

We have attempted to examine the very critical issue of corporate governance from the prism of the financial services industry. We have also drawn attention to the traditional as well as the residual (developmental) role of the financial sector in a developing country such as ours, which fact provided the basis for why the sector must lead the vanguard for the adoption of sound governance practices in the Nigerian corporate sector. Within the context of this expected role, big challenges lurk in the corners in consequence of certain well-known societal values that effectively hinder progress in this area. But these challenges only point to the need for greater diligence on the part of leaders of Corporate Nigeria, and especially those in the financial industry. There is need now, more than at any other time in the evolution of banking in Nigeria, for the financial services sector to be run on a set of immutable codes of conduct for boards, senior management and for staff members of the individual institutions in the industry. This should, in fact, include aspects of international financial standards, especially those that relate to assessment and management of risks, transparency and viability.

Developing countries now increasingly recognise that corporate governance is an essential tool for prosperity and economic development. As such, and in order to attract investments, both local and foreign, companies need to adopt and implement sound governance practices. In recognition of the centrality of the principle to economic and social development, several African countries have in the past few years adopted and generally codified the broad protocols on good governance, as agreed at the levels of international conventions. I strongly urge leaders of industry in the country to follow this example to fashion a set of guidelines for good governance practices for the country.

Being paper presented at the 18th Annual Directors Seminar of the Financial Institutions Training Centre (FITC) on the theme. "Promoting Good Corporate Governance: Issues and Challenges" June 2002.

Chapter 12

Ethics and Responsible Leadership in the Banking Profession

Introduction

May I prefix my presentation today with an expression of appreciation to the Financial Institutions Training Centre (FITC) for the privilege given me to be part of its Founders' Day celebration for the year 2000. This is the second edition of the formal celebration of the institutions Founder's Day since the founding of the F1TC in 1981.

The maiden edition of the FITC Founders' Day celebration in 1998 featured a public lecture in which Dr. Pius Okigbo was the lead presenter. You can, therefore, understand my trepidation at being invited to follow so closely in the footsteps of this intellectual giant of our time.

I will not attempt to compete with Dr. Okigbo for the elevated slot his lecture has occupied in this series. For to do so, with a man who has contributed to my intellectual development, would be absolutely presumptuous. Today, I would rather attempt to live up to the high standard he has set for me, if only to assure him of my willingness to learn even more from him. The organisers of the second FITC Founders' Day celebration have been very magnanimous in allowing me the latitude to choose the topic for my presentation today. After deep introspection regarding the choices open to me, I decided on the theme: "Ethics And Responsible Leadership In The Banking Profession"

If any issue strikes in me a continuing cord of concern about the future orderly development of this important vocation, it is the need for banking to be practiced on a defined set of immutable moral rules of engagement.

My concern basically stems from the fact that we have once again found ourselves at the crossroads of potentially momentous changes in our national economic life. The unique role of the banking system, in the context of economic change, can never be taken for granted. With the advent of the universal banking concept, the scope of the industry's role in national economic life has indeed widened dramatically. Modern banking now sits squarely at the nexus of virtually every economic exchange. That is why all of us should worry at this time about the state of the moral and ethical principles upon which the profession currently stands.

The Nature of Banking

The business of banking is fundamentally that of risk-taking, although a complete banking service includes other operations that are basically low risk in nature. The major raw material on which the banking industry thrives is deposits upon which its loans and advances portfolio are based. The differential in the cost of such deposits and its lending rates, otherwise known as spread, constitutes the basic motivation for the industry. But the industry has responsibility to a number of publics ranging from depositors, lenders and shareholders to regulatory authorities and the public at large. It is the desire to meet these responsibilities that shapes the conduct of banks and motivates them to act one way or the other in the economy. The extent to which a bank fulfils its obligations to these publics determines its place in the industry.

For instance, a bank would cease to bear that name as soon as it loses its ability to meet the expectation of its depositors which, simply put, is to have their money back whenever they so desire. Similarly, when the intermediation role of providing the financial needs of deficient economic units becomes impossible for a bank, be it as a result of Holding Action or whatsoever, it stops being a bank.

On the part of the shareholders, the bank has a responsibility to make reasonable returns. This is in addition to preserving their equity in the bank. These and other related responsibilities impose a set of conflicting objectives on a bank. This conflict is due mainly to the fact that liquidity and profitability are often pulling in opposite directions and both are critical for the survival of a bank. The ability of a bank to balance these objectives is not only a reflection of its creativity but also the hallmark of its professional depth.

Banking is a fiduciary relationship — a trust position and a marriage built on confidence. It is the combination of trust and confidence that motivates a man to put his entire life's savings in the care of an organization in which he may not be personally acquainted with even a single person.

How a bank nurtures this implicit expression of faith, though intricate, is crucial to ensuring that the critical mass of its patrons continues to repose confidence in it. But more important is the fact that how the critical mass of bankers discharge their professional obligations to the citizenry can become the deciding factor in the survival of an entire economic system.

The reason for this is not far-fetched. Money, we all agree, is fungible. Indeed, it is the most fungible of all the creations attributable to the human ingenuity. In the basic sense, the economic potency of money stems from its ability to continually play the twin roles of store-of-value and medium-of-exchange.

But by far, the most important contributory factor in ensuring the sanctity of these roles is the strength of the written and unwritten articles of faith binding generations of operators in the financial industry. And the term operators here is used in a generic sense to include those functioning in the regulatory capacities as well as those directly involved in the flow of instruments that, together, approximate money in its modern form. Of all the institutions that make up the financial industry, banks are the most directly involved in the critical processes leading to the creation and destruction of money. The banking industry, for this and other reasons, is also the most closely regulated and monitored all over the world.

The Banker as Trustee

Let me say, for the purpose of this discourse, that the term "bank" is used to describe a variety of institutions established for one or more of the following purposes:

- to make loans and extend credit,
- to facilitate the transmission of funds by cheques, bills of exchange and other forms of commercial paper;
- to receive and hold money in deposit and to disburse it; and
- to exchange the currency of one country for that of another, among others.

Banks, also acting in fiduciary capacities, provide vaults for the safe-keeping of valuables, buy and sell stocks, bonds and shares for their clients, and, in general, perform a variety of services not included in a strict definition of the term "banking".

Banking is basically a business involving the buying and selling of financial services. It is also a profession to the extent that it boasts a well-defined body of knowledge that is distinct from other aspects of human endeavour. Professionals in the many facets of banking agree that trust and reputation are the key ingredients of this vocation. This is why a banker should normally be conservative and well groomed both in character and appearance. His natural mien should be subdued and his attitude cautious. This is actually the origin of the pinstripe-suit characterisation of bankers from time immemorial.

As professionals, bankers need not be reminded of the impact of their actions on the public perception of their character, their values and their relationship with others. Hence, bankers should strive, in a general sense, to act and be seen to act in a manner that broadly reflects prudence and ethical correctness. Today, there are visible exceptions to this general norm which, in fact, I suspect makes the theme of this presentation all the more important and contemporary.

Ethics and Banking

In the Lexical sense, ethics is the branch of philosophy that is concerned with what is morally good or bad, or right or wrong. Another tag for ethics is actually moral philosophy. In banking, therefore, ethics refers generally to the accepted code of conduct basically designed to promote best-practice principles amongst banks and bank workers as well as to encourage strong commitment to high standards in the banker-customer relationship. Ethics in banking relates to a set of innate and learned moral codes of conduct reflected in the names, attitude and behaviour of individuals engaged in banking activities. Ethics focuses on moral correctness of behaviour.

In relation to the banking profession, ethics encompasses the totality of the written and unwritten norms, laws, processes and, in general, best-practice principles issued jointly and severally by the regulatory authorities and other institutions as guides in the day-to-day functions of the operators in the banking industry. The foregoing is, in addition to the natural knowledge of good and evil, embedded in every human being. It is in this respect, for instance, that the Chartered Institute of Bankers of Nigeria (CIBN) has a professional code of conduct which emphasises integrity, honesty and professional competence. In its developmental role in the industry, the Institute insists on its members taking full cognizance of this body of norms along with its Memorandum of Association, the Banks and Other Financial Institutions Decree of 1991 and other regulations relating to banks and banking such as the Failed Banks, Money Laundering decrees, etc, in all they do.

Equally important to the ethics of the banking profession is the reputation of the institutions as well as the integrity of staff members. Corporate reputation refers to the totality of an organisation's inspired personality, derived mainly from its values and brand perception. The organisation's corporate reputation is expressed in the form of its overall goodwill. And, as we are all now aware, goodwill is no longer that nebulous aspect of the firm's total dynamics. Instead, it can now be quite easily measured and thereby managed. Due to the fiduciary nature of banking, reputation is the number one element in the operators' watch list of critical success factors. Therefore, a bank that treats ethical issues with levity ought to be doing so at its own mortal peril. It should be only a matter of time, for it to reap adversity. But is that the state of affairs today in Nigeria? In an environment where ethical issues are brushed aside, this may not appear to be the case, but experience has shown that no solid institution can be built on false values.

Why have banking ethics become, in recent times, a foremost source of concern to regulators in the industry, policy makers and the public at large? Indeed, more than any other form of economic engagement, banking has attained the status of a truly global village industry. The reason is none other than the ability of money and its variants to transcend national borders and, therefore, regulatory restraints. This phenomenon is a product of globalisation. Today, money and financial resources can be moved literally at the speed of light from one location to another, leaving regulators and economic managers perpetually playing catch-up. We have seen the happier outcome of this phenomenon in America's New Economy. We have also seen the enactment of its less savoury side in the recent financial melt down in Southeast Asia. Money, and thereby banking, has always been an important nexus in the capital accumulation process. It has even become more so with globalisation. Hence the present need, more than ever before, to ensure that bankers act in a manner that conforms to the highest standards of moral correctness.

Here in Nigeria, the concern is of a more basic nature — a reflection both of the state of development of the economy and of the lessons from our recent history of distress in the industry. During the decade of the 90s, some 50 banks in the country were forced to close shop for various reasons directly or indirectly related to ethics. The result was a debilitating distress in the financial industry. In the process, the ability of the industry, to create wealth was curtailed, while individuals lost their life savings, suffered health and related damages and businesses collapsed. At the same time, the Failed Banks Decree was enacted and its provisions had a telling effect on the operators of the failed banks, bank debtors and the industry at large. Till this date, the industry is yet to recover from the consequent economy-wide shake up and its ripple effect.. Banking ethics is, therefore, of great importance if not for anything else, but simply to ensure a more orderly future development of the industry.

Of late, we have begun to witness a subtle replay of the less savoury aspects of banking that invariably brought distress to the industry in the 90s. There is, for instance, the unmistakable pressure on staffing as new banks are licensed, hitherto distressed banks are resuscitated and as more merchant banks convert to commercial operation in the wake of liberalisation. Under the circumstance, there is a real incentive to lower the standards in the staffing process. Invariably, experience is spread thin while the wage bill is bloated. In an economy with minimal growth and shrinking margins, this portends dire consequences, both for ethical considerations and the critical personnel competence requisite for the intricacies of sound banking..

Perception Vs Reality

Public opinion of the banking industry in Nigeria has remained very strongly critical. This historical fact is founded on reasons that are not too difficult to explain. It is generally believed that the state of banking in Nigeria and of financial intermediation in general, has been largely elitist in outlook. The average Nigerian business person, it is believed, has very severely limited access to credit, at least not on terms that could enable him grow his business and therefore create more wealth at the rate he would want.

The Small and Medium Enterprise (SME) sector is recognised the world over as a critical engine of the wealth creation process. In more efficient economies of the world, this important segment of the enterprise sector thrives on the availability of bank credit. Here in Nigeria, the SMEs are nearly completely cut off from their most important source of sustenance — short and medium-term credit. The result has been stifling, to use the language of lovers of metaphors. If we subject the evidence to critical examination, it may well be the case that Nigeria boasts one of the highest enterprise failure rates amongst its peers in the developing world. All these have rubbed off negatively on the banks such that in any popularity contest at this time, banks would almost certainly come out poorly.

But our analysis cannot carry the required depth if we ignore all the salient issues involved here. Public concern about banking and the practices attaching thereto should never be ignored. We cannot, however, fall prey to the fallacy that perception is reality. Being largely perceptual, public opinion can be, and is often, manipulated and misled. Many a time, public perception is found to be incongruous with the extant facts in an argument or situation. So it would seem in the case of the banking profession in Nigeria.

The clash between public perception and reality as they relate to banking is indeed a litany. Let us examine a few of the more popular stereotypes. Banking is looked upon today in Nigeria as a virtual threat to our national economic interest - milking the economy and the real sector dry, and in the process, declaring super-normal profits for its immediate constituents. It has been said in some quarters that, if one analyses the portfolios of a bank, it would be discovered that the huge resources at their disposal are channelled into trade and trade- related businesses to the detriment of the productive sector of the economy. Nothing concrete, they say, would be achieved unless banks show commitment and interest in the productive sector of the economy. I think this is a sad view indeed to take of an industry whose fortunes are very intricately tied to wealth creation in any national setting. And Nigeria cannot be an exception in this regard. The view of banks as economic parasites is an unfortunate generalisation even if it is derived from the antecedents of a few deviants. I believe banks are in business to fund business. They cannot single-handedly determine the direction to which businessmen channel their funds. Banks simply put money in the viable transactions brought to them by the actors in commerce and industry. Simply put; banks do not, on their own, decide where money goes in the economy.

The relatively high returns in banking, which is part of society's grouse with it, need also to be viewed in tandem with the dramatic gains in efficiency as seen in the general improvement in service delivery in recent years. It may not be an overstatement to take the perhaps immodest position that no other sector of the economy has worked harder than banking to extricate itself from the morass of the well-known Nigerian development conundrum through technology and training. But the job of weaning the industry to become more relevant to the cause of national development remains the prerogative of the monetary authorities. And in fairness to the banks, they have not been bystanders in this regard. The entry into the industry of people of questionable character should be seen in the light of years of lapses both in macroeconomic management and in the regulatory oversight function.

Deriving from the foregoing, bankers are also perceived as an arrogant lot, feeding fat on their customers and living in a cosy world of their own at a time when the fortunes of the real sector have declined dramatically. It is hard to sustain this notion in the light of reality. What one sees instead is a crop of aggressive and very hard-working young people daily roaming the open but uncertain market in search of mandates. The pressure with which they put up in this regard can only be imagined.

There is also the much-debated apparent wide gap between banks' deposit and lending rates. This matter touches on the fundamentals of the free market concept, especially in a situation of proximate market perfection. Like in any other economic situation, the pricing of banking instruments is driven by risks.
Put differently, margin expectations are a function of perceived risks. In reality, therefore, certain intervening factors outside of the banker's control have conspired to keep margins on banking transactions in Nigeria relatively high. Such factors include poor infrastructure, security and general high cost of doing business, and that high margins were in the past. Today as we speak, the margins are virtually non-existent.

While one would like to put up some defence for the industry, it is important to state that such a defence is not unquestioning. This speaker is not wont to put up such a defence. I would, therefore, admit very clearly that all is not well with the banking system in the realm of ethics. Our system is going through a corrosive tunnel. The banking industry is at the centre of every economic system and once the industry is degraded by unethical practices, the whole system is in danger of degradation. Why do bankers get into unethical practices?

Unethical Practices - The Push Factors

Perhaps it might be worth our while to ask ourselves, what induces unethical practices in the banking industry? In my view, bankers are pushed into unethical practices by two major sets of forces: internal and external, in addition to the national propensity to corruption.

Firstly, in a materialistic society like ours, individual attainment is put far ahead of societal advancement in the management of success. Primitive accumulation becomes the driving force for most individuals. And bankers are part of the society. It takes self-discipline and strong will to do otherwise.

The internal forces derive generally from personal characteristics — greed, family pressures and the like. To those who fall prey to this set of forces, the industry should regret harbouring them in the first instance. There is however, another set of forces — external to the professional — including shareholders' expectations, societal pressures from the banking public and the media in particular.

The fairly high returns, usually posted by banks, has attracted all kinds of investors, including those who want their investment doubled in a matter of days, to the industry. Shareholders have in many cases, pressured management to a feeling of inferiority by constantly comparing banks' returns without caring about the strategies adopted by each bank. I would like to say that while we must be interested in good results, we must also be concerned with how such results are obtained. To me, this is basic to the ethical practice of our profession.

The Nigerian media sticks out prominently in this search for results without a reciprocal concern for its sources and the quality of earnings. In all the banking reports one reads, what seems to be solely an issue is the level of profit a bank makes. Accordingly, we see such headlines as "The most profitable bank of the Year, The banker of the year, and such other high-sounding descriptions of a bank and its key players, only based on financial results. Would it be out of place for us to read something positive about banks not connected to high profitability? All these reports put pressure on operators, sometimes, though inexcusably, into cutting corners to meet such expectations.

This development is dangerous both for the health of the industry and those of its operators. It leaves the industry badly heated up while creating avoidable necessity for bank executives — the necessity of remaining the most profitable bank, for instance, once so described.

Bank Profit and Ethics

Profit declaration in celebratory fashion is not necessarily a bad thing for corporate organisations. For a bank, however, the most important index of success may not be found in profit and loss accounts. Instead, the state of the balance sheet ought to be a primary focus of attention for any bank analyst as it is for bank management. What is happening today, in defiance of the lesson from our recent history, is that information on banks' performance is disseminated to the public in such a way that the importance of the balance sheet is obscured. Such window-dressing is often the prelude to the lowering of ethical standards as financial institutions seek to out-do one another in the race for fanciful profit figures at the expense of fundamental considerations of underlying strength. Once the critical mass of institutions begins to adopt this focus, distress can only become the logical consequence.

This unrestrained celebration of banking industry profitability detracts from the need to critically address the economy's fundamental policy lopsidedness. It attracts negative sentiments for banks which are demonised for allegedly profiteering from the system at a time when the economy is contracting. Conveniently overlooked in this line of argument, of course, is the fact that industry is simply suffering from years of official policy that actively promoted commerce (or trading, to put it bluntly) to the detriment of real production even to this date. Here again, therefore, the perceived low point of a 'profiteering' banking industry collides violently with the reality of official policy failure.

Who Should Worry About Ethical Behaviour

The interesting thing is that for banks, just as it was for our Lord Jesus Christ, those who shout Hossanah today, almost always, are the same people who should crucify him tomorrow. Those who are praising banks on the basis of their profits today and thereby, as it were, leading them into temptation are already calling for the cross. In a newspaper of August 16, 2000, the headline in one of the major dailies read "Distress Signals in Banking Industry". The report stated that "signals akin to those that preceded the bank failures of the early 1990s are re-emerging". While calling for urgent action on the part of the authorities, the report identified some of the signals as the transfer of parastatals' accounts to the Central Bank, paper profits, investment mismatch, among others. The point is, if we suspect that the profit is paper profit, why do we give so much prominence to it?

We should all be concerned about unethical practices in the industry. While shareholders' funds are put at risk by such acts, the entire economic system is put on the line. An entire economic system, together with its government, could be at risk of collapse and social disruption emanating from a dislocated payment system due to bank failures. Above all, our cherished traditions, which honour truth and confidence, could come to naught if unethical practices are left to flourish.

There is real cause for us bankers as well as policy makers to worry about the so-called recovery of the industry from the distress of the 90s. My honest position is that all is still not well with banking here in Nigeria. And ethical issues remain at the heart of the matter. By the most recent account of the Nigeria Deposit Insurance Corporation (NDIC), cases of bank fraud have declined precipitately in terms of reported numbers from 573 in 1998 to just 185 in 1999. Yet, in terms of actual naira amount involved, we achieved a disturbing leap from about N3.2 billion in 1998 to N7.4 billion in 1999. This reflects an increase of about 132 per cent. In terms of actual or expected total loses arising from all reported fraud cases, the increase is by a truly phenomenal 300 per cent! These officially documented cases are indeed just a tip of the iceberg. A good number of these cases go unreported.

The true picture would, in fact, shake the faith of any true convert to the notion of a new dawn in banking in Nigeria.

Perhaps, the only happy picture emanating from these depressing moral statistics is that the top-bracket institutions in the industry no longer hold the premier position on fraud. In 1997 and 1998, the top ten banks accounted for about 97 per cent of the amount involved in fraud cases. The figure fell sharply to 65 per cent last year. What this means is that fraud is becoming a major source of resource leakage and outflow from among the smaller banks than was hitherto the case. It would appear from the available evidence that bank fraud has been democratised —just like the polity itself!

Instructively, however, the industry appears to be responding to this growing threat to their operation with something close to a collective shrug. In 1998, seventy banks out of the 89 then in business complied with the requirement for fidelity insurance cover for their staff. Of the 70 that complied, only 51 banks were adequately covered. In 1999, the picture changed sharply, albeit for the worse. Out of the 90 banks then in operation, only 54 complied by taking out fidelity insurance on their staff. Of the 54 so complying, only 34 banks procured adequate cover as prescribed by policy. In the light of the foregoing, therefore, I find it difficult to understand the source of the apparent confidence being displayed by the industry.

The Diamond Bank Example

I have no doubt whatsoever that there is much an individual banker (and indeed a banking organisation) can do to promote and nurture ethics in the profession. In this regard, I am informed by our own experience at Diamond Bank. Permit me, therefore, to share this experience with you.

Diamond Bank has been accorded a high level of respect for the close attention it has paid to ethical issues since its inception in 1991. This fact has been a particular source of pride to us at the bank. While we want to record rapid growth in our numbers, we are concerned not only with the results but also with HOW those results are achieved.

In furtherance of this unequivocal bank-wide ethical bias, the bank has developed a handbook on ethics that outlines clear principles to which every staff member must subscribe. Sanctions for deviation are swift and decisive, even for the first offender in certain circumstances.

By the provisions of this handbook, which is aptly titled Statement "Of Ethical Principles And Codes Of Conduct," all employees without exception are required to read and sign a letter from the Chairman/CEO confirming their full awareness of and intention to adhere to, this Statement. Each signed letter is kept in the employee's file. On an annual basis, the Bank's Company Secretary distributes certification letters to key management personnel to secure reconfirmation that they are keeping faith with the covenant entered into *ab initio*.

These documents are kept in the custody of the bank's Corporate Legal unit. The Diamond Bank handbook of ethics has been painstakingly put together by a committee that worked on its general outlines for close to a year. The handbook covers all critical issues in ethics, and contains sections dealing with the following aspects:

- Preserving the bank's Corporate Reputation;
- What amounts to 'undesirable business';
- Respect for competition and competitors;
- Non-acceptance of gifts, favours and business entertainment by staff members;
- Improper payments to secure business;
- Conflict of interest;
- Discrimination and affirmative action;
- Sexual harassment; and
- Confidentiality of clients' business information.

I would like to believe that some other banks have similar practice. I am convinced that if all banks should adopt this example and pursue its tenets with

due diligence and discipline, then we shall pretty soon begin to see the happier consequences reflected in the totality of the industry's practices. I am not in doubt that this lofty goal is achievable. What it requires is the collective will to do the right things.

Being paper presented at the Year 2000 Founders Day Celebration of the Financial Institutions Training Centre, Lagos, August 2000.

Part IV

Entrepreneurship and Corporate Governance

PART IV:

Entrepreneurship and Corporate Governance

The dual issues of entrepreneurship and good corporate governance have been identified as major contributors to national economic development. In addition to driving national output and income, these mutually reinforcing concepts also initiate and manage change in business and, *ipso facto*, in the society as a whole. While entrepreneurship performs these roles in the course of its relentless pursuit of business opportunities, corporate governance reinforces them by enthroning professional management, checks and balances in the business place. Where good political governance enthrones development, entrepreneurship and good corporate governance provide the difference between corporate advancement and failure.

The weakness of the Nigerian economy over the years has been largely attributed to the dearth of entrepreneurs and poor corporate governance in enterprises, especially the small and medium variants. Instances abound where poor leadership, lack of accountability, poor or no succession plan, inappropriate checks and balances by many a Board of Directors, have brought enterprises to their knees.

- So, how should we go about developing entrepreneurs?
- How do we develop and sustain leaders?
- How do we institutionalise good corporate governance?
- How do we develop institutions, that is, the rules of the game in both the private and public sectors?

These questions and many more are the purview of Part IV of the book and they are addressed under three lead papers:
- Entrepreneurship and Building Institutions
- Corporate Governance and Policy Challenges

- Thinking Tomorrow Today: A Paradigm for Leadership and Competence.

Chapter 13

Entrepreneurship - Building Institutions

Introduction

I would like to start by expressing my appreciation to the Executive Council of Lagos Business School Alumni Association (LBSAA) for giving me the privilege to address this distinguished gathering of industry captains, business executives and entrepreneurs both substantive and potential. May I also use this opportunity to congratulate the organisers of this Annual Conference for their efforts towards promoting the sharing of business development and management knowledge among the members of the Alumni Association. I have no doubt in my mind that this forum will contribute immensely to the achievement of career goals and personal fulfilment of members as well as the success of our various business interests.

The importance of the theme for this year, "Entrepreneurship-Building Institutions", cannot be overemphasised. The role of entrepreneurship in economic development involves more than just increasing output and income. It involves initiating and managing change in the structure of business and ultimately, of society itself. Positive change must of necessity be accompanied by the development of standards of behaviour and practice that promote productivity, economic exchange and the wellbeing of the larger society.

Notwithstanding the significance of entrepreneurship on personal and societal fulfilment, the deeper essence of 'institution building' in the entrepreneurial process is poorly understood. In fact, most entrepreneurs do not realise the need for building institutions as the fundamental guarantee for the long-term survival and success of their business organisations. As a result, many businesses fail not because of bad business ideas, but because the institutional framework required to sustain them were missing. In Nigeria, with many of our key national institutions in decline, the successful entrepreneur must pay particular attention to institution building, both in his business and the wider society.

It follows then that we need to pay greater attention to the subject of institution building as a vital component of entrepreneurship. To address the topic, may I start with an attempt to define the two main concepts: entrepreneurship and institution building. We will go further to define some other concepts that are related to and sometimes confused with these two concepts; i.e. organisation, capacity building and governance. Thereafter, we will look at the entrepreneurial process in two stages, viz. "starting a new business" and "growing the business". This approach, I hope, will enable us to establish the importance of institution building and the blocks for institution building. We will also examine the place of national institutions in the entrepreneurial process. To support our assertions in some cases, the presentation will draw extracts from the profiles of some entrepreneurs.

Crisis of Nomenclature

In a general sense, the term 'institution' has tended to engender much confusion. In its everyday usage, there is a tendency to treat the term as synonymous with the term 'enterprise' or even organisation'. It is, therefore, critical at this juncture to clearly identify these concepts so that, when we speak, we are in no doubt as to what we are referring to and the implications attaching thereto.

To guide us in this regard, we shall take recourse to Douglass C. North who is perhaps the most revered contemporary authority on institution building and institutional change in the world. North defines institutions as "the rules of the game in a society or, more formally, the humanly devised constraints that shape human interaction". By this definition, institutions are, therefore, the framework within which human interactions take place. As the soft underbelly of human interactions, institutions are perfectly analogous to the formal and informal rules of the game in a competitive sport.

On the other hand, organisations provide the physical structure for human interactions. They may well be likened to the players in our selfsame competitive sport. Organisations would typically include political bodies (political parties, the senate, local authorities, regulatory agencies etc.); economic bodies (firms, trade unions, cooperatives, etc.); social bodies (churches, clubs, etc.), and educational bodies (schools, vocational training centres, universities, etc.). In the long run, the evolution of these bodies and their success as going concerns are fundamentally influenced by the institutional framework. Organisations in turn influence how the institutional framework evolves through governance. In sum, therefore, organisations are constrained by the institutional framework of the society within which they operate. They are equally so constrained by their own internal institutional frameworks. In Nigeria, as in other societies, the effective entrepreneur works on both fronts-external and internal. To ascertain the significance of institutions in the affairs of man, we may need to answer the simple question: why do institutions matter? Institutions matter to the extent that they reduce uncertainty by providing a structure to everyday life. At the core of this matter lies the explanation for the differentials in the relative performance of organisations as well as national economies. Depending on the dynamics of the particular situation, institutions would work to dramatic positive outcomes; they may equally work in reverse.

And why, we may ask, should organisations and nations, for that matter, bother about certainty in their affairs? Stability is so central to organisational performance that it could indeed be regarded as the preeminent success factor. Without stability, the total cost of doing business (the so-called transaction and transformation costs) tends to rise in tandem. Stability, therefore, fosters initiative, risk taking and entrepreneurship.

Having attempted to resolve what we have called the crisis of nomenclature, let us return to first principle-the flagship theme - Entrepreneurship.

The word "entrepreneur" was first used by the wealthy Irish-born French banker and speculator, Richard Cantillon (1680-1734), to describe the risk-taking aspect of economic life. This reflected a big leap in the body of economic knowledge then because for a long time economists had theorised that the only factors of production were land, labour and capital. Cantillon used the term to draw attention to the process of bearing the risk of buying at prices that are certain with the intention of selling in the future at prices that are uncertain.

The definition was later broadened to include the concept of bringing together all of the factors of production. Early in the 20th Century, the concept of innovation was added to entrepreneurship. This innovation could be process innovation, market innovation, product innovation, factor innovation, and even organisational innovation. Later definitions described entrepreneurship as involving the creation of new enterprises and the entrepreneur as the founder.

In practical terms and as a tool for economic development, the following questions are instructive:-
For instance, who is an entrepreneur? Is he born or made? Can entrepreneurship be learned or is it one of those gifts of Mother Nature? If entrepreneurs are born, how do we identify them so

that we can provide them with developmental opportunities? If on the other hand they are made, how and where are they made? Is it in the business schools as some say or via apprenticeship programmes?

Answers to these questions are very crucial today in Nigeria, as they suggest the direction for our poverty eradication efforts or wealth. The best way to eradicate poverty is not to throw money at it but to grow out of it. To grow out of poverty, you need to create jobs. To create jobs you need entrepreneurs. For instance, one of the recommendations of the 8th Nigeria Economic Summit of 2001 is for the creation of 500,000 entrepreneurs in the next three and half years. It is assumed that if each entrepreneur so created employs 100 workers, a total of 50 million jobs would be created in Nigeria within this time frame. You can see the potential impact of our subject matter.

Considerable effort has also gone into trying to understand the psychological and sociological wellsprings of the entrepreneurship process. These studies have noted some common characteristics, among entrepreneurs, with respect to need for achievement, perceived locus of control, orientation towards creative thinking and positive attitudes towards risk-taking.

In order to include all types of entrepreneurial behaviour as much as we can, we shall adopt the following definition as the foundation of this presentation:

Entrepreneurship is the relentless pursuit of business opportunities without regard to the resources currently controlled by the entrepreneur.

This general definition of entrepreneurship has a number of implications directly attaching thereto:
- Entrepreneurship occurs in both large and small firms;
- Entrepreneurship occurs in any type of industry;
- Entrepreneurs have a unique approach to opportunities that could be described as the "Can-Do-It" approach; and

- Entrepreneurs accept the constant challenge of resource mobilisation and do not accept the limits placed by their own personal resources.

The decision to bring a business idea or concept into reality is usually not an easy one. It takes a great deal of energy and courage to create a new business, especially given the certainty of uncertainty. Yet, entrepreneurship and the actual entrepreneurial decision, have resulted in several millions of new business ventures throughout the world. Let us now examine the ingredients that make for success in the world of enterprise.

Foundation of Successful Enterprise

The desire and the possibility of starting one's own business must rest on a solid foundation of finding, evaluating, and developing an opportunity if success is to be achieved. Going through this process helps the entrepreneur to overcome the strong forces that stifle the creation of something new. This process also applies to any growth initiatives in an existing enterprise such as product innovation; process re-engineering; new market development; mergers and acquisitions; etc.

Starting a new business would normally entail a number of basic phases, although it is essentially an interactive process with considerable trial and error elements. The sequencing of these phases will therefore not follow as systematic a pattern as we have made out in the following sub-titles.

Identifying Business Opportunities

Most good business opportunities do not suddenly appear but rather result from an entrepreneur being alert to possibilities to trends that are emerging and to new means of technology and techniques.

Perhaps, we may profit from the examples of some entrepreneurs of our time who may help us illuminate the importance of alertness to possibilities in enterprise development. For instance, Irene Dufu - born in a traditional fishing village in Ghana returned to Accra from England where she trained as a nurse and had 13 years of professional experience. She joined, with a short-service commission, as a nursing officer at the military hospital in Ghana. During her military service, she was approached by a group of artisan fishermen seeking a loan to buy new canoes. Because they were illiterate and lacked collateral, they had been turned down by the banks. Dufu agreed to apply for a loan on their behalf, using her house as security. The loan was granted and repaid by the fishermen in six months.

The fishermen's example set Mrs Dufu thinking about establishing a fishing company. Consequently, she took to fishing and registered her fishing company in two years. She began with a small wooden vessel, a crew of 12 and 3 offices. Ten years down the line, she employed *65* fishermen, on three boats, including a 350 top deep-sea trawler an 80-ton tuna vessel and 12 sales and administrative staff. Turnover was over $1.2 million.

In some cases, entrepreneurs establish formal mechanisms to identify potential opportunities. Masayoshi Son, the Founder, President and CEO of SOFTBANK (a computer software development company) in Japan went through this process as he said: *"For a year and a half I did research and made business plans... I came up with 40 new business ideas from creating software to setting up hospital chains..."*

If that example seemed a bit far-fetched, there are numerous men and women in Nigeria, who have demonstrated that the ability to recognise and exploit opportunities is a key quality of a good entrepreneur. Such people include Chief Adeola Odutola, Chief Ugochukwu, Chief Ilodibe and young men like Aliko Dangote. The example of ABC Transport to provide comfortable road transportation in the face of the high cost of air travel and dwindling disposable incomes among Nigerians, is a classic case of opportunity identification, exploitation and development into a viable enterprise so far. In all these examples, it would appear that the characteristic essentials in an entrepreneur are:

- the capacity to appreciate opportunities,
- the ability to take risk — driven by initiative, and
- a passionate zeal to achieve success

It is the passion that drives the entrepreneur even when the first two features are waning.

Although most entrepreneurs do not have formal mechanisms for identifying business opportunities, some sources are often fruitful: consumers and business associates, members of the distribution system, technical people, and examples from other nations.

Evaluating the Opportunity

The evaluation of the opportunity involves looking at the source and nature of the opportunity, its real and perceived value, its risks and returns, its fit with the personal skills and goals of the entrepreneur, and the differential advantage in its competitive environment.

We may have something to learn from some of the success measures that Son used to evaluate his business ideas. He said:

- *"One success measure was that I should fall in love with a particular business for the next 50 years at least... I wanted to choose one that I would feel more and more excited about as the years passed.*
- *'Another factor was that the business should be unique. That was very important to me. I couldn't want anyone else doing exactly the same thing.*
- *"A third was that within 10 years I wanted to be number one in that particular business, at least in Japan.*

- *"And I wanted to pick a business where the business category itself would be growing for the next 30 to 50 years. I didn't want to choose a sinking ship.*
- *"I had all those measurements, about 25 in all, and 40 new [business] ideas. I took a big sheet of paper, and I drew a matrix and put down scores and comments for each. Then I picked the best one, which turns out to be the personal computer software business. That was the start of SOFTBANK"*

Notice that Son went through the process of creating several business concepts *mentally* as well as creating the successful SOFTBANK *physically*.

Developing the Business Plan

Once the business concept is defined, a good business plan must also be developed in order to exploit the opportunity defined. The business plan is a written document that describes all the relevant external and internal elements involved in starting and managing a new venture. It is often an integration of functional plans such as marketing, finance, operations/manufacturing and human resources. Thus, the business plan — or, as it is sometimes referred to, the game plan or road map — answers the questions:
- Where am I now?
- Where am I going?
- How will I get there?

Potential investors, even suppliers and customers at times, will request or require a business plan. A good business plan is thus not only important in developing the opportunity but is also essential in determining the resources required, obtaining those resources, and successfully managing the resulting venture. John Peterman alluded to this point when reflecting on the ultimate failure of his fast growing company. He pointed out that:

We had also, without realising it, planted the seeds for serious problems later on. All the thinking about the brand, the niche, the target market — it was intuitive for a very long time. I wish now that we'd written down our ideas, our concept - in detail - at the start. It was a long time before we put anything into words in that way, and by then I think it was too late.

Implementing the Plan

After resources are acquired, the entrepreneur must employ them through implementation of the business plan. The operational process of the enterprise must be dealt with. This involves implementing a management style and structure, as well as determining and embracing the key variables for success.

To identify opportunity is the key to entrepreneurial success but the capacity to confront opportunity separates the men from the boys. It is at this point that zeal and consuming passion come into play. Without such consuming passion, the entrepreneur will surely cave in at the daunting challenges that are naturally associated with the unbeaten path. Some entrepreneurs have difficulty managing the venture they create — one difference between entrepreneurial and managerial decision-making. Both qualities are, however, required for successful implementation.

Entrepreneurial Deepening

Statistics indicate that many start-up firms manage to struggle successfully through the first year or two of their existence. However, something happens soon after. Sales level off, margins decline, cash flow stalls, and competitors begin to pay attention to that early success. Only a few entrepreneurs survive this critical period, or in other words, manage to get over the "brick wall". This brick wall is the critical boundary between an Emerging entrepreneur and an Emergent entrepreneur. The brick wall arises from the fact that the entrepreneurial characteristics required to launch a business successfully are often not those required for growth and even more frequently not those required to manage it once it grows to a large size. The role of the entrepreneur needs to change with the business as it develops and grows but all too often he or she is not able to make the transition. In many cases, the key challenge is to manage a sound business concept through the stage of building a viable and sustainable institution. Not every entrepreneur is up to this task.

An extensive analysis of contributions of entrepreneurs during a series of entrepreneur symposia held between 1991 and 1992 in the United States revealed a consistent pattern of events that served as indicators for recognising the brick wall and the demand for change in their companies. Some of the key points the entrepreneurs made had to do with recognising the signs of the brick wall. For example, trying to do everything and getting burnt out, or working day and night but with no positive effect on sales, being unwilling to make the investments required to grow, etc. Frequently, entering and emerging entrepreneurs fail to realise that change must occur within themselves as well as to how they run their company. These necessary changes are presented in the following six Guiding Principles for ensuring entrepreneurial success.

Professional Management/Good Governance

This principle says that the entrepreneur must change his or her management style in order to get over the brick wall. Most successful entrepreneurs say this is the most challenging change they had to undergo. Hear Peterman:

> *It's tough to balance your own instincts as a founder and top manager with the desire to let the people you hired do their thing. Managing managers wasn't something I set out to do; it was a job requirement that was incorporated by default into my position because my original idea for a business was a good one. But I think I drew out of this experience the skills to do it well; I believe that next time around I will know how to step back from the fray, assess things objectively, and make the right call.*

Rather than concentrate on the day-to-day operations of the organisation, successful entrepreneurs entrust these details to the specialists, and work on aligning and focusing their employees in the right direction. This is what corporate governance is all about. With proper alignment and maintenance of the alignment processes, the entrepreneur still shares in the decision-making.

Re-inventing the Vision

Successful entrepreneurs said that the entrepreneurial vision must be re-invented continuously. They view their vision of the company as a guide or "big picture" that steers and aligns the activities of the company and the employees. They say that their visions changed as the company matured. Many Entering and Emerging entrepreneurs have a simple "vision" of a positive P&L statement.

The Emergent entrepreneur frequently has a more abstract picture of where he/she sees the company going. A clear, albeit abstract, vision is critical for providing direction for the entire company.

Re-inventing the vision is a must because time changes everything and the vision is not cast in concrete. It must be flexible enough to accommodate environmental adjustments. The difference, however, is that while the invention is the preserve of the visionary, re-invention can come from employees, partners or other stakeholders. An enterprise must focus on its vision, but a great danger awaits one that sticks inflexibly to it irrespective of the times.

Nurture the Entrepreneurial Spirit

Successful entrepreneurs nurture the entrepreneurial spirit in their top people. The entrepreneurs identified an ever-present need to maintain the drive and entrepreneurial mentality of their employees in the effort to overcome the brick wall because it is people's entrepreneurial spirit that creates and finds opportunities for growth. Successful entrepreneurs said that as the company grows, the encroaching bureaucratic, organisational hierarchy stifles the employees' entrepreneurial spirit and intensity and therefore, their spirit must be nurtured.

Customer Obsession

Successful entrepreneurs consistently indicated superior customer service as their core competitive advantage over the competition. A flexible and pro-active posture is necessary to satisfy the customer. In fact, it is necessary to maintain viability and achieve growth. Successful entrepreneurs said that the key is to make the satisfaction of customers the central focus of their company, with no boundaries on the imagination as to how or how much to satisfy customers.

Team Building

The successful entrepreneurs demonstrated and continually encouraged teamwork as the route to success. This encouragement filters through the company's employees, creating an appreciation and understanding of each other's roles. It is this strong sense of teamwork and focus that the entrepreneurs cited as the basis from which superior customer satisfaction is achieved and growth beyond the brick wall is made possible. It is necessary to see that everyone is working in the same direction rather than working independently.

Successful entrepreneurs said that teamwork is a way of getting the employees to feel they are a part of the company, not observers. It is a way of keeping a culture of smallness as the company gets bigger.

Success with Persistent Opportunism

Always keeping an eye open for opportunity and positive change is the hallmark of successful entrepreneurs. Such characteristics as persistently asking why deviations occur and how they can be prevented or exploited, and an incessant drive to move forward are typical of successful entrepreneurs. It is not a gambling type of mentality. It is a calculated opportunistic sense of action that is peculiar to successful entrepreneurs. The inclination of opportunity hunting is maintained throughout their career and does not end with the initial founding of the company. Successful entrepreneurs continually seek opportunities within and outside the realm of their current business to create growth essential for long-term success.

Institution Building and the Entrepreneurial Process

It should be clear at this stage that institution building is the critical factor that determines the long-term survival and success of any organisation. It is the difference between most organisations that fail prematurely and those that achieve significant and sustainable growth over the long-term. This can be deduced from our examination of the principles that enable the emergent entrepreneur to get past the threshold dividing the smaller emerging entrepreneurs from those who have fulfilled the promise of size and sustained growth.

From our discussion thus far, the following blocks can be identified for building strong and credible and effective institutions:

(i)   Vision;
(ii)   Professional management;
(iii)   Good corporate governance;
(iv)   Capacity building;
(v)   Continual process re-engineering; and
(vi)   Effective succession planning.

Vision

Successful entrepreneurs use the vision to create common purpose that tells their people where they want to take their organisations. Their employees are motivated and aligned toward a common purpose to create a unified front. A focused group of employees, with everyone moving in the same, desired direction, is a key factor in the building of any institution. Such a vision reflects the values and character represented by the customers and employees — the greatest assets of the company. In turn, the response of customers and employees reinforces the company's vision.

Deriving from the vision is the clear business imperative for a well-articulated corporate strategy towards pursuing the vision as well as support achievement of overall business goals and performance objectives.

Professional Management

The entrepreneur who starts a business with a fresh idea — to make something better or less expensively, to make it in a new way or to satisfy a unique need — is often not primarily interested in making money. The visionary wants to do something new because it is interesting and exciting, and because it may be meeting a need. Once the business begins to have some success, then the nature of the processes needs change.

At this stage, the infant business experiences its first set of challenges:
- How does the visionary entrepreneur transfer the skills and the inspiration that made the little enterprise a success into something larger?
- How does the business deal with cash flow constraints?
- How does it obtain the legitimacy necessary to enable it to borrow?

Often, the entrepreneur is not interested in these issues. Visionaries can be notoriously poor at supervising staff, negotiating with investors, or training successors. The business now needs a professional management focus, which calls on a different set of skills, to manage and sustain growth, that are distinct from the skills necessary to start an enterprise and promote a vision.

Applying management skills allows the adolescent enterprise to continue to do well, but the business culture begins to change. The emphasis of management is on:

- Organisation structure, describing the operating blueprint including;
- Service delivery models and enterprise management architecture;
- Organisational arrangements with respect to responsibility of the constituent parts of the organisation;
- Policies and procedures relating to human resources management, service delivery and management, other internal operations, and general administration.

Corporate Governance

With professional management comes the next challenge: the maturing enterprise now requires credible corporate governance to create checks and balances and to ensure that the management focus is effective. At the same time, it is to ensure that the management focus does not become too powerful to overwhelm the entrepreneurship necessary to create rapid growth and access new markets. Good corporate governance is very crucial and not easy to come by. It determines how an institutional framework evolves. It can frustrate or enhance the functioning of the structure, policies and procedures of an organisation. The governance of an organisation rests squarely with the entrepreneur or the board and executive management as the organisation grows.

The governance must be such that creates a system of values that is favourable to satisfying customers and guiding employees in doing the right thing. It must also create a system of accountability and ensure effective oversight for cost and performance as well as the enforcement of a system of reward and sanctions. This system incorporates financial and performance management, including the budgeting and budgetary control process.

Upon developing into an institutionalised company with appropriate governance structures, the business encounters a new set of challenges:

· How does the business preserve its vision?
· How does it balance growth, risk, and profitability?
· How does it establish a governance system that holds management accountable without undermining its independence and flexibility?

Capacity Building

The resources needed for taking the opportunity in terms of material resources and human capital must be accessed. The required resources at different stages of the development of the enterprise must be acquired. This process starts with an appraisal of the entrepreneur's present resources. Care must be taken not to underestimate the amount and variety of resources needed. The downside risks associated with insufficient resources should also be assessed, and this is often very high. Acquiring the needed resources in a timely manner is an important step in the entrepreneurial process.

Institutions are developed over time and should continuously be strengthened to remain relevant in a dynamic environment and meet the challenges of growth. Capacity building for this purpose involves:

· Continuous development of employees;

· Management renewal;
· Filling positions with competent people; and
· Adequate funding.

One of the critical problems confronted by the entrepreneur is securing financing for the business. While this is a problem throughout the life of an enterprise, it is particularly acute at start-up stage. From the entrepreneur's perspective, the longer the venture can do without outside capital, the lower the cost of capital in terms of interest rates or equity loss in the company. Thus, the entrepreneur should be committed to investing his personal savings and ploughing back profits from the business as much as possible. After all internal sources have been exhausted; the entrepreneur may find it necessary to seek additional funds through external financing.

Continual Process Re-engineering

Process re-engineering is akin to vision re-invention. The success of a business is largely dependent on its ability to meet and surpass the level of competence displayed by the competition. This ability is reflected in superior service delivery, value-added products and services and consistency of quality. To sustain its high standards of quality, an enterprise must continually re-examine itself to ensure that it keeps up with the needs of its customers — external and internal — over the change continuum.

Process re-engineering looks at the technology, the processes the techniques and the procedures of service delivery to effect repairs and renewals to meet the needs of a changing environment. This includes the management of both income and expenditure, cost control and allocation, product refinement as well as physical and psychological restructuring — include public perception management — to concretely position the company to compete favourably.

Succession Planning

This is one aspect of enterprise building that most Nigerians either take for granted or would love to wish away. Perhaps, the thought of retiring from the driving seat of a major activity embraced with faith and passion is contributory to this attitude. But the cost is very high. It is no longer news that many successful enterprises in Nigeria die with their founders. This is indeed a vexation.

Although it is now generally accepted as a rarity where wealth lasts longer than the third generation in a family, our own case is that the second generation hardly sees the wealth. Meanwhile, such international corporate giants as Guinness, Heinekens and SG Warburg are still growing stronger. Why?

There are three major stages in the development of an enterprise, namely: creativity state, direction stage and delegation stage. The entrepreneurs at the helm of successful companies always obey the requirements at every stage of the development of the enterprise.

Accordingly, we must move from creating the enterprise to directing it and then to delegation. It is at the delegation stage that the problem of succession manifests itself. Although it is not generally agreed as to which stage of the enterprise succession planning should begin, entrepreneurs must begin to decontrol, decentralise and assign responsibilities once the dream has become a company. They must begin to concentrate on strategies — corporate governance — so that one does not stand in the way. Again, Peterman put it succinctly: ... "at some stage, the business you nurtured takes on its own momentum and you just get swept along by it". At this stage, it is expected that successors would have been identified, nurtured and put on the learning curve. All that is appropriate for the entrepreneur at this point is to take hold of the brakes — systems and structures — and apply them when necessary.

Any enterprise that disregards the need to build succession does so at its own very high risk. An entrepreneur can only assure lasting success through building and developing successor management and enduring institutions.

The Other Dimension of Institution Building

Institution building is two dimensional namely, internal and external. The internal dimension concerns one's own organisation, culture and team. The external dimension involves the industry and national structure (including key national institutions) which in turn shape the competitive environment and foster risk-taking because they bring stability and predictability. In Nigeria, however, most people in the private sector work on the internal dimension and generally ignore the external dimension. It is about time that this situation is remedied if Nigeria has to achieve the necessary environment for meaningful and sustainable economic development and growth. The private sector has a responsibility and a role to play in nation-building and public institution building. The tendency currently and in the past has been to regard this as the sole responsibility of the government. In this regard, the efforts made by the Vision 2010 project and the ongoing efforts of the Nigerian Economic Summit Group are laudable and should be sustained.

Public Institutions

The holistic nature of society emphasises its political, sociocultural and economic dimensions.

These are closely interwoven and influence one another in a dynamic manner. Corporate organisations pursue their objectives within this dynamic environment and so:

(a) They seek to achieve results under the prevailing political, sociocultural and economic settings that prescribe the available opportunities;

(b) They do so in the context of laws, rules and regulations, conventions, attitudes and practices which form the 'rules of the game' and which affect them and are in turn affected by them.

Public institutions mainly define this context. It follows that credible public institutions and sound decisions emanating there from help to create the enabling environment for developing corporate institutions. In other words, the way public institutions respond to the objectives, strategies and results achieved by corporate bodies provide a feedback mechanism which conditions and guides future behaviour.

Societal norms and standards are greatly influenced by public institutions. Strong institutions and the rule of law encourage honesty, integrity, transparency, accountability and effectively coordinated and implemented government policies, as well as ethical rules for doing business. Taken together, all these contribute to opening up opportunities for entrepreneurship to thrive as well as create a conducive environment for strong corporate institutions to emerge.

The policies, rules and regulations of any society, which contribute to its enterprise culture, reflect the credibility of the public institutions. It is no wonder that more companies are formed in countries where the government gives priority attention to the provision of economic infrastructure such as roads, communication, transportation systems, utilities, and economic stability to support the viability of new ventures and ideas. Countries that have a repressive tax structure can suppress company formation since a significant monetary gain cannot be achieved to compensate for the social, psychological, and financial risks.

One of the factors responsible for the collapse of Adesemi Communications International, a company launched in Tanzania in 1993, relates to government regulations. According to Monique Maddy:

> *Licensing problems that had plagued us for years in Tanzania began to spin out of control. Central to our business model had been the assumption that Adesemi would receive a commission on the thousands of additional phone calls it generated each day on the network of the national phone company, Tanzania Telecommunications Company Limited (TTCL}. Such an arrangement is the industry norm throughout the world. But no matter how much we pleaded or cabled, TTCL refused to pay us any commission. We realised that in Tanzania, the high returns we had forecast wouldn't materialise for a long time.*

What we have in this nation are weak institutions, which have largely been manipulated by political office holders and influential individuals. Also, corruption that pervades all facets of our society has made nonsense of the institutions. Although corruption is a worldwide phenomenon, the level of corruption and the brazen disregard for rules and regulations in most of our public institutions have impacted negatively on the operating environment and national development.

Poor resource allocation and management have also contributed to the weakening of important institutions of government such as the Judiciary, the Police, the Civil Service, and the Military. Successive governments failed to define national priorities properly and allocate resources in building the capacity for these institutions to serve their essence. The Judiciary still employs outdated methods of recording evidence, causing undesirable delays. The Police Force lacks operational vehicles, facilities and basic communications equipment. This adversely affects its capacity to fight crime and protect the citizens. The poor conditions of service and inadequate funding of the Civil Service, the Judiciary and the Police Force invariably encourage corruption.

It follows that like entrepreneurs, our political office holders need to get their priorities right and build strong institutions that will facilitate national development. This is where good public governance comes into play. Good public governance will facilitate the building of strong public institutions. Such public institutions will in turn facilitate the development of public codes, standards and practices for corporate governance. Leading public institutions that impact directly on corporate governance, include the Corporate Affairs Commission, the capital market authorities — the Nigerian Stock Exchange and the Securities and Exchange Commission, the Central Bank etc. Good corporate governance rests squarely on strong and enduring corporate institutions.

Conclusion

In the foregoing submissions, I have deliberately taken liberty of the space given to me by the organiser's choice of theme. I have not only tried to read the minds of the organisers; I have liberally proceeded on a course that I can only relate to in a most passionate way. Short of institutions, there could be no value addition to entrepreneurship or even the larger issue of nation-building.

Entrepreneurship, the enterprise culture and enterprises do matter. They provide society with the physical semblance of progress and wellbeing. But these concepts can only become meaningful in the context of the credibility conferred by a supportive institutional framework.

We cannot see, feel, touch or even measure institutions since they are essentially constructions of the human mind. But institutions are a solid part of our existence, and, indeed, provide the explanation for the relative performance of nations (and enterprises) across the globe. We can only view the continuing near-stagnation in Nigeria's overall economic performance (including the performance of our enterprise system) through this very prism.

Let me conclude my submission today by returning to Prof. Douglass North:

> *Institutions provide the basic structure by which human beings throughout history have created order and attempted to reduce uncertainty in (social and economic) exchange.*
>
> *Together with the technology employed, they determine transaction and transformation costs and hence the profitability and feasibility of engaging in economic activity. They connect the past with the present and the future so that history is a largely incremental story of institutional evolution in which the historical performance of economies can only be understood as a part of a sequential story.*

Being paper delivered at the 6th Annual Conference of Lagos Business School Alumni Association, November 2001.

Chapter 14

Corporate Governance and Policy Challenges

Introduction

The twin issues of capacity building and good corporate governance in the Nigerian banking industry cannot be more relevant at any other time now that the system is once more faced with perceptions of distress, both real and imagined.

As was the case in the bank failures of the early 1990s, issues of capacity of the operators and the organisations themselves, as well as the kind of corporate structures and governance that have been put in place to ensure the success of banking enterprises, are now being called to question. This, therefore, makes the topic of this presentation both contemporary and critical. The relevance is buttressed by E.V.K. Jaycox in a paper he presented on *Capacity building: The missing link in African development* at a seminar by the African American Institute in 1993. He concludes that, "anybody who is involved in economic development anywhere in the world, but obviously in Africa, knows how critical human and institutional capacity is to the development effort and the chances of success".

The central focus of this paper is an analysis of the concepts of capacity, capacity building and good corporate governance in Nigerian banking experience. The paper will examine what constitutes capacity, how capacity is developed or built at the individual and corporate levels, the essential attributes of good corporate governance and their roles in the success of a banking organisation.

Quite a number of authors have offered a definition of capacity building. A few of these will, however, serve our purpose. Morgan (1993) sees it as "the ability of individuals, groups, institutions, organisations and societies to identify and meet development challenges over time," while Berg (1993) regards capacity building as being characterised by three main activities: "skill upgrading— both general and job-specific; procedural improvements; and organisational strengthening." He comes to the conclusion that capacity building is broader than organisational development in that it includes all types of skill enhancement and also procedural reforms that extend the boundaries of a single organisation.

There is a close similarity between these two views. They both see capacity building as the development of appropriate skills and abilities at the individual and corporate levels to ensure the performance of organisational tasks in an effective, efficient and sustained manner.

Professor Cohn Trickier is credited with coining the term "Corporate Governance". In his most definitive reference to the concept, Trickier stated that "if management is about running business, governance is about seeing that it is run properly." The Cadbury Report defined it as "the system by which companies are directed and controlled". My good friend and the eminent former Commonwealth Secretary General, Chief Emeka Anyaoku, who delivered the Diamond Bank Tenth Anniversary Lecture last year, obliged us with a broader definition as advanced by the Commonwealth Association for Corporate Governance: "corporate governance is essentially about leadership: for efficiency, with responsibility, and leadership which is transparent and accountable".

Generally, therefore, corporate governance is about providing effective and accountable leadership in such a manner as will enable the realisation of the organisation's overall mission.

Capacity Building in the Nigerian Banking Industry

The upsurge in the Nigerian banking environment in the early 1990s led to a huge demand on available human resources in the industry. In order to fill the vacant positions, many bankers, who were relatively new in the industry and just learning the ropes, found themselves in managerial positions. Indeed, the practice then was to move through as many banks as possible. The more one moved, the faster one rose in the hierarchy. Thus, we had people without the requisite experience and exposure occupying very senior and strategic positions in several banks in the country.

It is open for debate whether the distress that followed shortly afterwards resulted mainly from management inexperience and lack of proper training. However, except in few cases, most of the banks that went under were under the management of this crop of bankers. The recent Central Bank of Nigeria (CBN) directive requiring bank employees to have attained a certain number of years, before assuming senior management positions in banks, gives credence to the view that training and experience are essential elements for good corporate governance.

From the definitions given earlier, capacity building both at the individual and the corporate level is an imperative for any organisation's survival. Morgan underscores the link between capacity building and institutional development with a definition of what he calls "capacity development". This, he says, is the "ability of individuals, groups, institutions, organisations and societies to identify and meet development challenges over time". Morgan uses capacity development to focus on the process aspects, while capacity building would seem to connote starting from scratch. He uses the analogy of building a house to explain this. Once the structure is completed and the house is standing then the development of the property continues.

In other words, development could be regarded as an ongoing process of building on the existing capacity of the human asset. There is thus a close relationship between human resource development and capacity development and an evolving relationship between training and capacity development.

J.C.N. Mentz of the University of South Africa says development refers to that gradual increase in the capacity of the individual. That is the socialising process. This explanation is applicable, for instance, to the university graduate who enters the banking industry where the emphasis would now be on the continuous sustained development of the individual's skills and expertise, which fact is equally applicable to bankers with many years of experience. But my view is that capacity building and development not only include institution building but also human resource development. Human capacity building ultimately leads to institutional building.

As I said earlier, capacity is the ability to do something at the individual and at the corporate levels. This is, however, developed in a sustained manner as to enable the building of a reservoir of knowledge, experience and expertise. The individual and organisation can draw on this reservoir to carry out tasks. As the experience and knowledge of these tasks grow, the individual's capacity and that of the organisation also increases or develops.

It is assumed that a new recruit in the banking industry already has an inherent capacity to do a particular job. As time goes by, and with formal and informal training, this capacity should increase through experience, which a person gains by performing those functions and responsibilities attaching to his position. However, certain factors could inhibit the enhancement of the capacity, including attitude of the supervisor, *patrimonialism*, lack of motivation and delegation of authority, among others. Given this scenario, our concern should be how to ensure that this inherent capacity is developed to ensure that full potentials as well as individual and organisational goals are realised. We must ensure that, at the time of joining the industry, the recruit is placed where his present capacity is best suited for and where he is likely to grow this capacity. He must then be given the requisite motivation, supervision, training and all to enable him to develop his personal capacity.

At the corporate level, good structures must be put in place for the organisation to provide the context in which personal capacity is developed. Managements must equip staff understanding, skills and access to information, knowledge and training that enables them to perform effectively. They must ensure that management structures, processes and procedures, not only within organisations but also the management of relationships within the different organisations and sectors including private, public and community are aimed at developing the bank's potential. It must evolve strategies that will ensure the development of the company's capacity to preserve and grow its market share and market power. Areas to look at in this regard include managerial and administrative capacities, planning, research and development capacities, marketing techniques, networking/relationship building, customer service, relationship management, domestic and foreign operations, credit operations, assets and liability management, cost control measures, and financial analysis/interpretation. Others include: effective budgeting systems, product design and development, performance measurements, branch expansion, etc. This, of course cannot be done in isolation from a good organization, including ownership and operational structure.

The Demand for Good Corporate Governance

Permit me once more to make reference to Chief Anyaoku's position on Corporate Governance and Enterprise Culture. He is of the opinion that the importance of corporate governance has been further buttressed by the position of the Commonwealth Business Forum in its 1997 resolution to the effect that "capacity should be established in every Commonwealth country to create or reinforce institutions to promote best practice in corporate governance; in particular, codes of good practice establishing standards of behaviour in the public and private sector should be agreed to secure greater transparency and the reduce corruption".

He summarises corporate governance to cover three essential areas, including conformance, performance and consensus: Conformance of company managers to high standards of transparency, probity, accountability and responsibility, the Performance of board of directors in providing the strategic leadership which will sustain their companies' competitiveness locally and in the global market; and the Consensus which maintains the harmonious and productive relationships between the company and its host society.

Perhaps it is right to say that of the three, *Performance* has received less attention in the corporate governance debate. But this aspect is also of critical importance. It is only the ability of the board of a company to provide the needed strategic leadership that would ensure that company managers conform to high standards and that the company remains afloat and relevant. Good corporate governance will lead to probity, efficiency and effectiveness of the banking industry. The influence of the regulatory authorities should not be enough in achieving good corporate governance. Organisations on their own should adopt and pursue good corporate practices in running their businesses. A few banks, I am happy to note, have introduced an ethical code of conduct for their staff in a bid to ensure transparency and accountability in the discharge of their duties.

Good corporate governance is not relevant to the corporate organisation alone. It is equally important in national governance. It will not only lead to efficiency, increased productivity and accountability in companies but will also help enthrone good governance and achieve growth in the economy and other areas of national life. The setting of appropriate standards for corporate governance will encourage foreign investment in the country as well as local investors.

Conclusion

Capacity building and good corporate governance are powerful tools for ensuring the efficiency of organisations and that of national life. In whatever field of endeavour, effectiveness can only be achieved if the right capacities are built at the individual and corporate levels. Inherent capacities of the individual must be developed alongside enhancing the operational and capacities of the company. With this and good corporate governance in place, an improved performance and profitability of private and state enterprises will be achieved.

In reality, the two concepts of capacity building and good corporate governance must work together in order to achieve the best outcome in terms of organisational deepening and, ultimately, performance. Corporate governance sets the tone for capacity building to the extent that it is the former that gives impetus to the latter. But in order to put these concepts to full effect, capacity building should indeed be seen to be relevant beyond the organisation and, in fact, the industry in focus. Thus for banking, the following sub-sets of the larger society must as of necessity be considered in tandem if capacity building is to yield optimal results:

(i)   The Government;
(ii)   The Regulatory Authorities; and
(iii)   The Banking Public.

I am certain that even in these times of waning public confidence in the banking industry, trust can be restored with increased capacity building and the adoption of good corporate governance attributes.

Being a paper presented at the Institute of Directors' Forum, Eko Hotel, Victoria Island, Lagos, April 2002.

Chapter 15

Random Thoughts About Corporate Governance

I am pleased to be here this evening to share fellowship with the members of the Institute of Directors, and also to share my thoughts — random thoughts on a subject, on which the Institute is regarded as the authority. I am referring to *Corporate Governance*. However, in discussing it, my attention would not be on what it is and how it should be implemented, but on those issues, which I think could make its enthronement in Africa quite difficult.

Introduction

The theme of corporate governance has come under greater international focus in recent years. The highly publicised collapse of the American energy giant, Enron Corporation, those of WorldCom and Global Crossing have contributed in no small measure to the new attention on the subject. These widely reported corporate failures have caused serious ripples in diverse economic sectors across the world, with the financial services industry shouldering much of the untoward consequences.

They have also caused global investor attention to shift from the traditional analysis of financial numbers with its emphasis on profitability ratios and shareholder value. The new rage is on corporate governance and corporate responsibility. Investors now investigate and analyse companies on these new areas to ascertain their soundness as a first principle in the investment decision process. The traditional priority, given to the interest of directors and shareholders, in the management of organisations, has come under serious review. A clear paradigm shift is therefore taking place in favour of managing corporate organisations for the benefit of a much diverse stakeholder constituency.

The Enron experience has indeed helped to accelerate a process that had begun to emerge with the globalisation of economies. With globalisation, there has been a growing consensus that the competitiveness of businesses, especially in emerging and developing economies, will be enhanced the more they are perceived to be:

- fair
- transparent
- accountable, and
- socially responsible.

Therefore, in order to grow and to compete effectively in the global marketplace, it is imperative that businesses are run on the principles of sound corporate governance.

The level of compliance with corporate governance principles required of organisations would normally vary from one country to another. Though recent corporate failures like Enron's have highlighted the continuing need for vigilance, corporate governance issues are more generally taken for granted in the developed countries as they have:

- strong judiciaries and rule of law
- stable and robust national institutions with integrity
- powerful institutional investor community

On the other hand, concern over corporate governance has grown in intensity with respect to emerging economies which are typically characterized by:

- weak judicial/legal systems
- fragile institutions, and
- capital markets that lack depth.

In their eagerness to attract investments, both foreign and otherwise, developing countries are generally more likely to ignore certain issues of potential consequence for corporate governance.

My intention in this paper is not to reinvent the wheel. That job has already been taken care of by experts in the field. What constitutes good corporate governance practices, the roles of the board of directors, management and the varied stakeholder constituencies have been fairly well publicised in various reports and findings. Amongst these would readily be included: the Cadbury Report, the King's Report (otherwise known as Code of Corporate Practices and Conduct), and the Principles for Corporate Governance in the Commonwealth as articulated by the Commonwealth Association for Corporate Governance (CACG), just to mention a few.

At this point, I would like to address the issue of corporate governance as it concerns the emerging economies with Africa as my specific point of reference. In this regard, I intend to identify the major constraints that work against the evolution of a strong corporate governance culture in the African continent and in Nigeria in particular.

The African Experience

Historically, the concept of good governance has not fared well in the African corporate environment for a number of reasons. In the first place, it is a relatively new area of focus. Even on a global scale, the connection between good corporate governance and wealth creation, both at the micro and macro levels, has only recently become generally accepted, thanks mostly to the pioneering work of Professor Douglas North of the Washington University in St. Louis. In Africa, most entrepreneurs are inclined to regard with scepticism the supposed salutary effect on the bottom line arising from the application of corporate governance principles. It is worth bearing in mind that we are, in fact, talking about businessmen with no direct or formal relationship with the multinationals that are by their very nature run on lines more closely aligned to the good governance tenets. Because it is not generally applied, corporate governance is ironically but certainly viewed as a potential source of loss of competitive advantage.

In Africa, the basic structure of business remains largely that of the small and medium enterprise (SME) format. The typical African enterprise is run as a virtual extension and embodiment of its promoter. The going-concern precept is still evolving even if tortuously so. At issue here is the fact of the continued existence of the primordial relationships built around the extended family system, clannish and ethnic bonding, amongst others. These relationships exert pressures of considerable magnitude on managers and directors in enterprises. In consequence thereof, wealth creation, which is presumed to be an integral part of the corporate governance concept, is not given the priority it deserves.

Corruption continues to loom large in Africa's corporate environment. This is the outcome of the inter-play of several factors. For one thing, the state is very central in the typical African economy. In Nigeria, for instance, the state constitutes as much as 70 per cent of the economy. I am sure that the recurring issues in contemporary governance in Africa are fairly familiar to this gathering. To wit, one can point at such issues as weak, and in many cases, non-existent legal and institutional frameworks; inconsistent audit standards; poor banking practices, including the near-primitive payments system; rudimentary capital markets; disregard for minority interests; and the very important matter of scarce competencies at board and management levels. This latter point has been identified as a contributory factor to the emergence of interlocking positions which have implication for conflict of interest.

The relationship between corruption and the other issues of fragile structures and law enforcement are often viewed in the chicken and egg sense: corruption breeds weak structures and poor enforcement of rules. But these self-same factors may also be fuelling corruption. The question has often been raised as to which is a more important factor impeding the general application of the corporate governance principles: corruption, or the weakness of national institutions (including of course the legal framework)? I would readily take the position that it is indeed the fact of weak judicial and legal system that has bred the type of brazen disregard for due process and grand corruption that is prevalent in many African economies today. If the law was seen as impartial both in principle and in practice, it would over time begin to serve more and more as deterrence that they are meant to be in the first place. At the moment, we are still very far from this ideal.

At this juncture, it is pertinent perhaps to examine in some detail the 'character' of the impediments to corporate governance by looking at the various levels of its manifestation.

Levels of Constraints

The difficulty in nurturing and sustaining the corporate governance culture in the typical African environment can be examined from two prisms, namely at the national level and at the corporate level. In adopting this approach, the solution to the problem would, hopefully, become self-evident.

National Level

I shall use Nigeria as my focus. As a society struggling to build institutions that provide the basis for global best practice principle, Nigeria, we have agreed, is yet to make appreciable advances in corporate governance. Issues relating to transparency, accountability, probity and stakeholder rights are still largely observed in their breach rather than in their observance. Cases of insider abuse have not become a thing of the past, even though concerted efforts are being made to bring about the much-needed improvements.

The question then is, why has corporate governance been slow in taking root in Nigeria? This question is important since an accurate diagnosis of a problem brings one much closer to addressing the problem itself. Corporate governance is by its very nature a performance-driven concept. Accordingly, in failing to bring it to full realisation in our corporate environment, the untoward consequence can be seen in terms of overall discount on performance both at the individual corporate level and at the level of the macro-economy.

Perhaps, the most important single factor militating against the enthronement of good governance in Nigeria's corporate environment is the inadequate capacity of our institutions. Good governance in the enterprise sector has much to do with the fidelity of the existing rules of engagement as they relate to property rights, etc. and the capacity of the judicial system to pursue and enforce the principles of rule of law. In Nigeria, discretionary practices, even on matters of contractual relationship, are still quite high.

Perhaps arising directly from the lack of institutional capacity is the fact of the high level of corruption in the country. In the past several years, Nigeria has ranked quite high on the corruption index of Transparency International (TI). Corruption, as we all know, is the nemesis of good governance for the precise reason that it thrives on discretion as against well-defined rules and principles. The direct consequence of corruption is a high and spiralling cost of doing business.

There is also the problem of infrastructural inadequacies. This is a major source of inhibition to good corporate governance practice as it carries grave implications for the cost of doing business. In Nigeria, serious shortcomings continue to be the norm in the basic but critical areas of energy, communication technology and transport. These would tend to impact quite negatively on the ability of corporate leadership to exert itself optimally in the area of governance. Today in Nigeria, the Internet remains an elitist concept. To that extent, the gains accruable from this invaluable modern tool of management are still largely unexploited in the great majority of enterprises operating in the country.

A very important factor in the inadequate application of good corporate governance principles in Nigeria has been the lack of depth and breadth of the domestic capital market. The capital market in Nigeria is still relatively small and shallow. The culture of grassroots or mass equity ownership, and the critical role of shareholders and institutional investors in encouraging good governance in individual organisations is, therefore, very much lacking. Most companies wishing to raise capital rely quite heavily on debt financing by banks. But the banking industry's capacity to 'enforce' greater adherence to corporate governance principles in client-organisations is limited for reasons that are only too obvious.

Corporate Level

The self-same factors at play at the national level would naturally be evident at the corporate level. But a key issue at this level would seem to be the relatively underdeveloped private enterprise sector. Several salient considerations are noteworthy in this respect, and I shall sum these up as follows:

- The private sector is largely informal, and operates under a set of principles that run counter to those that underpin due process. Where a semblance of the formal private sector exists, of course outside of the multinational and their subsidiaries, they are often non-institutionalised.
- Most indigenous entrepreneurs adopt opportunistic rather than institution- building approach to evolve and develop their organisations.
- Again, most organisations revolve around a single founder who would usually equate his/her own private interests with those of the organisation. In

such a setting, decision-making tends to generally lack objectivity.

There is equally the issue of dearth of competencies as earlier stated. Instances abound where the same crop of so-called technocrats become virtual recurring decimals (some would use the word "clones") within the corporate environment. This turns the enterprise system into a veritable breeding ground for conflict of interests and insider abuse.

In the all-important banking sector, the problem is not made any lighter by the continuing lack of depth of the payments system. The entire economy remains very much cash-based. This has direct implication for corporate efficiency and performance.

Conclusion

I have attempted in this short interaction to highlight the very critical issue of corporate governance in any economy, but with special focus on the continuing need for its enthronement in the developing economies and Africa in particular. The realities of a globalising world economy make this needed transition urgent and imperative. As is evident from the argument presented, big challenges lurk at the corners in consequence of the several impediments arising both from the society at large and from the nature and maturity of the enterprise sector itself. But these challenges only point to the need for greater diligence on the part of economic leaders within the countries in question. There is need now, more than at any time in the evolution of the corporate sector, for organisations to be run on a set of immutable codes of conduct for boards, senior managements and for staff members. The Commonwealth has, through its various arms, pushed the frontiers of advocacy in this direction.

Many developing countries now increasingly recognise that corporate governance is an essential tool for prosperity and economic development. As such, and in order to attract investments, both local and foreign, companies need to adopt and implement sound governance practices. In recognition of the centrality of the principle to economic and social development, several African countries have in the past few years adopted and generally codified the broad protocols on good governance as agreed at the levels of international conventions. This is a trend that must be nurtured and sustained with the much needed encouragement and support from the Institute of Directors as a body and by your membership on an individual basis. But how should the Institute and its members foster the principle of corporate governance in Nigeria? It is my considered opinion that this should be done, not only by mounting seminars and workshops on the subject, but in addition by each of your members living the principle. You should all be the role models of what you preach. The Americans have a saying — "you cannot sell from an empty wagon". Members of this august body must live their corporate lives so that each of them can shine and stand out as an epitome of good corporate behaviour as you preach it — modelled on global best practice.

Being paper presented at the Institute of Directors' Year 2002 Annual Dinner at the Shell Main Hall, Muson Centre, Onikan, Lagos, December 2002.

Chapter 16

Thinking Tomorrow Today: A Paradigm for Leadership and Competence

Introduction

As we all know, human resource is the most critical of all resources of any organization. It is in this light, that we have to appreciate the theme for this conference, which is: "Complacency to Competence". The environment of today's organisations has changed a great deal due to a variety of driving forces. Increasing telecommunications, for example, has 'shrunk' the world substantially. Much of the developing countries have also joined the global marketplace, creating a wider arena for sales and services. Remaining complacent in today's competitive environment will result in failure for any organisation.

Many successful companies are beginning to understand for themselves what kept Lewis E. Platt, the retired CEO of the Hewlett-Packard Company, up at night:
'Whatever made you successful in the past will not in the future'.
So, profitable companies can become victims of their own success. Complacency breeds content. Finding solutions to the new and immediate problems become more pressing than opportunities for market-transforming innovations.

Leaders and managers of organisations need practical ways to recover entrepreneurial initiative and stimulate the innovation of their organisations, in order to stand the test of time. This is the thrust of the topic — *"Thinking Tomorrow Today: A New Paradigm for Leadership and Competence"* — on which I was asked to share my thought.

Transformation of Leadership Management

Management practices have laid so much emphasis on improved analytical and administrative tools. But these alone will not be enough for survival in the future, because they are geared primarily to improving the efficiency of present operations. The new business leaders will be those who can stretch their minds beyond the management of physical resources. They will have the capacity to conceptualise broad new philosophies of business, and translate their vision into operations. To the traditional skills of managing people, material machines, and money, they will add a challenging new skill management of ideas arising from thinking tomorrow today.

A profound change in the main task of top management is emerging as a result of the accelerating dynamics of technologies, markets, information systems, and social expectations of business performance. If this projection is correct, the threat of obsolescence of managers will pass swiftly from today's conversational shocker to tomorrow's operating reality. Executives best prepared to survive this challenge will turn out to be those equipped to think tomorrow today or do what I call strategic thinking, a type of intellectual skill not ordinarily developed in business schools or by the common work experiences of middle management.

Historical Development

The roots of this radical transformation of the general management job can be identified in recent business history:

- Resources — up to about the last two decades the main task of top management could fairly be described as the efficient administration of physical resources. The focus was essentially short-range and unifunctional, and, of course, the dominant decision criteria were largely economic. The highest demonstration of management skill was the successful manipulation of revenues and costs in the production and distribution of materials, machines and products.

- People — Beginning in the 1930's this concern with managing physical things was enlarged by a growing interest in managing people. This was enlargement, rather than change, because the ultimate goal of effective people management was still much the same as physical resource management, whereby top executives extended their grasp over resources by means of their ability to organise and motivate people. The focus of management attention remained within short-term horizons and unifunctional activity.

- Money — After World War II, in a business environment marked by rapid growth in corporate size, product and market diversification, accelerated technological development, and shortened product life cycles, the principal task of top management evolved from concentration on physical and human resources to a major concern with money. This shift was accompanied by an extension of planning horizons and a transition from a unifunctional to a multifunctional view of a company's activities.

In contrast to physical resources, money is inherently neutral. To be used, it must be transformed into physical and human resources. Money also is flexible through time. For example, it is capable of expansion and contraction, as well as of rapid shifts in the forms, risks, and costs of financial instruments. These characteristics of neutrality and flexibility encouraged a broader management view that encompassed many functions within a company as well as longer- term planning horizons.

· Ideas —We are now beginning to sense that a focus on managing money, although broader than the earlier focus on physical and human resources, still fosters a dangerous sort of tunnel vision. The world of management is in a revolutionary phase. Within the company, racing technologies destroy both their own foundations and inter- technological boundaries. Outside the company, the environment is moving faster (in market evolution and consumer behaviour) exploding in geographic scope (from nation to world) and reflecting the demands and constraints of a new society in which the traditional role of private business and traditional criteria of management performance are challenged by new concepts and standards.

At the same time, new analytical techniques, largely quantitative and computer- based are presenting a management opportunity that is unique in at least three important ways. First, they provide an administrative capability without parallel in breadth, depth, and speed. Second, for their full and efficient utilisation, they press management to establish a unified command over the totality of a business, including the dynamic interface of external environment and internal activities. Developments in information technology have also provided access to a minefield of information through the information superhighway called the Internet. These changes are defining a novel view of management itself as a universally applicable resource, readily transferred from one business to another, from one industry to another, from one technology to another and from one country to another.

As a result of the forces driving change, organisations are required to adopt a "new paradigm" to increase their sensitivity, flexibility and adaptability to the emerging demands and expectations of all stakeholders. Today's leaders and/or managers must deal with continual, rapid change. Management faced with a major decision can no longer refer back to an earlier developed plan for direction. Management techniques must continually notice changes in the environment and organisation, assess these changes and manage them for survival into the future.

Managing change does not mean controlling change; but rather anticipating change, understanding change, and pro-actively adapting to change. This requires intellectual vision, with the ability to transform vision into operating results through the flexible administration of physical, human, and financial resources in any environment. This might be described as applied conceptualisation or, more simply, as the management of ideas.

Central Focus on Ideas

Thinking tomorrow today is all about generating and manipulating ideas. It is the ability to universalise from here and now to everywhere and always. If it is true that top executives in the years ahead are going to be tested above all by their ability to manage ideas, then they are going to have to understand what it means to think like philosophers and develop skill in doing so. This has implications for management education, training, and selection, especially at the higher levels of administration. It also carries a substantial threat of obsolescence for managers now holding broad responsibilities whose talent, education, and experience have not equipped them to use their intellects in this manner.

The implications are not limited to the purely intellectual demands placed on general managers. They also extend to corporate purpose, organisation, and function. A business devoted to the identification of central ideas and the formulation of strategies for moving swiftly from ideas to operations will differ in structure and activity from a business primarily concerned with management of money, or of physical and human resources.

Management of ideas also goes beyond the concept of strategy. Just as there are alternative strategies for attaining an objective, so there are alternative strategies for executing an idea that defines the central purpose of a business. Focusing on the management of ideas contributes to more realistic planning, more appropriate objectives, and more relevant strategies.

New Ways of Thinking

Thinking in terms of such ideas, from initial concept through to full implementation, is a difficult intellectual task. It is no assignment for second- rate minds, or even for first-rate but narrowly oriented minds. Moreover, it demands the special intellectual ability to visualise the translation of ideas and strategies into controlled operating systems responsive to dynamic change. The need for these unusual talents is the inevitable outcome of radically new conditions within and outside organisations.

The critical new condition is acceleration in the rate of change and is of such magnitude that change itself becomes the central object of management attention. Up to now, with rare exceptions, the administration of change has been handled as a supplement to the administration of established ongoing activities. In this context, the future evolves from the present to a controllable pace, and it is reasonable for managers to concentrate mainly on targets of efficiency and to treat adapting to market challenges as a subsidiary element within a larger administrative responsibility.

At this point, it becomes more important to make correct decisions about the direction, timing, and implementation of change than to attain a high level of efficiency in administering steady- state operations. However, few business organisations have been designed to give primary support to this unfamiliar ordering of goals. In most companies, the values, organisation, responsibility, control systems, information networks, and performance standards are not well adapted to this requirement.

Most companies, including many with reputations for being well managed, are organised primarily to administer yesterday's ideas. In these organisations, investments and operations are measured by efficient performance, with relatively short-term targets for achievement, and a primary focus on the administration of existing resources and markets. This was an appropriate corporate design concept when the rate of change within and outside the company was slow.

The weakness of such organisations is revealed, however, whenever a single department senses a new opportunity or a forced adaptation. Invariably, the expected rapid exploitation of new markets usually increases production costs, and is regretfully resisted by managers whose performance will be adversely affected in any shift in ongoing efficient activities, irrespective of the overall impact on business development. Less common, but equally possible, is resistance from the marketing people to innovation in production technology with its risk of cost, quality, and delivery uncertainties. But even this view is simplistic. For in spite of the current touted commitment to a marketing orientation in management, the performance record in many companies suggests that leadership by the marketing function frequently generates little more than better adaption of existing products to better define existing markets. This may be a move in the right direction in the short run. But it is not good enough in a period when new technology may erode established market positions or capture untouched markets "overnight".

Inherent in the concept of core ideas for top management is a total business orientation, rather than a market-oriented administration (or a technology- oriented or any "other-oriented" administration). A total business orientation views the company as a system of physical, financial, and human resources in dynamic interaction with a changing environment. It views swift response to opportunities and problems as more important for long-term success than efficient control of current operations. It values the future above the present. Such an orientation has revolutionary implications for many management tasks. Such orientation will task an individual ability to forecast the future today and in the process arrive at a reasonable outcome for tomorrow based on utilisation of sophisticated and scientific tools of analysis. *Thinking tomorrow today* therefore requires skill and competence levels for issues of uncertainty.

Planning for Uncertainty

You may say that uncertainty in Nigeria — in the economy, society, politics- has become so great as to render futile, if not counterproductive, the kind of planning for the future most blue-chip companies still practise: forecasting based on probabilities. Yet, executives have to make decisions that commit to the future current resources of time and money. Worse, they have to make decisions not to commit resources — to forgo the future. The lengths of such commitments are steadily growing: in strategy and technology, marketing, manufacturing, employee development, or in the time it takes to bring a new plant on stream. Every such commitment is based on assumptions about the future.

To arrive at these decisions, traditional planning asks 'What is most likely to happen?' We may however start our thinking for tomorrow or planning for uncertainty instead, by asking the question: 'What has already happened that will create the future?' The first place to look, for instance, is in demographics. Everybody who will be in the labour force in Nigeria in the year 2015 is already alive today. There have been two revolutionary changes in the workforce of Nigeria: the explosion of advanced education and the rush of women into careers outside the home. Both are accomplished facts. The shift from blue- collar labour to knowledge and service workers as the centres of labour force gravity is irrevocable.

Business people need to ask: 'What do these accomplished facts mean for our business? What opportunities do they create? What threats? What changes do they demand — in the way the business is organised and run, in our goals, in our products, in our services, in our policies? And what changes do they make possible and are likely to be advantageous?'

The next question is: 'What changes in industry and market structure, in basic values, and in science and technology have already occurred but have yet to have full impact?' Closely related is the next question: 'What are the trends in economic and societal structure and how do they affect our business?'

The answers to the question 'What has already happened that will make the future?' define the potential of opportunities for a given company or industry.
To convert this potential into reality requires matching the opportunities with the company's strengths and competence. It requires the analysis of the 'core competence'.

'What is this company good at? What does it do well? What gives it a competitive edge? Matching a company's strengths to the changes that have already taken place produces, in effect, a plan of action. It enables the business to turn the unexpected into advantage. Uncertainty ceases to be a threat and becomes an opportunity.

There is, however, one condition: that the business creates the resources of knowledge and of people to respond when opportunity knocks. This means creating and maintaining resources for the future in people and their development. They enable a business to make its future — and this is the challenge we will now throw our searchlight on, in the next section of this presentation.

Personnel Management Challenges

Management must assume responsibility for strategising, for choosing and modifying the company's vision and mission, for developing new competences, for validating the choices made, and for energising the values and aspirations of organisation members at all levels to sustain those choices.

At the heart of this process are learning organisations and learning persons. There is resurgence in the development of organisation capability not only in management ranks, but wherever creative contributions to future competitive advantage can be sparked and developed. This extends beyond training and encompasses appropriate incentives, careful career planning and placement, decentralisation, delegation, an open and supportive climate for learning, and the nurturing of teamwork and collaborative entrepreneurship.

Link to Human Resources Development

The emerging dominance of ideas, as a central concern for top management, raises critical questions about the education, selection, and development of
candidates for high-level assignments in the years ahead. Neither business school education nor in-company experience is presently structured to emphasise the strategic thinking concept. Rather, the principal thrust in school and company environments is toward new analytic techniques, both quantitative and qualitative, and their application in rational decision-making and control.

There is good reason to doubt that students in professional schools are at a stage of their intellectual development where they would benefit from a major emphasis on the role of central ideas in top management responsibilities. Moreover, the relevant technical input to their education is so important and growing so rapidly that any sharp curtailment would constrain their ability to handle management tasks in junior executive positions.

The education of middle-level managers is another issue, however. There are opportunities at this stage to expose selected high-potential executives to the significance of core ideas in the design of future corporate strategies and in the adaptation of organisation and resources to their implementation. The opportunities arise in planned job experiences and management education programmes, both in-house and at known business schools. Imaginative action at this level will produce two important benefits. One is the preparation of a cadre of potential top executives for the broad new responsibilities that the future business environment will thrust on them. The other is a new selection criterion for top-level positions, based on specific performance in mind-career assignments, where the ability to think conceptually and to relate ideas to applied management can be tested.

Today's development programmes give principal emphasis to new techniques for analysis and control in functional areas, and to strategic planning of resources utilisation at the general management level. It would be desirable to curtail the technical content to some degree and to introduce material on dynamic environmental change (markets, technologies, social, political), on the role and manipulation of ideas, and on the impact of change on corporate strategy.

Of equal importance is the need to enrich idea-management experience on the job and also to test executives' abilities below the top management level. This would require giving such executives more opportunities for assignments that require imaginative projection, assessment of the total environmental outlook, and relevant strategic decision. Companies that move in this direction will fortify their management ability to cope powerfully and speedily in a radically new business world.

Link to Incentive Structure

Very often, firms resort to the budgeting and financial control systems, thus falling into the trap of short-term accounting-driven control instruments. Therefore, the ability of the organisation to generate, evaluate, monitor, implement, and control strategic ideas for the future is almost entirely lost.

Strategically thinking organisations devote considerable attention to devising measures of performance and control for strategy implementation. Much more creativity is required for measuring the long-term impact of strategic ideas, and monitoring the progress of strategic programmes and the deployment of strategic funds. Both the budget and the reporting systems should be designed to express this dichotomy between operational (for ongoing businesses, short term) and strategic accountability.

Rewards and motivational systems should also be devised to allocate appropriate weights between short and long-term performance. Most organisations suffer from the use of short-term measures of performance to reward high-level managers, who are mainly responsible for strategic actions. Japanese companies are noted for tempering this bias and for emphasising rewards for long-term performance as well. Strategically managed organisations are trying to develop more balanced reward systems.

Among other systems, the strategic factors approach involves the identification of the critical success factors governing the future performance (profitability) of the business and the assignment of proper weights depending on the inherent characteristics of the organisational units. Some relevant factors might include:

product quality measures, client-satisfaction/market demand measures, productivity levels, product development measures, and personnel development measures.

There is no doubt that performance measurement, accountability and incentives are integral to the successful introduction and implementation of the strategic thinking process. The difficulty of devising such systems must be acknowledged. However, it is a necessity for the strategically managed organisation.

Link to Human Resources Allocation

Thinking tomorrow today is distinguished by its emphasis on providing strategic criteria, for resource allocation, that depart from marginal, ad hoc or trend increases. It ensures that resource allocation decisions are taken in full view of long-term consequences of resource redeployments. Thus, strategic thinking enables institutions to embark on manpower planning concentrate their human resources development efforts on the areas and skills that hold great potentials for the future, and to gradually withdraw resources from old and less productive ones.

"Sloughing off yesterday" is particularly important in turbulent times and businesses have to think through the changed circumstances in which they operate. Precisely because results in service organisations are not easily measured, there is a need for organised abandonment of marginal and resource-consuming activities of the past. In turbulent times, an institution needs to be able both to withstand outside contingencies and to avail itself of sudden unexpected opportunities.

Although commonly neglected, as a resource for strategic allocations purposes, managerial and staff skills and their knowledge about the future of their clients and the environment, are now increasingly recognized as the scarcest organisational resources. Financial resources are easier to measure and deploy;

and can be borrowed, but the scarcest resources for us to find are entrepreneurial managers and innovative engineers to run our most challenging businesses. Not surprisingly, in professional services organisations like banks and high-tech companies, the highest priority for the attention of top management is the recruitment, placement and development of human resources.

Integration into Strategic Thinking/Planning

The above challenges to human resources management imply the need for HR professionals to be integrated into the entire strategic thinking/planning process. The human resources manager will then be in a position to understand, draw up and advise on the human resources implications of management thinking for the future. To enable an HR professional to be effectively, he must be:

- Knowledgeable and interested in the core business of the organisation.
- Informed about developments in the operating environment that will impact on the business to enable him to contribute meaningfully to strategic issues and earn the respect of his other colleagues.
-

Conclusion

From this presentation, we have come to the conclusion that management teams face a period of unprecedented dynamic transformation of the operating environment, which is throwing up tremendous business challenges. Tomorrow will not be the same as yesterday for large, medium or small business enterprises as changes need to be managed in a pro-active manner. Management must, therefore, modify existing management practice and culture, and take on methodologies more appropriate to tomorrow's rapidly changing environment.

In short, management must recognise, grasp and achieve some fundamental objectives to secure a firm basis for competitive success in national, international and global markets. Among such objectives are:

(i) A continuous watch on trends and cross impacts of development in the operating environment, for early warning of new opportunities and risks to ensure prompt responses.

(ii) The effective access and use of technology to satisfy customers' strategic needs and improve productivity.

(iii) The use of competitive and time effective management processes to review, update, integrate and implement visions, decisions and plans for tomorrow, whether expansionary or recessionary times.

(iv) The effective use and development of more competent, knowledgeable and business driven top management and support teams.

Being paper presented at the Annual Conference of IPMN on the theme: Complacency to Competence, October 2001.

Part V

Key Sectors and Issues

Key Sectors and Issues

In the ever continuous effort to understand and solve national development problems, a major and effective borrowing from navigation has been the principle of triangulation – a navigation technique that uses the trigonometric properties of triangles to determine a location or course by means of compass bearings from two points to a known distance apart. In the social sciences and development planning in particular, triangulation enjoins us to seek solutions to a problem by choosing and attacking it from three points or strategies. By so doing, the chances of resolution are enhanced because one, two or a combination of the three strategies would hit 'the bull's eye'. Yet, the challenge that remains is where to begin and/or which points to choose.

In the quest for Nigeria's economic development, practitioners and leaders have raised several issues. The final part of this book is focused on three sectors that are considered germane to Nigeria's

- Education, with an appropriate title – Education: Universities and Convocation Ceremonies
- Oil and Gas, with emphasis on financing projects in the sector
- Transportation, with a focus on the so called 'soft infrastructure' – Fleet Renewal.

Arguing that the nation missed the train (the *'festival years'*) in the thirty years of military rule *(the masquerade years')*, during which the education system and national ethos were bastardised, the paper on education and university convocations enjoins all to seize the opportunity encapsulated in democracy if we must *'dance in the sun again'*. While focusing on strategies of financing oil and gas projects, the section also concludes that it is vitally imperative to leverage global best practices in managing the sector if we must reverse the oil curse. Finally, the section draws attention to the import of transportation as a veritable means of diversifying production, expanding trade, coping with population growth, reducing poverty, improving environmental conditions and ultimately, enhancing economic development.

Chapter 17

Education: Universities and Convocation Ceremonies

Introduction

The yearly convocation for the conferment of laurels on graduating students provides an opportunity for a close-up on a rare festival. It is a snapshot trade fair of the knowledge community in a state of self-adulation and backslapping. It reflects the climax in the parade of excellence as the academy turns its products loose on a society that almost invariably would be waiting with open hands for these products. Convocation equally provides a rare opportunity for serious introspection. Most importantly, it provides a unique opportunity to challenge the institution, its graduates and supporters to return to foundation principles and make a firm commitment to rebuild our system of knowledge delivery. This challenge places on the university a pivotal role in the march to a great society.

In the great ancient tradition since Plato, the academy is by its very nature the place of truth. This is so for the primary reason that it is the place where knowledge is sought and imparted. Knowledge and truth are like Siamese twins. They are inseparable. Thus, you cannot find one without the other. That is why every society, that is desirous of pursuing progress, places emphasis on knowledge acquisition and capacity building.

At every convocation ceremony, therefore, we tread the hallowed path beaten by men whose very mention conjures awe and inspiration. We are inspired by the over-arching vision of these men in their attempt at establishing a constructive pattern for societal development that is rooted in institution- building. But the history of our country is replete with the destructive counter-poise to institution-building. Nigeria has been under military rule for close to 30 years out of our 40 odd years as an independent nation. There are very few discerning individuals today who are still in denial that, from an institution-building point of view, those 30 years have mostly been wasted. The convocation ceremonies of Nigerian universities can be likened to 'festivals, masquerades and dancing in the sun'.

Some Definitions

'Of festivals, masquerades and dancing in the sun', is a somewhat audacious concession to satire. For come to think it, isn't convocation — even of the academic variety — *a festival* of sort? Does the rainbow coalition of *dramatis personae* that gather for the great occasion not give a collective sense of an assemblage of *masquerades?* And is this festival dance not going to be enacted under the direct gaze of the *sun?*

A brief lexical exploration would throw more light on the theme, and thereby enable us to wade through its essence. The New Lexicon Webster's Dictionary of The English Language defines FESTIVAL as "a joyful celebration or occasion; a local season of entertainment, often annual, when cultural works are produced or performed ..."The same authority defines MASQUERADE in the well-known spirit of revelry:" A ball at which masks are worn; a false show for pretence or concealment of the truth". The Webster's Dictionary defines dancing in the following terms: "To move rhythmically, along or with a partner or other dancers to music or drumming." The SUN hardly needs an introduction, but just in case. It is "the controlling body of the solar system, lying at the principal focus of all planetary orbits..."

The constituents of the satire also find strong expression in our folklore system. To that extent, they are mostly native African, nay Igbo, expressions that spice a great number of our proverbs, legends and mythology. But in terms of giving allegorical expression to our current play on satire, one cannot but take recourse to the near-term historical antecedents of the Nigerian nation. Within these antecedents can be identified the undulating phases that has marked the nation's chequered epochs. The immediate pre- and post-independent period (circa 1950-67) could be likened to Nigeria's era *of festivals* (the good old years!) when the polity was notable for relative policy stability, incremental economic growth (even with an underlying weak base), good external image and healthy competition within a truer federal structure of governance. Simply put, we were building a great nation based on traditional institutions and practices that have typically been successful elsewhere. In contrast, the late 1960's up to the eve of the inception of the present democratic dispensation could be likened to the era of the *masquerades.* This was the time of considerable experimentation and failure to adapt to changing times. During this period, Nigeria witnessed some of the most unwarranted official policy onslaughts on the national economy — the deleterious outcome of which still haunts us today: the white elephant projects that have continued to exact a terrible toll on our capacity to compete globally; the cement armada phenomenon; essential commodities; Champagne breakfasts in the rarefied precincts of Western capitals; disappearing windfall revenues from crude oil exports; and, of course, the jumbo loans contracted, incidentally, at the precise moment that the country was awash with petro-dollar. It was also the time of great distortion of our national values under the military, the emergence of men of dubious antecedents in the leadership scene, contrarian business culture like the 419 phenomenon, sycophancy and the near-complete absence of standards at all spheres of national life. In the ensuing melee, those who thought themselves dealt out in the national scheme took to robbery amongst other forms of violent inclinations.

The period from May 29, 1999 to the present time clearly marks the era of *dancing in the sun,* with democracy offering us yet another chance to re-engineer and restructure the polity for the better. The ensuing euphoria was evident in the generalised explosion of native emotions that greeted the advent of democracy. Resulting from the years of deprivation and lack of political space in our multi-national polity, various sections of the country literally mounted serious challenge to the sovereign authority of the government at the centre. Hence, the birth of what I would simply refer to as the new octopuses: *Bakassi, Odua Peoples Congress, Egbesu, Arewa Peoples Congress,* etc. The situation got so bad that the country was seemingly being run at the time by a troika at daggers drawn. There is no doubt that democracy has brought great expectation and euphoria in the land. In this state of affairs, we have characteristically ignored the depth of damage wrought on the system in the course of the past several decades. We have moved on without due introspection as to the amount of energy and exertion needed to pull us out of the mud of history.

The frank diagnosis of what currently afflicts, and continues to afflict, the Nigerian nation is an abiding absence of moral leadership and authority at the critical strata of society. This is precisely the reason why ethnic cleavages have sharpened perceptibly within the nation, even with our newfound democratic space (or perhaps due to it!). This is also at the root of the lack of buy-in by Nigerians across the ethnic divides for government's key policy initiatives both on the political and economic fronts. The idea of moral leadership here is not that which flows only from the Presidency, but the more generalised variant that brings together the entire cadre of our ruling elite. What has clearly happened is a massive, albeit silent, no-confidence vote on national leadership arising from a palpable perception of a moral discount where it matters the most.

It is difficult to find a better way of defining the threshold of the task at hand than done in the foregoing paragraphs. What is next is to proceed into territories both charted and otherwise. Let us first take a look at the University of Nigeria, Nsukka, and whose unique design — like Paris; Bologna, Oxford and Cambridge — had *sought* the progress of ALL OF HUMANKIND (Note the accent on the past participle). Next, let us look at the knowledge industry in the global context. This will help to situate our country, Nigeria, in the comity of nations and the race for material and mental advancement amongst the peoples of the world. Finally, we must define the challenge we face and what the UNN community can do about it.

The University of Nigeria

The first item of note in the above sub-title would, of course, be the accent on the definite article THE. There is indeed a sense in which one can assume, without fear of contradiction that we are all standing on sacred ground. The uniqueness of the University of Nigeria, Nsukka is one of a mental, physical and mythological (even mythical) dimension. Even with the establishment in 1948 of the University College, Ibadan (the fore-runner to the University of Ibadan), the under-current of native yearning for a truly African institution of higher learning was palpable. It is no exaggeration that the University of Nigeria, Nsukka amply filled that niche in terms, especially, of the philosophical impetus behind its founding. Let us take a brief look at that history.

The UNN was legislated into corporate legal existence in 1955. Several years before this landmark enactment, however, the very outline of this great institution had been taking shape in the minds of several Nigerian leaders. By far the greatest inspiration behind its conception was the towering personage of the then Premier of Eastern Nigeria, Dr. Nnamdi Azikiwe. Till date the legend endures, albeit in tatters. But the force that saw to the realisation of the dream of a mighty academy was none other than the then burgeoning thirst for knowledge in Nigeria, nay Igboland.

The documented historical facts about the institution tell the story of incredible grit and collective determination. The very speed with which plans for the university were made to crystallise into reality would amaze most of us today. One of the first steps taken by the Eastern Nigeria Government, toward actualising the dream of a truly national institution of higher education, was the invitation to educational and physical planning authorities from the U.S. and the U.K. In 1958, under the joint auspices of the Inter-University Council for Higher Education and the International Co-operation Administration (now the United States Agency for International Development or USAID), a delegation comprising Mr. J.W. Cook (Vice Chancellor of the University of Exeter), Dr. John A. Hannah (President of the Michigan State University) and Dr. Glen L. Taggart (Dean of International Programmes at M.S.U.) visited the country.

The delegation surveyed and endorsed the proposed site at Nsukka. The outcome of the team's efforts, including an extensive investigation of salient factors in the establishment of the new university, was encapsulated in a White Paper published by the Eastern Nigeria Government on November 30, 1958. The team had concluded thus: "... that the development of the University of Nigeria based upon the concept of service to problems and needs of Nigeria, is a desirable project and one that should receive support from any source which could help to make it a sound endeavour". The delegation's recommendation for a provisional council to "draw upon the technical and consultative resources available throughout the world for help in planning the institution" was quickly implemented by the regional government in April 1959, and vested with full powers to establish a sound institution. Reflecting the internationalist concept on which the institution was founded, the council was made up of Dr. Nnamdi Azikiwe as Chairman, and Dr. T. Olawale Elias, Dr. Okechukwu Ikejiani, Mr. J.S. Fulton (U.K.), Dr. Margueritte Cartwright and Dr. Eldon Lee Johnson (both of the U.S.) as members.

The university was formally commissioned on October 7, 1960, while classes began on October 17 of the same year with a student enrolment of 220 and a 13- member academic staff compliment. Thus was born a unique institution whose founding marked a watershed not only in the development of higher education in Nigeria but also (and perhaps more significantly) in the political dynamics of the country.

The philosophy of the university was etched in the immutable legend: TO RESTORE THE DIGNITY OF MAN. It encapsulated the African developmental ideology, summing up the thoughts of Casely Hayford, Edward Wilmot Blyden, Marcus Garvey, our very own Nwafor Abyssinia Orizu and others as subsequently articulated by Dr. Azikiwe in *Africa Renascent*. The black race must move out of the handicaps of history and restore its dignity through authentic development based on a value system founded on relevant knowledge. Looking down both ancient and recent history, was the idea that gave birth to this philosophy not a prophetic dash of inspiration? Were the authors merely looking at the decades of deprivation visited on the black race? Or were they equally stricken by the premonition that there would come a time when the people at the epicentre of the founding of the institution would lose their collective dignity and esteem within the Nigerian milieu? In that case then wasn't this institution assigned the hallowed duty of restoring, as well as preserving, the dignity of this core constituency? These are questions that deserve deeper introspection than we have so far been willing to concede.

It follows, therefore, that education at Nsukka, as conceived by the university's founding fathers, must be closely related, first, to the Igbo, and then the Nigerian, African and universal development and reality. The school was built on the land-grant model that proved very effective in the U.S. Its underlying operating philosophy was designed to achieve a direct connection with its immediate environment and society. Dr. Nnamdi Azikiwe, as the University's first Chancellor, summed up this fact in his address entitled

"Heroes and Heroines of a New Nigeria" at the institution's inaugural convocation on October 13, 1960: "The founders of the University of Nigeria aimed at relating its activities to the social and economic needs and the day-to-day life of the people of Nigeria". This was how accountancy, home economics, surveying, management sciences, journalism, fine and graphics arts, etc. became its core courses — a scheme still then undreamt of at the British-oriented universities in the country.

Within four years of its founding, the university's student enrolment grew phenomenally to 2,940 compared to the federally-funded University of Ibadan (founded 1948) which in 1964 had an enrolment of 2,284 students. The University of Nigeria is, therefore, paramount in our discourse today because its idea was conceived and nurtured within a specific developmental *nexus*. It represented both an historical and cultural watershed. It was built on a firm foundation. Unfortunately, today what is left of that vanguard is an abiding sense of a stultified dream and of the consequent nostalgia. We must ask why and look for the way forward for recapturing that dream.

Values and the Age of Knowledge

If there is one point on which most discerning observers of the affairs of our country are overwhelmingly agreed, it is that socio-economic progress has largely eluded us since we gained sovereign status in 1960. Among the recurring indices in this state of affairs has been the painful distortion of our system of values, especially in regard to knowledge acquisition. This situation had become quite acute following the devastating Nigerian civil war, and has been made worse still by the advent of oil as the key national money-spinner. Paradoxically, oil has funded many bad practices, which have undermined our economic progress and fostered decline in our values.

Our values are basically inert qualities that are nurtured in the context of our socio-cultural existence. With the benefit of hindsight, it is possible to identify about four historical (even if potential) centres of excellence: the academia, the business class, the bureaucracy and the political class. In the past, the differentiating attributes of these centres of excellence were well known and respected. For instance, the university teacher was under no illusion as to his capacity to acquire wealth by magic. The bureaucrat was under no illusion regarding his capacity to achieve a breakthrough in the scientific arena. Today, all these attributes have blurred beyond comprehension. The civil servant is a (potential) politician, academic and a business mogul all rolled into an untidy whole. The academic is a budding businessman with the potential to make questionable millions outside his immediate calling.

Our value system has undergone a sea change to the detriment of our progress as a people. This has impacted most adversely on our system of knowledge delivery. And because our education has suffered precipitately, our material progress has become the logical victim and hostage.

Historically, every age of man is an age of knowledge because knowledge has always been a critical ingredient in the quest for progress by mankind through the ages. In the 21st Century, however, knowledge has become the ascendant force for progress, dethroning the forces of intuition and dogma. Being a universal property, knowledge cannot be an exclusive preserve of any one nation or people. At any given time, nations and peoples are in direct and fierce contest for dominance in the great theatre of knowledge. To gain a strong foothold on the knowledge threshold, therefore, a nation must of necessity learn to harness knowledge for the benefit of its citizenry. Herein lies the challenge for our political leadership and for our institutions of higher learning.

It is a matter of deep irony that whilst many nations have achieved rapid progress in living standards through the manifestations of purposeful education, others such as Nigeria have witnessed major relapses even in the gains registered in their early years of nationhood. Most are perpetually disabled from mobilising their potential capacities to save their peoples from endemic poverty and the attendant loss of self-respect and dignity. Today, our country is a true testimony to this phenomenal regression — even with democracy now in place.

The challenge of national leaderships in these countries is captured in Gilbert Highet's Man's *Unconquerable Mind (1954):*

> *Anthropologists sometimes talk as though they believe it is impossible to compare one society with another. Yet they would agree ... that a nation whose children died in infancy or grew up weak and sickly was inferior physically to a nation, which kept its children alive and contrived for them a long and healthy life. In the same way, there can be no doubt that a superior nation is one which uses the minds of its people, giving them a constant flow of challenges, ensuring that no class or group is kept from acquiring knowledge because of sex, colour, caste, religion or poverty, stimulating the free, fresh production of ideas, respecting those who record and transmit knowledge, keeping open many demands of communication within (and beyond) its frontiers.*

If the Highet principle is used to gauge the progress of nations, then Nigeria has fallen short on virtually all its critical aspects. The more cherished route to popular acclaim and esteem in our country today would easily be identified as primitive accumulation. However, primitive material acquisition has long ceased to be the most important source of respect in the world of today, except perhaps here in Nigeria. America's Bill Gates, one of the wealthiest men in the world today, enjoys global acclaim primarily by virtue of his creation of the Microsoft Corporation - a true model of the infinite capacity and genius of the human mind. Mr. Gates' billions of dollars in assets get mentioned only as an adjunct to the fact of his association with Microsoft. Yet, there are scores of equally rich individuals but who do not come close to Gates in terms of popular acclaim and respect in spite of their considerable wealth.

The difference lies in how money is made to impact on the larger society in an enduring sense. Knowledge-bound wealth and development, which truly elevate human dignity, are evidently much sought after in the world today, except in Nigeria. The global accent is on the knowledge industry because it is the way to a meaningful progress for us and for posterity. All over the world today, it is men of knowledge and (therefore) character who preside over the affairs of nations, not men of wealth and material means. Today's leaders, at whatever level in society, must not only be highly educated; they must be champions of education for the mere reason that education is the most functional, viable and enduring source of power in the present age.

Education, in the sense we canvassed here, must not be equated to the mere acquisition of degrees. The latter simply describes an educated illiterate — one with education but without the benefit of its deeper morals. Indeed, in the words of William Penn, the American civil rights leader, "knowledge is light, it is wisdom; it is, in other words, another country where everything is done in reverse proportion to the practice in the land of ignorance. To possess it is a key to an understanding of nature and life".

Crisis in Our Education

Nigeria's educational system has witnessed what would rightly be termed concentric cycles of crisis. Successive Nigerian administrations (with emphasis on the military) have displayed a robust disdain toward the elevation of our system of knowledge delivery. The operating philosophy has obviously favoured the proprietary theory of the state whereby the blind expropriation of the collective wealth for the ruling class is received wisdom. In other words, the political class (the military inclusive) has not recognised the critical precepts of knowledge and social communication as enunciated by Gilbert Highet.

In the circumstance, education has suffered in the hands of the most surprising of assailants — the national leadership cadre. Anti-academia sentiments have been especially high under military rule. But it has not fared dramatically better under the civil democratic dispensation. Witness, for instance, the plethora of truces brokered between the government and the Union of Academic Staff of Universities since May 29, 1999. The spirit and letters of these pacts have been observed more in their breaches on the part of the government. Against the current of good reason as expressed in the highest principle, those who record and transmit knowledge have since ceased to count for much in our national scheme of things.

The benign neglect of education has its immediate origin in the series of schemes under military rule aimed at emasculating the academia, which had emerged as a prominent voice against political misrule and resource mismanagement. At issues were the obvious interference in the administration of universities, sustained depletion and inadequacy of physical infrastructures, irregular payment of salaries and direct selection of top university administrators by the government. University administrative and faculty leaderships are nearly as a rule selected on basis other than merit. Today, only fleeting thought is spared even in the circle of the discerning, for the deeper reasons behind the explosion of occult tendencies in campuses across the nation. The exodus of our best teachers to foreign lands no longer makes headline news.

All of these reflect a vicious shift of paradigm away from the deeper essence of the role of education in the making of nations. The sense of a system in chaos had, in fact, proceeded from our primary and secondary education. School enrolment at these levels has fallen sharply, the result (no doubt) of mass poverty among the working class and rural populace. The most conspicuous index of the neglect of education in Nigeria is seen in vivid relief in the low ratio of public spending on education, health, etc, relative to other countries as shown in Tables I and II in the appendices section of this paper. Not only has the country performed dismally in comparison with the advanced nations of the world. We have fared no better in relation to many poor countries in sub-Sahara Africa.

The picture gets even worse when more detailed data on our higher education are subjected to close scrutiny. Tables III and IV in the appendices section show yearly enrolment of university freshmen and the award of first degrees, respectively. Giving allowance for the four-year average duration for most first- degree courses, what comes out clearly from these schedules is the incredible rate of attrition (drop out) at our institutions of higher learning.

Students who enrolled to pursue first-degree courses in 1990, for instance, should (all things being equal) have left school with their diplomas by 1994, while those admitted in 1991 should be out of the undergraduate programme by 1995. What is, however, obvious from these two tables is that between the year of enrolment and supposed year of graduation, the rate of graduate turnout relative to enrolment continues to deteriorate alarmingly: it was 19.26 per cent in 1993/94; 8.5 per cent in 1995/96; *3.9* per cent in 1996/97; and 2.3 per cent in 1997/98. Now, I have no reason whatsoever to doubt the veracity of these figures given that they were taken from government's official records.

Additionally, a recent World Bank study of Nigeria's educational system has highlighted the precipitate decline in that all-important sector. According to newspaper reports, the study, which was conducted in conjunction with the Nigerian Institute of Social and Economic Research (NISER), covered the period spanning the past 15 years. The study raised particular concern about the poor mastery of the English Language and lack of requisite skills among Nigerian graduates. These deficiencies, it said, made these graduates most unfit for the labour market and even the larger society. The simple verdict of the study is that "Nigerian university graduates are poorly trained and unproductive on the job, (and that) graduate skills have steadily deteriorated over the past decade".

The message from the foregoing insights is incontrovertible: our education, from all indications, is in deep and sustained crisis.

The Challenge We Face

In the intervening years of nationhood, Nigeria seems to offer the perfect counterpoise to the Le Chatelier's Principle: *that when a system in equilibrium is subjected to a stressful pressure, it tends toward a new state of equilibrium that opposes the effect of the stress*. Unless somebody in this distinguished gathering is in a position to offer a contrary set of explanations, and convincingly too, one is virtually sold on the idea that we have steadily failed as a nation to properly equip ourselves for the tough challenges of the future. The sustained onslaught on our education, the only assured route to national progress, has proceeded in giddy fashion without much effort at affecting a turnaround.

In the circumstance, therefore, the great centres of knowledge that were conceived by the visionaries of yester-years now lay prostrate before us. The basis of the cultural decay that has now caught up with our system of education is both macro and micro in outlook. At the macro level is the grand failure of leadership within the ubiquitous structure of governance in our country. At the micro level is the family together with the structure of learning at the formative years. Several watersheds have conspired to reshape this latter milieu, and none for the better. First, is the steady breakdown of moral authority that flowed from the family structure. Second, is the eclipse of the missionary school system in the aftermath of Big Government. And third expurgation of the system of moral instructions that was an integral part of the early learning experience. All of these precede the collapse of the mighty vanguard built around our Timbuktus at Nsukka, Ibadan, Zaria and even their later-day variants.

How do we resolve the problem of knowledge acquisition in a world in which education has become the guarantor of a nation's reckoning in a fiercely competitive market place? How prepared are we for the inevitable changes that will define the character of the peoples and nations of the world? Is our system of knowledge delivery in the proper state to support an all-round and internally consistent developmental ethos?

Today, Nigeria's very precarious standing in the world's progress chart reinforces the urgency in the above questions. Nigeria has been formally rated among the poorest nations on the global human development index. Education is a key variable of this index. In fact, on several variables within the basket, our dear country is just within whiskers of the stark bottom. The situation has not been made any easier by certain mental fixations that tend to hobble us in a state of dubious self-adulation. For instance, contemporary development paradigm clearly rejects our ancient romance with the largely nebulous legend "our vast human and material resources". Nations such as Japan, South Korea and (ironically) Nigeria have since blown the myth that the quantum of resources available to a nation has any direct correlation with its ability to progress materially.

As long as Nigeria wants to survive as a sovereign entity, she must carry the burden that goes with that aspiration. The burden is that of devising creative means of achieving greater collective focus on the imperatives for rapid progress. The pivot of needed action is the reconstruction and reinforcement of the superstructure that is the Nigerian nation. For this to happen, we must stand firm on the premise that the survival of any nation now depends on how well it is able to cue in on to the global scheme of things. In this regard, there is a big lesson to be learned from the harrowing fate of the mighty dinosaur. Not even the size and might of this specie was sufficient to save its kind from total extinction once it failed to adapt. A similar fate awaits any nation that fails to prepare itself and its people for the new global-village reality. At both the corporate and individual levels, the reward system has changed irreversibly in favour of the knowledge man. The same transition ought to be taking place at all levels of our national life. In other words, we must refocus once again to emphasise learning just as the great Zik and other visionary leaders in the land taught us not quite long ago. This is because knowledge is the new common denominator for progress in our time.

Time is not on our side since the knowledge gap will continue to widen until we take forceful and concerted action to rebuild our knowledge institutions over many generations to come. My view is that we must address our minds to four priorities, which, if properly implemented, will set in motion the process of reversing the effects of the years of decline:

- First, we must put pressure on governments (Federal, State and Local) to fund education at all levels, with particular attention to payment of salary scales that will attract the best and the brightest back into teaching.
- Second, in the tradition which UNN has fostered, the curriculum in our universities must be refocused on science, engineering, management, healthcare, etc — the practical courses which help us become competitive both as a nation and as individuals. In this regard, both undergraduate and graduate programmes must be upgraded to global standards.
- Third, it is time for the university community to mobilise private funding to support the facilities and research that create the enabling environment for both knowledge acquisition and adaptation to our practical needs in Nigeria. Specifically, priority must be given to technology transfer and development.

. Lastly, we must put increased effort into continuous learning since what graduates learn after they graduate is critical to their success in the competitive marketplace. This is particularly important if we are to close the gap with the rest of the world, especially given the precipitate decline in standards that Nigeria has experienced in the last several decades.

These four steps are but a minimum starting point and they, by no means, replace the critical need for Nigeria to adopt policies that lead to sustained economic growth at accelerating rates. We face a chicken or egg situation. Knowledge is an imperative if we are to develop but development also is the source of funding knowledge acquisition and capacity building.

Conclusion

This paper has attempted to trace the reasons for the decline of our education system against the backdrop of knowledge as the driving force behind all successful societies today. I have raised the challenge for UNN to lead the way in a permanent reversal of institutional decay and pointed out the four key priorities that must be addressed both urgently and forcefully. It remains to return to my theme and re-emphasise the key message it contains.

- The time of FESTIVALS *1950* - 1967 was a hopeful time with Nigerian institutions largely based on historical practices, which have stood the test of time. This was a time of progress with value system support of Nigeria's development.
- The time of MASQUERADES (1967— 1999) was one of destruction, particularly in tearing down and constraining the very educational institutions, which are the drivers of a nation's development and competitiveness. These wasted years have created a legacy that will take massive effort over generations to reverse and put right.

- Now, we are DANCING IN THE SUN and it is not yet clear whether we realise the nature of the education crisis we face and the implications for our future development. The gravity of the situation makes it imperative for the UNN community to rise up and take the lead. Our noble traditions have provided the foundation on which to build and now we need to have all hands on deck.

Epilogue

In concluding, permit me to close by returning to the UNN legend — TO RESTORE THE DIGNITY OF MAN. In pursuit of that noble course, one would like to borrow liberally from a book used by American universities many years ago to drive home to their freshmen the enduring essence of progress. The reference in question is none other than Charles Beard's treatise on *The Idea of Progress:*

> *An enquiry into the (minds) of those who originated ... the theory of progress shows at the centre of their thought the concept of the good life as the end of the progressive endeavour, the genius which is to preside over the searches and labours of explorers and experiments. The good life for the multitude, not for a superior minority living in the land of illusion ... This is the kernel germinating at the heart of the concept of progress. To see life whole ... to sound its deep, to illuminate its possibilities and to make the noblest and wisest use of material resources in realising its purpose. This is the sum total of the idea of progress — a grand end, conceived in the light of universality, appealing to mankind, seeking high destiny and striving for mastery over the instrumentalities to be employed along the way. Anything less than this is a caricature of the idea.*

The above submission by Charles Beard takes me once again back to the theme of this paper, and another variant of our play on satire to boot. The great theatre of the comity of nations can be likened to a vast FESTIVAL of human possibilities *sans frontiers*. In this over-arching continuum, the nations of the world are indeed the MASQUERADES in play. There are the big masquerades, and then again there are the smaller ones - all in a perpetual state of motion as in a DANCE.

The unique instance of our country Nigeria, would seem as if we are living under the Chinese curse: *may you live in interesting times!* We are all painfully aware of the great opportunities that we have failed to rise up to as a nation in the past. In the near-term, however, democracy has acutely heightened a curious sense of euphoria and urgency for the consequential dividends. Curious because the great lesson of our immediate past history seems all but lost in the heat of our vision of a near-utopia in the shape of our new democracy. True, our new democratic space must yield for us - its latest constituents the minimalist's agenda of a conducive environment for knowledge delivery; a functionally competitive economy, and strong institutions that guaranty basic rights — including, of course, the right to the good life for the greatest number. But we must not delude ourselves regarding the extent of work needed to bring about this happier denouement. Otherwise that sense of euphoria will soon yield valuable space to despondency. That we possess the inert capacity to be sufficiently shocked into adopting a more fanciful dance step is not in doubt. In all of history, such turnarounds represent a constant index of the human spirit. Nigeria has the capacity and potential to enact a turn-around of its own, especially given its stupendous endowments. Ponder these issues in the true spirit of love for our country, and to commit to position the UNN at the epicentre of the vanguard to really RESTORE THE DIGNITY OF MAN.

Appendices

Table 1: National Public Expenditures On Education

	Country	Year	% of Public Ex penditure/GDP
1	Nigeria	1991/92	1.7
2	Ghana	1991	5
3	Burkina Faso	1990	3
4	Canada	1990	6.1
5.	Chad	1990	3.8
6	E. Guinea	1990	2.6
7	Guinea	1990	2.9
8	S. Africa	1990	3.8
9	U.S.A.	1990	6.3

Source: UNICEF, 1995

Table 2: Social Spending in selected Developing Countries

Country	Popu-lation	Health	Education	Debt service	% of population living on <$1 ($2)
Angola	12m	1.4%GDP	4.9% GNP	33.0%GNP	NA —
Cote d'Ivoire	14.5m	14%GDP	5% GNP	13.5%GNP	12.3% (49.4%)
Ghana	1.85m	1.8%GDP	4.2% GNP	7.7%GNP	78.40%
Kenya	29.3m	2.2%GDP	6.5% GNP	4.8%GNP	26.5% (62.3%)
Malawi	10.5m	2.8%GDP	5.4%GNP	4.7%GNP	42.10%
Mozambique	16.9m	2.1%GDP	4.1%GNP	2.9%GNP	37.9/.(78.4%)
Nigeria	120.8rn	0.2%GDP	0.7% GNP	3.4%GNP	70.2% (90.8%)
South Africa	41m	7.1%GOP	7.9%GNP	4%GNP	12%(36%)
Tanzania	32.1m	1.3%GDP	3.4% GNP	2.O%GNP	19.9% (59.7%)
Uganda	20.9m	1.8%GDP	2.6%GNP	2.4%GNP	36.7%(77.2%)

Source: The African Debt Report by Jubilee 2000

Table 3: Total Student Enrolment In Nigerian Universities By Major Disciplines

DISCIPLINE	1990	1991	1992	1993/94*	1994/95*
Administration	10,969	12,746	15,469	12,674	11,790
Agriculture	10,919	12,002	13,803	12,170	12,765
Arts	24,302	25,339	27,348	22,646	22,981
Education	29,996	34,834	31,506	31,012	30,544
Eng. & Tech	15,226	17,984	20,971	22,080	23,767
Env. Design	5,655	6,394	7,049	7,763	7,805
Law	9,284	9,524	11,291	9,765	10,516
Med/H Sc	11,162	12,565	13,956	17,118	18,304
Pharmacy	2,290	2,661	2,716	5,003	5,420
Sciences	30,083	34,819	40,068	41,504	41,823
Social Sc.	21,622	25,363	30,830	24,163	25,164
Vet. Med.	1,403	1,528	1,643	2,084	2,558
Others	6,577	5,015	8,679	20,017	22,744
TOTAL	179,488	200,774	224,879	227,999	236,261

Source: Statistical Abstracts (1996 and 1998), Federal Office of Statistics
*Federal University Only

DISCIPLINE	1993	1994/95*	1995/96*	1996/97	1997/98
Administration	12,674	11,790	13,210	16,305	20,603
Agriculture	12,170	12,765	14,925	20,340	21,251
Arts	22,646	22,981	21,976	22,477	25,188
Education	31,012	30,544	30,133	29,940	30,722
Eng. & Tech	22,080	23,767	27,108	31,904	35,808
Env. Sciences	7,763	7,885	9,548	9,506	10,784
Law	9,765	10,516	11,524	11,169	12,389
Med/Health Sc	17,118	18,304	19,962	22,067	22,563
Pharmacy	5,003	5,420	5,786	4,964	5,450
Sciences	41,504	41,823	47,728	54,307	57,368
Social Sc.	24,163	25,164	28,077	34,101	36,946
Vet. Med.	2,084	2,558	2,742	2,159	2,318
Others	20,017	22,744	20,402	-	-
Remedial	-	-	-	7,696	9,396
Sub Degree	-	-	-	10,565	11,783
TOTAL	227,999	236,261	253,121	277,500	302,569

Source : National University Commission

Note * Federal Universities only

Total Enrolment in Federal Universities by Major Discipline 2001/ 2002 to 2006/2007

DISCIPLINE	2001/02	2002/03	2003/04	2004/05	2005/06	2006/07
Admin Mgt. Sc	29,407	29,741	45,247	47,886	29,757	43,808
Agriculture	18,557	27,201	30,457	26,455	22,022	22,604
Arts	31,182	31,456	35,585	38,589	33,998	37,652
Dentistry	-	-	-	-	-	727
Education	33,782	33,798	48,230	48,889	49,247	52,988
Eng. & Tech	47,278	50,983	51,816	59,702	57,824	56,421
Env. Sciences	10,864	14,676	18,036	18,853	17,968	18,065
Law	14,395	13,896	15,430	18,506	16,299	15,008
Medicine	26,360	25,426	28,001	31,540	25,884	26,338
Pharmacy	5,727	5,873	5,967	5,538	4,740	5,261
Sciences	59,361	74,933	78,761	97,724	75,187	76,704
Social Sc.	45,320	38,154	54,450	52,924	56,725	53,946
Vet. Med.	3,474	3,365	7,273	3,771	3,735	3,066
TOTAL	325,707	349,502	419,253	450,377	393,386	412,588

Source : National University Commission

Table 4: First Degree Award by Nigerian Universities (Year Ending June)

DISCIPLINE	1992	1993/94	1995/ 96	1996/97	1997/ 98
Administration	1,898	1,483	2,118	2,607	328
Agriculture	728	1,846	1,995	2,028	186
Arts	2,416	5,818	6,637	6,396	637
Education	4,215	8,962	10,887	9,995	591
Eng. & Tech	1,397	2,425	2,991	3,296	643
Env. Design	330	422	854	795	171
Law	1,220	867	1,314	1,585	142
Med/H.Sc	718	1,422	1,851	2,142	502
Pharmacy	174	353	374	364	-
Sciences	2,047	5,271	6,041	6,747	692
Social Science	3,087	5,243	5,843	6,781	1,433
Vet. Med.	80	151	216	240	-
Others	94	-	-	-	-
Total	19,204	34,577	41,121	42,976	5,325

Source: National University Commission
*Note *   No session for 1994/95*

Graduate Out-turn of Bachelor's Degree by Discipline, 2001- 2005

DISCIPLINE	2001		2002		2003		2004		2005	
	Male	Female	Male	Female	Male	Female	Male	Female	Male	Female
Administration	3,294	2,298	4,727	3,413	6,380	5,321	4,089	3,201	2,521	1,843
Agriculture	1,086	604	1,381	705	1,366	873	1,268	828	299	167
Arts	2,732	2,351	2,938	2,982	3,672	3,963	2,706	2,746	1,687	1,495
Education	4,129	4,117	3,221	3,248	3,560	3,391	2,361	3,008	2,352	2,095
Eng. & Tech.	4,194	581	4,558	679	5,425	800	4,182	689	1,061	116
Env. Science	932	375	1,079	395	1,201	560	940	368	643	243
Law	1,558	990	2,112	1,781	2,846	2,664	1,901	1,461	1007	626
Medicine	1,200	568	1,538	613	1,489	903	1,219	721	359	230
Pharmacy	242	78	312	138	186	144	320	235	12	10
Sciences	4,743	2,494	4,461	2,840	5,839	4,347	4,390	2,581	2,190	1,379
Social Science	5,021	3,223	8,459	4,996	8,187	5,658	6,017	4,220	2,893	2,296
Dentistry	-	-	45	22	67	30	48	21	-	-
Vet. Medicine	68	19	99	47	155	54	47	21	30	6
Others	583	311	1,059	457	879	401	617	214	273	209
Total	29,782	18,009	35,989	22,316	41,252	29,109	30,105	20,314	15,327	10,715
Grand Total	47,791		58,305		70,361		50,419		26,042	

Source: National University Commission

Being paper presented at the 40th *Anniversary Convocation Lecture of the University of Nigeria, Nsukka, April 2001.*

Chapter 18

Financing Oil and Gas Projects in Nigeria

Introduction

The exploration of natural resources will guarantee overall economic development of the state through industrialization, employment generation and infrastructural development. Against the background of oil accounting for 85 per cent of gross foreign exchange earnings accruing to the Federal Government, I fully subscribe to the view that we have a duty to formulate policies and strategies that will attract investments in this vital sector of our economy.

From petroleum, which includes crude oil (its liquid state) and natural gas (the gaseous state) comes a variety of products amongst which are: fuels, asphalt and oil, gas, petrochemicals (used largely in the plastics, paint, detergent, antiseptics, cosmetics, synthetic rubber and fibres, fertilizers, etc).

The dependence of our local industries on imported raw materials has led to uncompetitive pricing of the final products, in the face of significant devaluation of the local currency against the world's major currencies. It is a truism that the West African trade route in modem times, stretches from Onitsha Aba, Nnewi, Idumota to, Cotonou, Douala, Ougadougou, Lome and Abidjan. As we forge alliances with these economies, our long-term objectives should not just be the creation of mega cities but also the creation of competitive advantage for our local entrepreneurs based on local sourcing of vital raw materials. This is not out of sync with events around us, given that total world oil consumption particularly by industrial concerns is projected to grow by about 36% from 490 million tons to 630 million tons of oil equivalent between *1995* and 2010, in the developing countries.

The mandate I have is to discuss the Financing of Oil and Gas Projects. However, in order to appreciate the dynamics of the financing options, it is important to remind ourselves that the petroleum system consists of the generation, migration and entrapment of hydrocarbons. Oil and natural gas are generated in rocks containing a sufficient amount and types of organic materials. When the source rock is subjected to a high temperature over a long period of time, oil and natural gas may be generated and expelled.

The conclusion from the above therefore, is that the petroleum industry is characterised by the following procedures:

- Acquisition of mineral interest rights
- Exploration (including prospecting)
- Development
- Production of crude oil and gas

These are generally in the area of the upstream sector, which is very capital intensive and where there is also the high probability of not discovering oil in commercial quantity.

Overall, the cost elements to be considered include:

- Mineral rights acquisition costs
- Exploration and drilling costs (seismic data acquisition/ interpretation/ storage)
- Development costs (rig provision, drilling chemicals and environmental services)
- Production costs (engineering, procurement, construction, operations/ maintenance and host community costs)

· Support equipment and facilities costs (pipeline construction/ maintenance) and finally
· General costs (logistics, etc.)

Financing Vehicles

In order to mitigate the risks attendant in this high- risk enterprise, several operating arrangements have evolved, particularly in the developing economies where growth in consumption has been more profound. This is not a coincidence, for hydrocarbon reserves are also concentrated in developing countries-only a mere 5 per cent of total proven oil reserves and 9 per cent of proven gas reserves are in the industrial countries.

Therefore, as business opportunities in the oil and gas sectors of industrialized countries diminish, energy companies are shifting their attention to the energy investment requirements of developing countries. In the circumstance, orthodox financing vehicles have yielded way to new initiatives, leading to scarcity of investible capital.

Driven by the huge demand for oil in the 1970s - which led to high oil prices, host governments became heavily involved in the petroleum sector ostensibly to take control of the "commanding heights" of their economies. This effectively reversed the previous practice whereby major petroleum projects were financed wholly, by the big multi-national oil companies.

Consequently, funds for oil and gas projects were appropriations from budgets, borrowings, financial institutions and prospecting oil companies. In recent times, due to the liberalisation of economies, the increasing need to address fundamental social/ economic crises and dwindling revenues, most governments have juggled priorities. The dilemma though is that the fear of possible expropriation remains an albatross, for wholesale participation by the oil majors.

The most viable option therefore revolves around private investors, financiers (local and offshore) and government.

We need to address the concerns (political and commercial risks) raised in the preceding paragraph in order to judge our preparedness for the journey to financiers' vaults. Thereafter, we shall examine the various available options.

Generally, risks associated with oil and gas projects can be grouped as commercial and political. By way of summary, these risks are in the areas of cost overruns, uncertainties in demand and prices, delays in project execution due to civil unrest, community disturbances, fear of expropriation, price control legislations which impact, the pay-back period, arbitrariness in tax and royalty legislations. Similarly, the tendency towards abuse of the judicial process and or neglect of due process and the rule of law creates uncertainties in the event of arbitration. In a way, these concerns have been addressed through guarantees and assurances from the host government in addition to co-opting the services of individuals and influence peddlers.

We shall now examine the issues relating to financing in broad terms. In order to mitigate the risks associated with petroleum exploration, companies get into Joint Venture arrangements or Mineral Conveyance agreements. Under the Joint Venture situation, there is a collaborative effort by two or more mineral interest owners commonly called the Joint Venture partners. A Mineral Conveyance on the other hand is a direct transfer of any type of ownership interest in minerals from one entity to another with the lessor retaining a royalty interest. This usually takes the form of Production-Sharing Contracts, Farm- Outs, Carried Interest, Unitisation, etc.

Whereas the Joint Venture partners absorb costs based on participatory interest, under a Production-Sharing Contract, the contractor bears all associated costs.

Options

Financing oil and gas projects is best undertaken through medium and long- term instruments, it is appropriate to state at this point, that a combination of debt and equity will be most ideal in order to achieve efficiency of funds utilisation and financial discipline. In recent times, private capital has merged with public funding through governments' deliberate dilution of interests in commercial enterprises.

Financing opportunities are offered by several Multi-lateral lending institutions and Export Credit Agencies (ECA), namely:

- The World Bank(strictly for public sector)
- International Finance Corporation (IFC)
- Multilateral Investment Guarantee Agency (MIGA)
- EBRD/ECGD (United Kingdom)
- US-EXIM
- FMO (Netherlands)
- AFREXIM
- JAPAN-EXIM

In addition, private sector institutions, such as banks and the capital markets, provide a veritable sources of funds – whether long, medium or short term.

We may articulate the World Bank's agenda in terms of Direct Lending, Guarantees, and Technical Assistance. Following a shift in policy, the World Bank's lending activities in the oil and gas sector (which averaged $1 billion in the late 1990s) are beginning to decline. Focus is now on basic infrastructural developments and technical assistance.

As you are probably aware, the EEC and Shell International recently approved a Niger Delta Contractor Finance Scheme in collaboration with a local bank. This alliance will create a $30m lifeline specifically to finance activities of SHELL contractors in diverse areas.

It is hoped that this initiative will provide funds at concessionary rates to the local contractors in addition to
- Development of executory capacity
- Aiding capacity building
- Development of human capital
- Asset stock addition.

It is envisaged that the other oil-producing majors in Nigeria will emulate this novel project and join the consortium. This will over time, convert our portfolio- carrying contractors to known names, with capacity to bid for and execute contracts in the international oil industry. Funding of oil and gas projects by local financial institutions has been restrictive. This has been attributed to inability to source long-term funds for on-lending. Reliance has been on traditional sources of funds and the money market resulting in high/unattractive cost of funds.

The emerging opportunities in the oil and gas sector will compel Nigerian banks not only to develop competency in the area of energy financing, but also help them to forge strategic alliances with off-shore institutions that can provide leverage for funds mobilisation.

Process Definition

A crucial point to make as we wrap up is that funding agencies are very discerning and meticulous. Articulation of qualifying projects and their presentation would have to go through rigor in the following areas:
- Project feasibility study
- Identification of project development partners
- Agreement on funding mix (debt/equity)

· Determination of funding agencies (including building consortium and syndication)
· Management

Conclusions

It is imperative that we leverage global best practices as we seek to develop our natural resources to achieve efficiency and profitability of our enterprises. Gone are the days of unplanned borrowings. The running of government businesses is progressively falling into the hands of acknowledged entrepreneurs and those with a private-sector background. This explains the surge in commercial sources of finance such as commercial bank loans, private bond placements and sale of equity in the capital market.

What this calls for is sophistication of our capital markets and growth in expertise of the human capital, even as they collaborate with experts from the developed economies. Training and exposure will help to address the current paucity of expertise in structuring complex financing arrangements.

Similarly, enterprises requiring funds from the lending institutions and capital markets will have to ensure professionalism in the management of those enterprises for in the final analysis, financial discipline, in all its ramifications, will be crucial to the successful execution of projects. Compliance with loan covenants, timely servicing of obligations and rendition of reports are minimum expectations. Political considerations and interferences are no longer fashionable if we profess to be part of the new economic order.

The degree of state participation will necessarily be determined by the project— type, tenor, political and economic environment although it must be said that involvement in the upstream projects should be reduced to the barest minimum. Given the World Bank's focus on infrastructure and technical assistance, funding and guarantees for properly packaged projects are assured.

Being a paper presented at the Oil and Gas Investors' Forum, July 2001.

Chapter 19

Fleet Renewal:
The Pivot of Luxury Bus Business

Introduction

The Importance of Road/Bus Transportation

It is difficult to conceive of any situation where transport does not play an important role in the life of an individual, community or nation. The importance of transportation is better conveyed in the postulation of *Robinson* and *Bamford* (both are economists) that *"as standard of living in individual societies increase and economy becomes more complex, the reliance becomes almost totally dependent on transport"*.

Thus, transport is an indispensable catalyst for activating and stimulating the tempo of the economic, political, social and strategic development of any society, be it developed or a developing one. By implication, the development of an efficient, flexible and dynamic transport system is very crucial for the occurrence of meaningful socio-economic and political transformation and development, and also for binding and unifying the various component parts of any society ranging from the village to global levels.

The relevance of transportation in an economic system also includes,

· The provision of job opportunities;

- Generation of revenue to the government in various forms of duties, rates, rents, tariffs and licences — this revenue is used to fund other economic, social and political development agendas of the government; and
- Creation of positive impact and contribution to growth of the national economy through economies of scale and the multiplier effects it exerts on the overall economy.

The most important sub-sector in the transportation industry in Nigeria today is road transportation. It accounts for more than 90 per cent of internal passenger and freight movements. The operation of road transport business is to a large extent left in the hands of the private sector in view of its ability to provide road transport services more efficiently and effectively than the government. A pointer to my assertion is the moribund state of most of the transport corporations established by state governments to provide intra and intercity transport services.

An important aspect of road transportation, where private operators have been most successful in Nigeria is in the area of road transportation. Bus transportation forms the backbone of most urban and intercity transport systems. This is because buses are affordable means of transportation, as it is cheaper than other modes of transport, even in the road transportation subsector. It also provides a high degree of flexibility and convenience, as it can render "door-to-door" service. Buses also play a major role in providing access to, and integrating with, other transport modes such as trains, ships and airplanes etc.

In most countries, there is a distinction between the buses used for intra and inter-city transport. The buses used for inter-city transportation are usually fitted with comfortable interior accessories (e.g. comfortable chairs, arm and headrests, etc.) to guarantee a reasonable level of comfort for long distance travel.

Critical Success Factors of Luxury Bus Business

The emergence of luxury buses as a mode of transportation in Nigeria dates back about three decades, led by very few operators. The business has gone through different stages of development. Today, luxury bus transportation is big business with great potentials. The success of the business could be ascribed to effective route and fleet selection, consistency and high standards of service.

Route Selection

Most of the luxury bus operators started on the eastern routes, conveying traders on the Lagos route. The most viable routes then were the Lagos-Onitsha and Lagos-Aba routes. Subsequently, the routes were extended to Port Harcourt and later to Abuja in the North. Currently, most of the major operators, with large fleets, have extended their routes to most parts of the country and even to some West African states. In general, buses need to be well utilised throughout their period of operation; that is high load factors need to be sustained in order for the business to be cost effective. Effective route selection guarantees adequate load factors.

It has to be understood that a bus operator is in the business of supplying a perishable commodity. The commodity is a bus seat and it perishes at the end of a trip. If the bus seat is not taken on a trip, it is a loss to the operator. For instance, if an operator running a 45-seater bus on the Lagos-Ibadan route undertakes a trip with 30 passengers, the revenue that would have accrued from the 15 untaken seats would be lost. Thus, a significant indicator of performance of a bus is the number of passengers carried in relation to the capacity of the bus.

The right size of bus is very important in this regard as it will have implications on optimum output and customer satisfaction. On routes of low demand, buses need to be small if they are to be well utilised. An operator of a large bus on such a route would be faced with two alternatives: to operate partly empty, or at full capacity (which may result in excessive waiting and customer dissatisfaction). Both situations may result in losses to the operator.

It also has to be noted that there are costs associated with route development. Developing a new route involves some costs, particularly at the initial period.

These are associated with creating awareness and attracting patronage to the new bus route. Within that period, the buses will often run at less than capacity and incur losses from unsold seats. Unfortunately, wear and tear and other operating costs and overheads will still arise.

Fleet Selection

Some operators of the business have attained success by also making the right choice of fleet. Operating costs, particularly the cost of maintenance, are greatly influenced by the choice of vehicle. A major determinant of the cost of maintenance, as well as the performance of the vehicle, is the availability of genuine spare parts. Where genuine spare parts are not available, the buses are likely to be off the road for long periods waiting for spares or cannibalised for lack of spare parts. The resulting loss of productivity is particularly damaging to any viable bus transport business.

Because of the operators' knowledge of road conditions, level of demand, and operating costs, their choice of vehicles is usually based on cost effectiveness and appropriateness for the Nigerian roads. Accordingly, I would be correct to deduce that Mercedes Benz brands, having remained the Number I choice of most operators, is cost effective in terms of suitability and ruggedness, and availability of spare-parts and specialists.

Bus Availability

Another determinant of the viability of a bus transport business is the availability of buses on the relevant route. Uncertainty about the availability of buses will negatively affect the image of the operator and hence patronage.

The proportion of a bus fleet that can be put on the road each day has a direct bearing on bus availability. Bus availability is an indication of the effectiveness of bus maintenance, spares and procurement, as well as staff management. With adequate maintenance and good administration, it should be possible to achieve fleet utilisation of between 80 per cent and 90 per cent. Fleet utilisation may fall well short of this range due to lack of maintenance facilities, skills, and problems over supply of spare parts and fuel.

Standard of Service

In selecting their fleet, some operators have been able to respond more effectively to the preferences of passengers, which range from vehicles offering basic conditions at low fares to more comfortable vehicles at higher fares. Expectedly, as income rises, a transport company needs to include more attractive and comfortable bus services in order to sustain patronage. In line with this expectation, some of the major operators have been able to segment their market by acquiring "business class" buses with air conditioner, TV, VCD and/or bar closet and other conveniences for first class travel.

To improve the standard of service, many operators have improved the quality of operational management by adopting formal operational structures and employing graduates to head their operations, e.g., LSTC.

Fleet Renewal

It is important that units of a luxury bus operation be maintained at a high level of fitness. This is achieved through consistent repairs, renewal and replacement.

Fleet renewal involves not only outright replacement, but also preventive and scheduled maintenance. While the scheduled maintenance comprises periodic servicing, preventive maintenance consists of parts replacement or engine overhaul. Fleet renewal entails a systematic and consistent sustenance of routes by ensuring that vehicles are constantly provided, maintained and replaced on time to sustain high standards of service. In the attainment of this objective, three main parties come to mind — operators, financiers and government.

The Role of Operators

Operators are expected to carry out preventive and scheduled maintenance on their buses after respective minimum distances of travel. This is because vehicles that are poorly maintained usually perform poorly and have a short life span. I am aware that some operators have their own garages for maintenance and repairs, manned by their employees and well stocked with spare parts. This is done to curtail the cost of maintenance.

However, it is rather disappointing that only very few operators renew their fleet in good time. The failure of many operators to carry out timely maintenance of their fleet is responsible for the high rate of breakdown and accidents on our roads.

Most operators wait for as long as 15 years before they scrap vehicles. They resort to putting older buses on the less viable routes, while newer buses are operated on more viable routes. After about 15 years, the buses are sold to marginal operators. The main problem militating against fleet renewal in the Nigerian bus transport business is the under-utilisation of available financial resources. Operators are not accessing and effectively utilising the financial resources and options available.

Most bus operators are yet to adopt more sophisticated financial management systems as their operations expand and business grows. As a result, scarce financial resources are inefficiently allocated. Moreover, the operations of many bus companies are fraught with financial leakages. It has become increasingly apparent that the main skill, which remains for the bus transport companies to acquire, is a sound understanding of financial matters as it relates to transport business.

The financial management activities of a bus company should transcend beyond sourcing of funds for financing its fleet and operational activities. It should also include efficient or cost-effective utilisation of the funds raised. This implies that financial management is needed for shaping the fortunes of a bus company since it involves decisions on how financial resources are allocated. In view of this, the financial management activities of a bus company should involve:

Investment decisions : These include decisions on the allocation and commitment of financial resources of the company to fleet maintenance and renewal, and other areas of operations.

Financing or capital-mix decisions : These involve the decisions of when, where and how to acquire funds to meet the company's investment needs through the best financing mix.

Dividend decisions : These involve the decisions on whether to distribute all profits, retain them, or distribute a portion and retain the balance for ploughing back.

Liquidity management : These relate to how the operations of the bus company should be carried out or its assets managed efficiently in order to safeguard it against the dangers of illiquidity and insolvency.

It is clear that the possession or acquisition of financial management skills will go a long way in facilitating the financing of fleet renewal in luxury bus business.

There are various internal and external sources available to bus operators to finance fleet renewal. Some of the sources are internal. For example, bus operators could provide funds for financing fleet renewal from private funds, direct income and retained profits. Private funds include personal savings and this is mostly used at the commencement of operations of a company. Direct income comprises the bus fares. Retained profits are the proportion of profits made from operating a bus company that is ploughed-back to grow the business.

Bus fares typically provide the single largest source of internal finance. Generally, the most effective costing systems are those that tend to cover all operating costs, including depreciation of the fleet, repair and renewal through bus fare revenues and associated income from activities such as advertising and courier services.

However, the recovery period of a fleet cost is long, and the cash flow system of a bus company must be such that will guarantee adequate funds for the maintenance of the fleet as well as to cover indirect costs. For this reason, it is expedient to finance new fleets, at least partially, from external sources, especially as the business grows over time. Usually, the company is expected to contribute a proportion of its financial requirement for fleet renewal by external financiers. These underscore the importance of good financial management for the success of a transport business.

The external financiers and facilitators of fleet renewal include the banks, assembly and manufacturing plants. I will review the different roles of these institutions seriatim.

The Role of Banks

One of the major sources of external finance for fleet renewal is bank finance. Bank finance may be through commercial or development banks. Such finance could be taken in the form of term loan, leases or overdraft facilities. Such loans could be packaged in various forms to meet an operator's funding requirement. For example, it could be a revolving term loan. It is mostly the major players that easily access this source of finance.

Most of the major players finance their fleet renewal by borrowing short-term funds from commercial banks. However, since this type of finance is usually short or medium-term, the new fleet does not repay the loan, but rather repayments are made from the overall company operations. This option may, therefore, hinder adequate cash flow for operations, and thus result in illiquidity and insolvency.

Banks could provide foreign exchange credits to bus operators. Some development banks and multilateral agencies have granted credit lines to some Nigerian banks for the benefit of Nigerian entrepreneurs. Diamond Bank has IFC and USEXIM Bank credit lines, which can be utilised by the luxury bus operators to finance fleet renewal. The advantage of this financing option is that it could be utilised as long-term loans, such that the revenue from the new fleet would be the source of repayment. However, the exchange rate risk may render this option less viable.

Banks can also assist the operators to raise long-term funds either in the form of shares or debentures in the capital market (as a corollary to providing advisory services on capital mix). Share capital can be raised by issuing new shares through rights issue, private placement or public offer. Loan capital can also be raised through the issue of debenture stock or bonds on the Stock Exchange or by private placement. It should be noted, however, that while investors in debentures and bonds get the status of lender, shares provide ownership rights to the investors in the bus company. Our desire for ownership exclusivity has hindered the share capital option in Nigeria.

Further, banks can provide lease finance to the bus operators. Leasing is a form of contract between the owner of the assets, called the lessor (say a bank), and the user of the asset, called the lessee (a bus company). There are two major types of leases — finance and operating leases. However, the type of lease that the banks can effectively provide is the finance lease. Under the finance lease, a bus operator (as the lessee) can specify the type of buses it wants, and the banks (as the lessor) will buy the specified buses. The bank will then sign an agreement to lease the buses out to the operator for periodic rental payments. At the end of the lease period, the bank offers the lessee the option to purchase the bus at a residual price.

Leasing is the most veritable source of financing a new fleet. This is because lease finance allows an operator to make a down payment of a small proportion of the total cost of a new fleet and pay the rest in instalments. The instalmental payment can be structured in line with the expected cash flow streams from the use of the fleet. Thus, it will afford a bus company the opportunity to acquire a greater number of buses and/or free their revenue for the maintenance of existing fleet and expansion of business.

The banks can also help the bus operators to rectify the problem of poor financial management systems by rendering financial advisory services to the operators on capital budgeting, capital mix, liquidity and cash flow management.

The Role of Assembly and Manufacturing Plant

The assembly plants can play a significant role in developing the bus transport business. They can do this by providing lease finance, as well as maintenance, educational and enlightenment services in addition to supplying the vehicles.

The assembly plants can provide finance and operating leases to the bus operators. It should, however, be noted that under a finance lease, the operator (as the lessee) would be responsible for the maintenance and insurance of the buses, as well as bearing the risk of obsolescence. On the other hand, the assembly plant (as the lessor) is responsible for maintenance and insurance costs on the buses and bears the risk of obsolescence under an operating lease.

I would like the audience to note that an operating lease assumes that a bus would have a substantial and quantifiable residual value. Thus, rentals on the bus will be lower (than under finance lease) since the cost will be amortised, not at 100 per cent, but at 90 per cent, or less, of the initial cost of the bus. The assembly plant is expected to either lease the bus for further periods, at the end of the initial lease or will earn cash from the sale of the bus after the operator (lessee) has used it.

Today, the difference between finance and operating lease is not quite distinct anymore. This is because hybrid leases can be structured. A plant like ANAMMCO can provide the leasing services through a number of options such as establishing a subsidiary leasing company, a tripartite lease arrangement among ANAMMCO/transport company/bank, where the latter mainly guarantees payment; or directly between the transport company and ANAMMCO.

To facilitate the participation of ANAMMCO in lease finance, the company will require credit finance from other sources. This can be from the banks that may prefer the credit risk of ANAMMCO to that of the transport companies. Thus, the whole arrangement can be structured in a way that will benefit all participants in the sector.

Other sources of finance that will enable ANAMMCO to participate effectively in lease finance are the technical partners. They can supply buses, chassis and components to ANAMMCO on credit and allow instalment payments over a reasonable period of time. As helpful as this last option may sound, exchange rate risk may constitute a major obstacle.

The assembly plants can provide better maintenance services for the operators due to their technical competence. Their alliance with foreign technical partners, who are most times the main manufacturers, would enable them to acquire genuine spare parts that could be sold to the operators. Further, the assembly plants should organise more enlightenment programmes, like this conference, to educate all stakeholders about developments and the important role of individual stakeholder in the industry.

The Role of the Government

The government, as one of the major stakeholders in the transport industry, is an important source of financing fleet renewal. Government finance is usually provided through government grants, subsidies and co-financing. The subsidies may come in the form of operating or capital subsidies.

Operating subsidies are the subsidies provided by the government to operators, which may be in the form of grants, tax holiday, tax relief, etc., to render transport services at lower prices than the commercial price. On the other hand, capital subsidies are provided by the government, in the form of leases, duty relief, soft loans, etc., to support the operators in acquiring a new fleet.

Subsidies are usually provided to public transportation, thereby assisting the low-income segments of the population, or to promote public transit use. In several countries, government-owned bus operators depend on both operating and capital subsidies. In recent years in Nigeria, the Federal Urban Mass Transit Agency provided capital subsidy, in the form of subsidised buses (provided on a soft loan basis) to beneficiaries. It is however unfortunate that most operators have misused this subsidy as they defaulted on the soft loans provided through the scheme.

Co-financing can be done between different tiers of government and/or between the government and the private sector.

This option is exemplified in the unsuccessful Federal Mass Transit Scheme, which was a co-financing venture between the Federal Mass Transit Agency (public sector) and transport operators (private sector).

In most parts of the world, the government serves as the regulatory body of the transport industry, providing system administration and planning, and transport infrastructure. The Nigerian government needs to increase its presence in playing this important role. The government needs to realise that its regulatory function is an essential element in assuring that the public receives the level of service it expects.

Conclusion

It should be noted that the major factors that can ensure timely and suitable fleet renewal is effective and efficient financial and operations management.

The various roles of stakeholders in fleet renewal have been identified. The list is certainly not exhaustive. It is my hope that all stakeholders, including the operators, government, banks, ANAMMCO and the technical partners will further explore ways in which they can be more relevant in fleet renewal and the development of the sector in general.

Being a paper presented at The Year 2001 Mercedes-Benz National Bus Conference, February 2001.